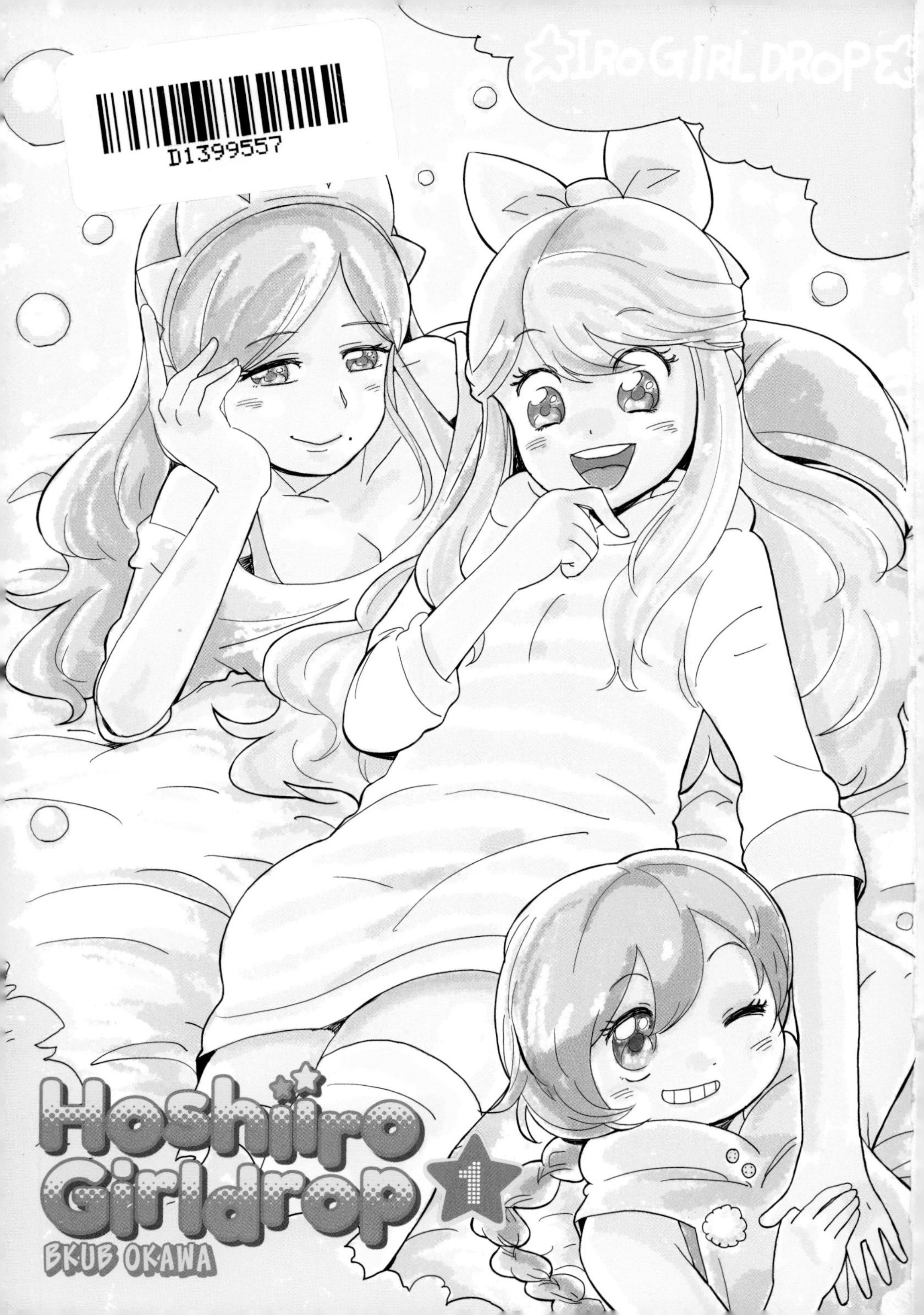
IRO GIRLDROP
Hoshiiro Girldrop 1
BKUB OKAWA

Kiro girldrop 1

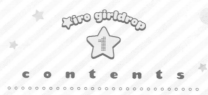

contents

CHAPTER 1 "I'LL ONLY TELL YOU!"

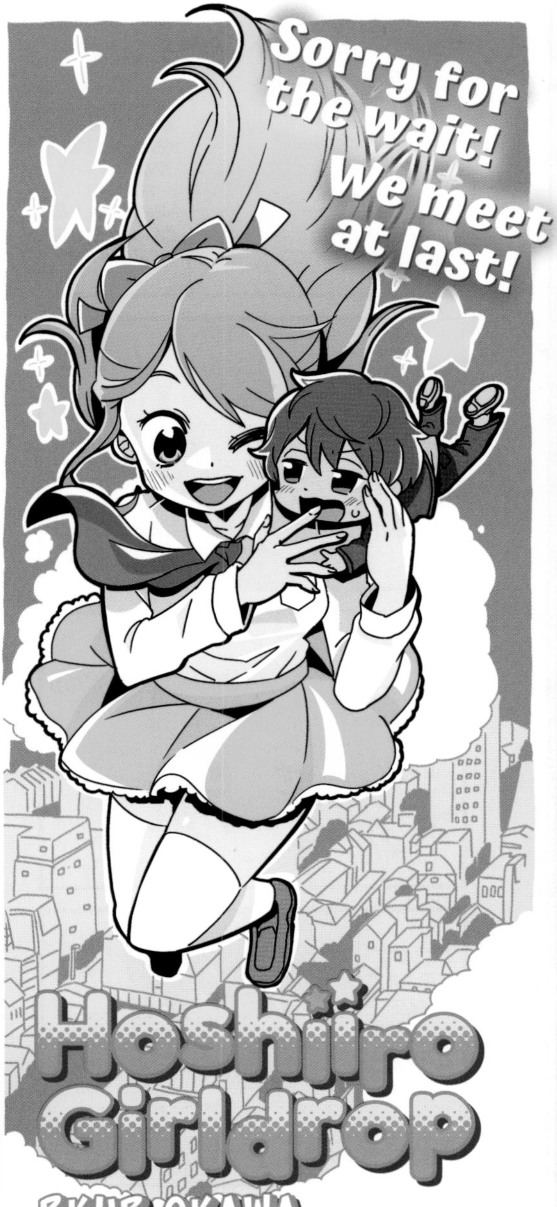
Sorry for the wait! We meet at last!
Hoshiiro Girldrop
BKUB OKAWA

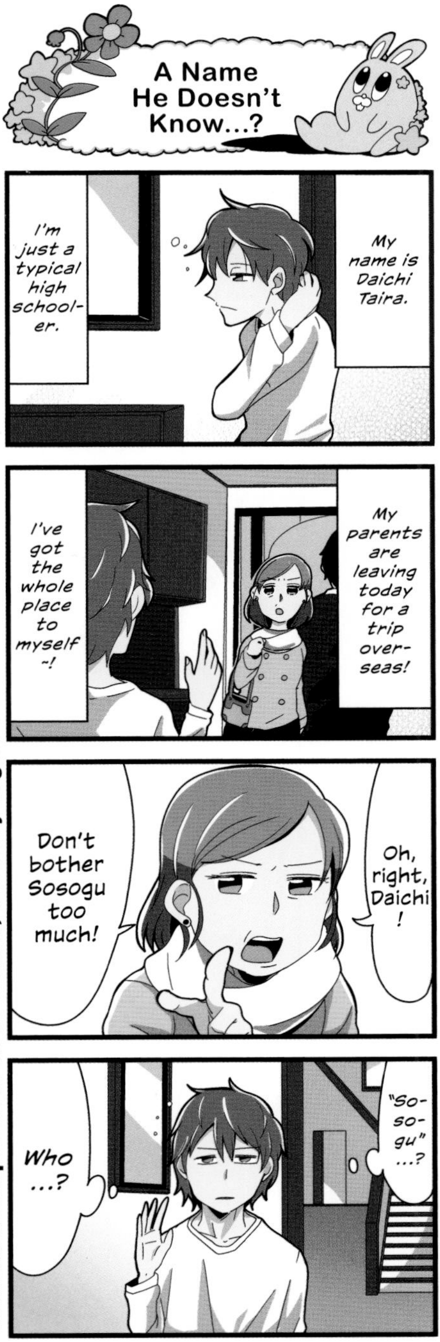
A Name He Doesn't Know...?
My name is Daichi Taira.
I'm just a typical high schooler.
My parents are leaving today for a trip overseas!
I've got the whole place to myself~!
Oh, right, Daichi!
Don't bother Sosogu too much!
"Sosogu"...?
Who...?

With the anticipation of an encounter, the story begins...?

A Sudden Encounter

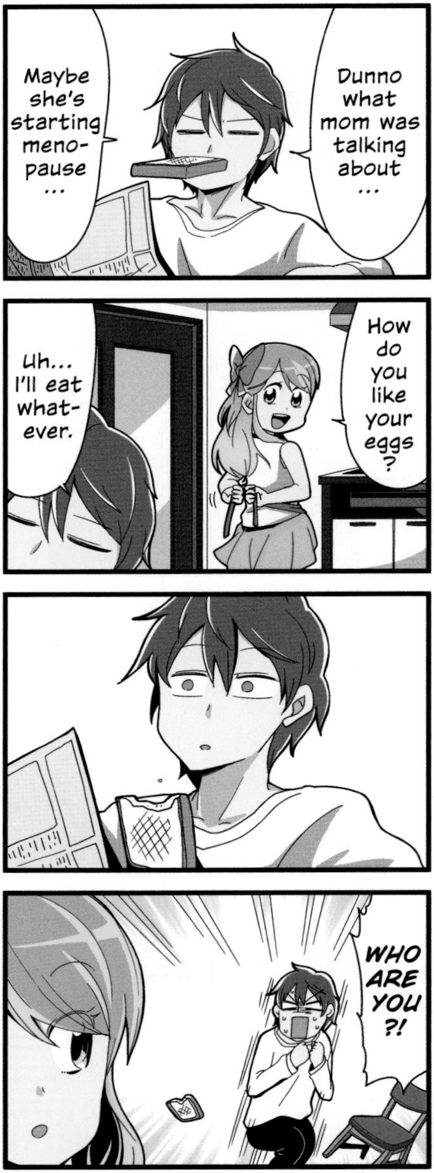
Dunno what mom was talking about...
Maybe she's starting menopause...
How do you like your eggs?
Uh... I'll eat whatever.
WHO ARE YOU?!

Childhood Friend?

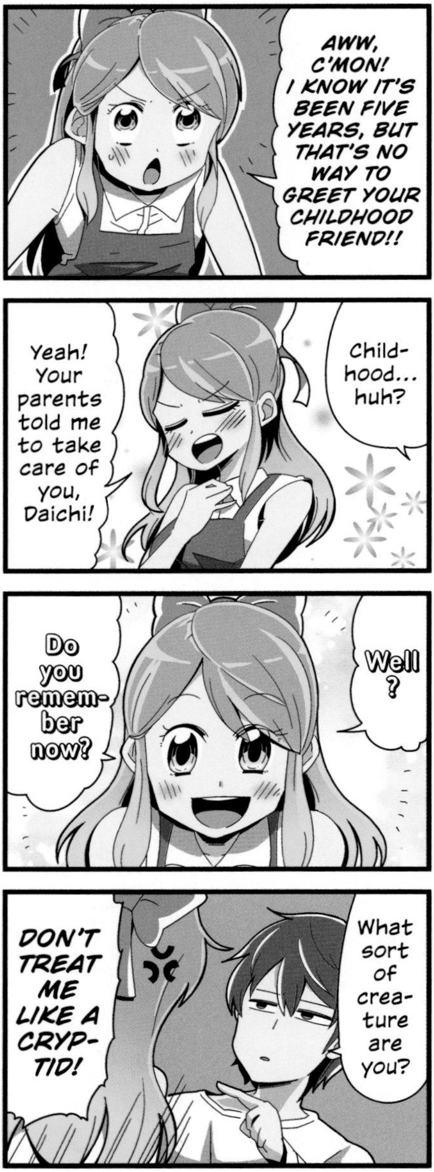
AWW, C'MON! I KNOW IT'S BEEN FIVE YEARS, BUT THAT'S NO WAY TO GREET YOUR CHILDHOOD FRIEND!!
Child-hood... huh?
Yeah! Your parents told me to take care of you, Daichi!
Well?
Do you remem-ber now?
What sort of crea-ture are you?
DON'T TREAT ME LIKE A CRYP-TID!

An Important Promise

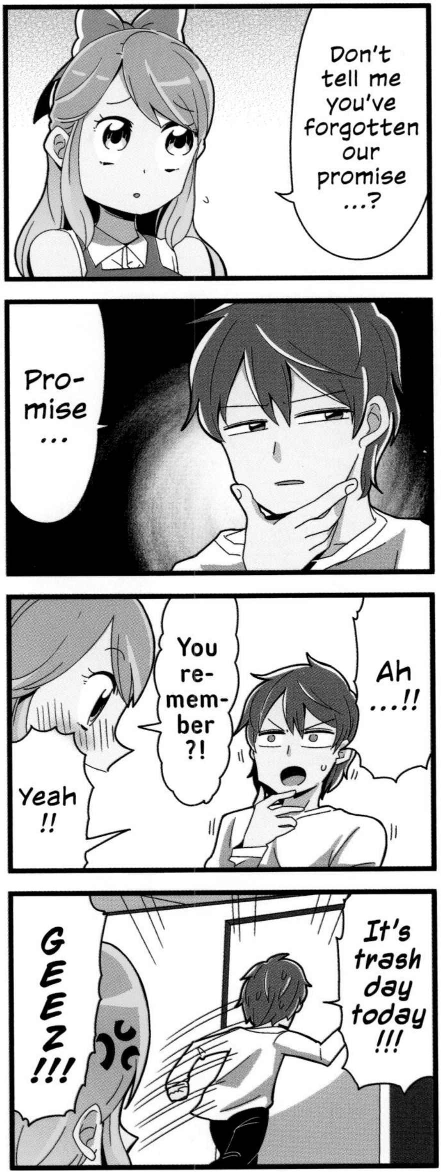
Don't tell me you've forgotten our promise ...?
Pro-mise ...
Ah ...!!
You re-mem-ber ?!
Yeah !!
It's trash day today !!!
GEEZ!!!

I'm Home!

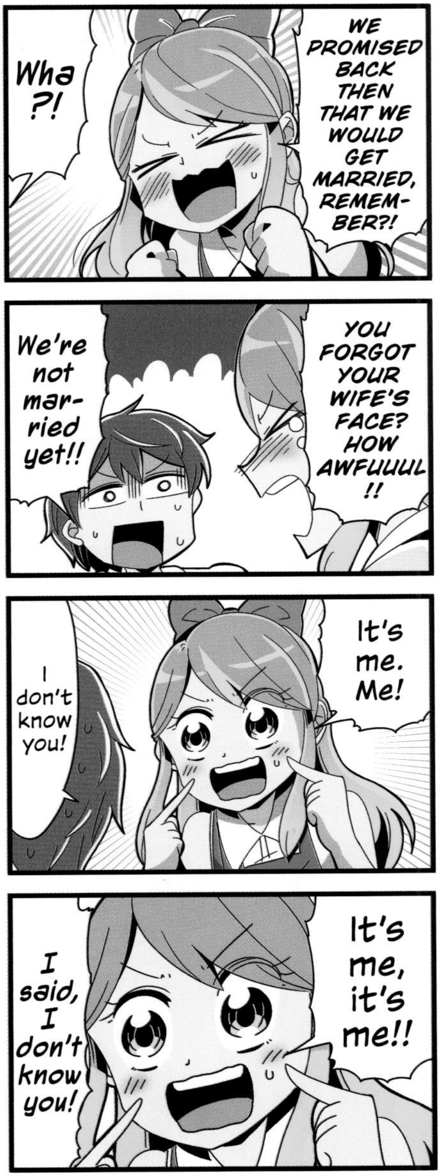
WE PROMISED BACK THEN THAT WE WOULD GET MARRIED, REMEMBER?!
Wha ?!
YOU FORGOT YOUR WIFE'S FACE? HOW AWFUUUL !!
We're not married yet!!
It's me. Me!
I don't know you!
It's me, it's me!!
I said, I don't know you!

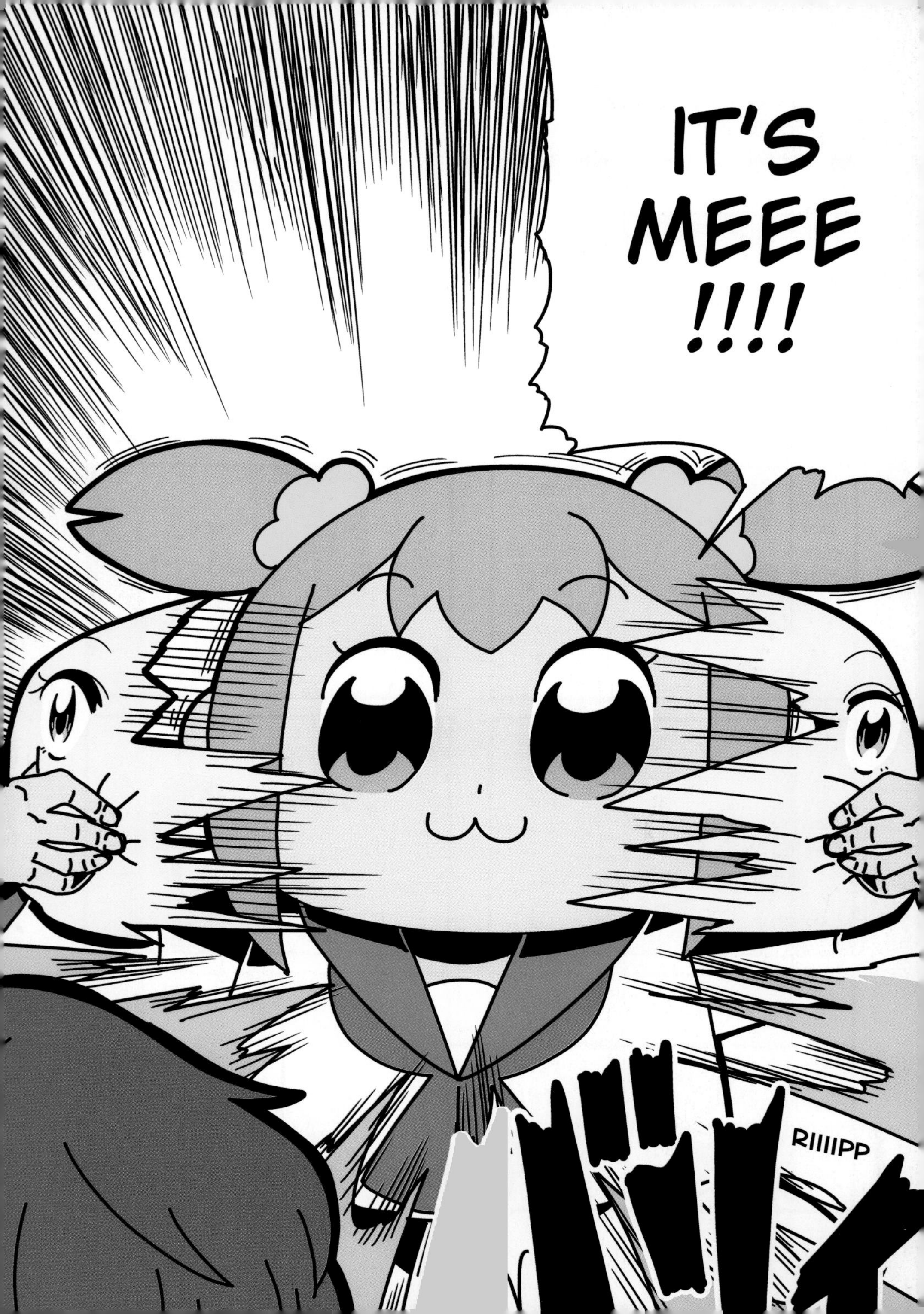
IT'S MEEE !!!!
RIIIIPP

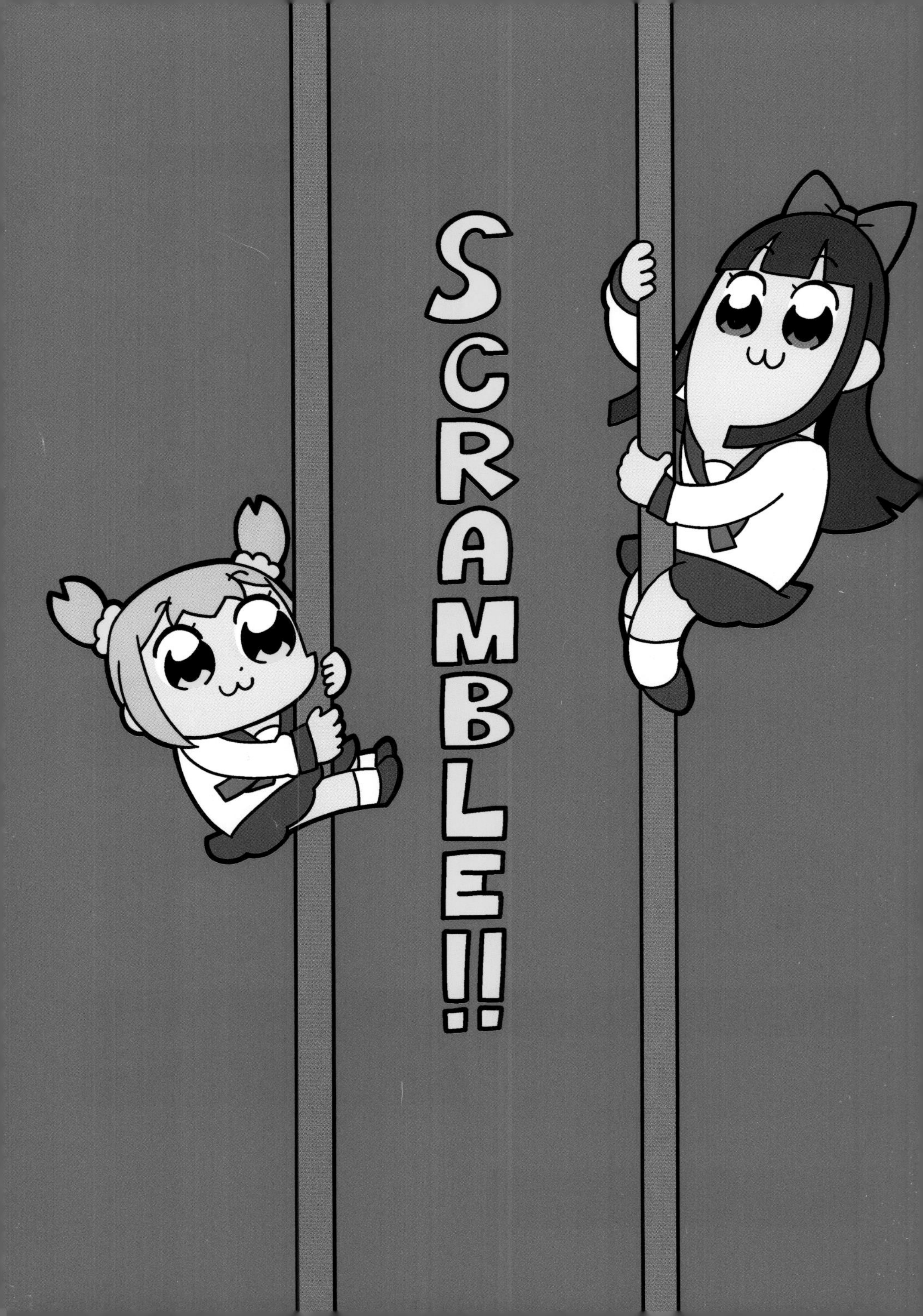
SCRAMBLE!!

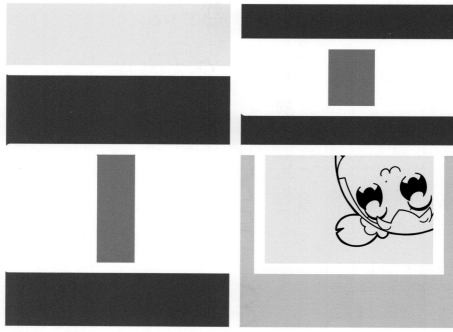

166

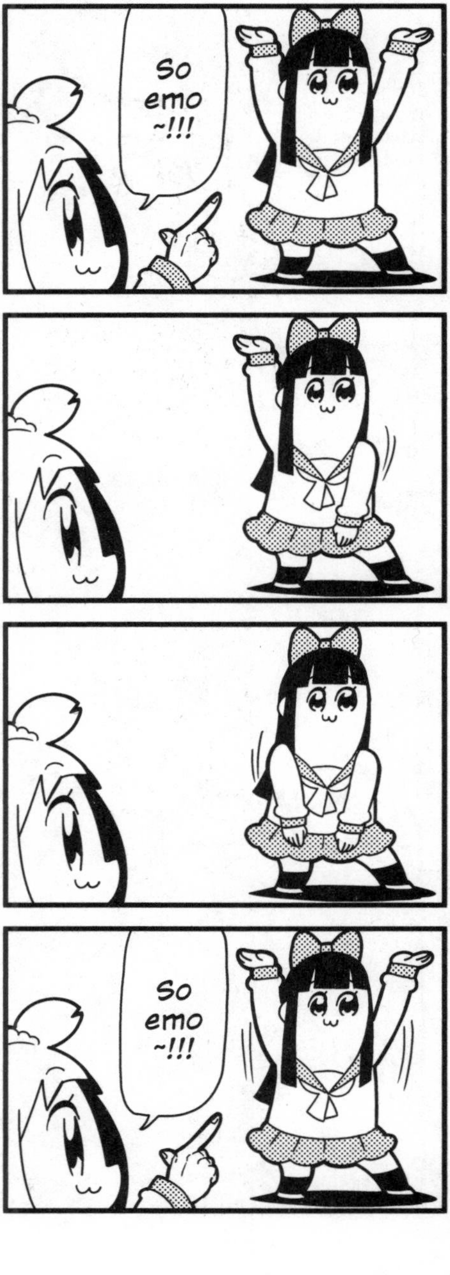
So emo ~!!!
So emo ~!!!

167

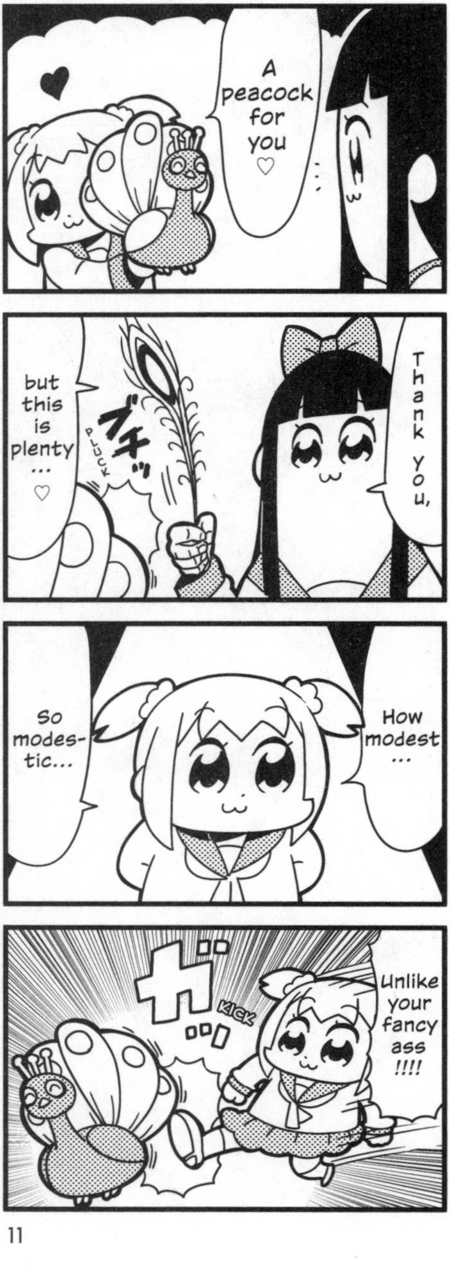
A peacock for you ♡
Thank you,
but this is plenty... ♡
ブチッ
PLUCK
How modest...
So modes-tic...
Unlike your fancy ass !!!!
KICK

I've run out of content to use for emojis, so I've resumed the serialization.

168

パカラッ
CLOPPITY
パカラッ
CLOPPITY
Hey, dahlings !! It's Valen-tine's Day!!!!
パカラッ
CLOPPITY
パカラッ
CLOPPITY
Buy some chocolat !!
ファサッ
SWISH
Huh ...?
パカラッ
CLOPPITY
Huh ...
パカラッ
CLOPPITY

169

Sliding along the banister is super fun~!!
WOOOOOOO
Move it, move it! Outta my way !!!
ゴロゴロゴロ...
ROLL
ROLL
ROLL...
BANG
!!!

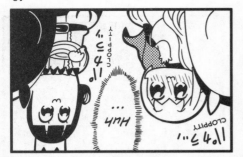

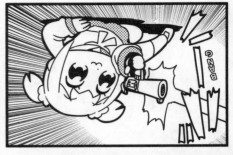

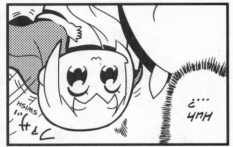

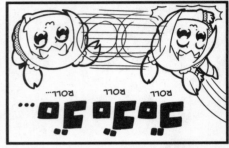

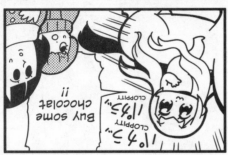

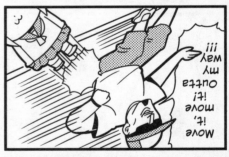

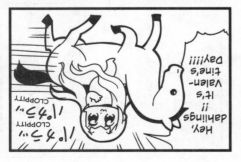

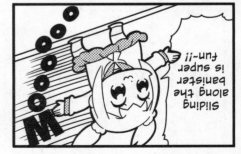

(170)

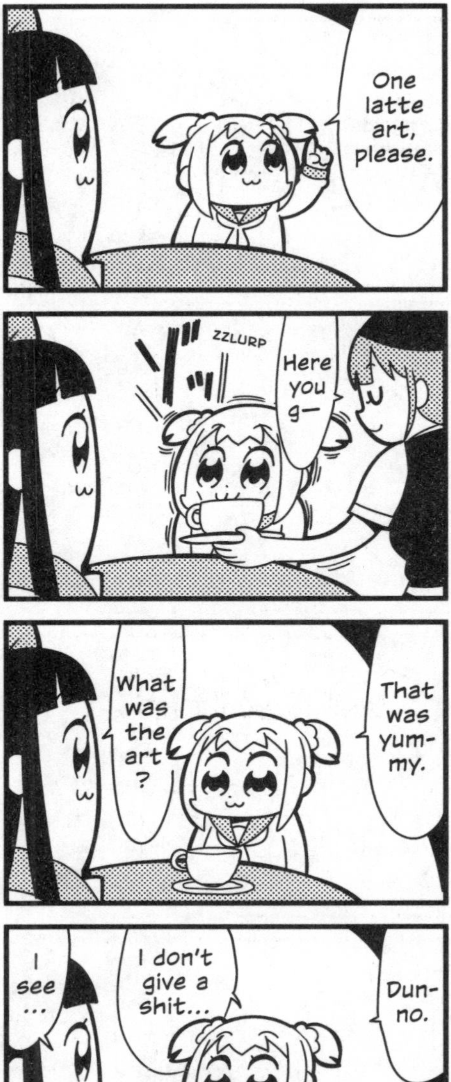
One latte art, please.
Here you g—
ZZLURP
That was yum-my.
What was the art?
Dun-no.
I don't give a shit...
I see...

(171)

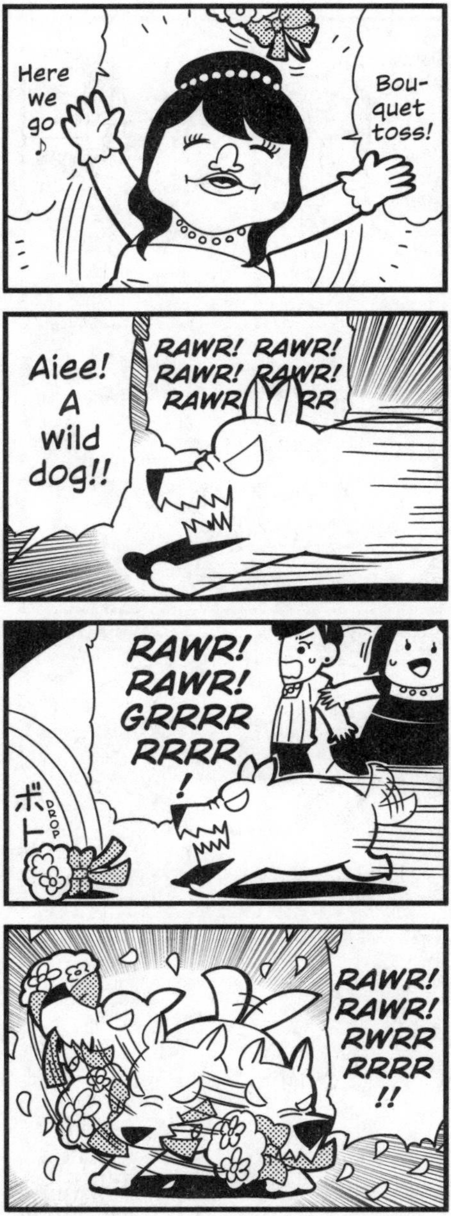
Bou-quet toss!
Here we go ♪
RAWR! RAWR! RAWR! RAWR! RAWRRR
Aiee! A wild dog!!
RAWR! RAWR! GRRRR RRRR!
ボト DROP
RAWR! RAWR! RWRR RRRR!!

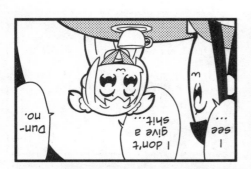

172

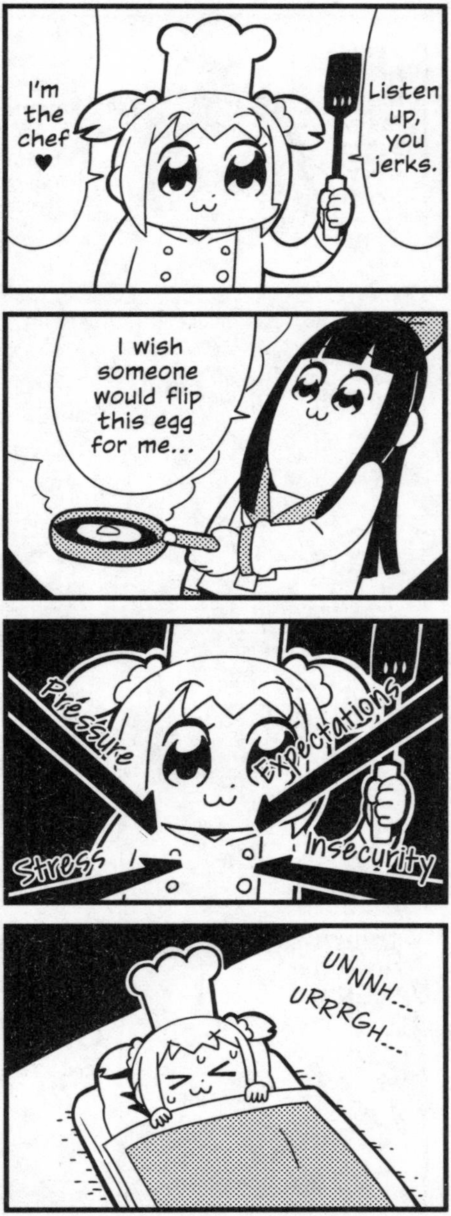
Listen up, you jerks.
I'm the chef ♥
I wish someone would flip this egg for me...
Pressure
Expectations
Stress
Insecurity
UNNNH... URRRGH...

173

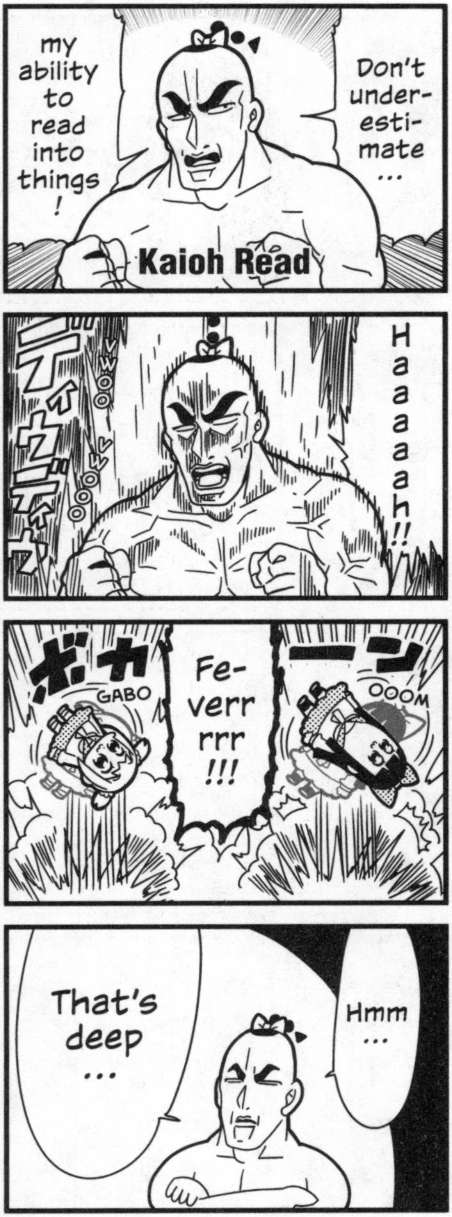
Don't under-esti-mate...
my ability to read into things!
Kaioh Read
Haaaaaah!!
ボカ
GABO
Fe-verr rrr!!!
ーーン
OOOM
Hmm...
That's deep...

174

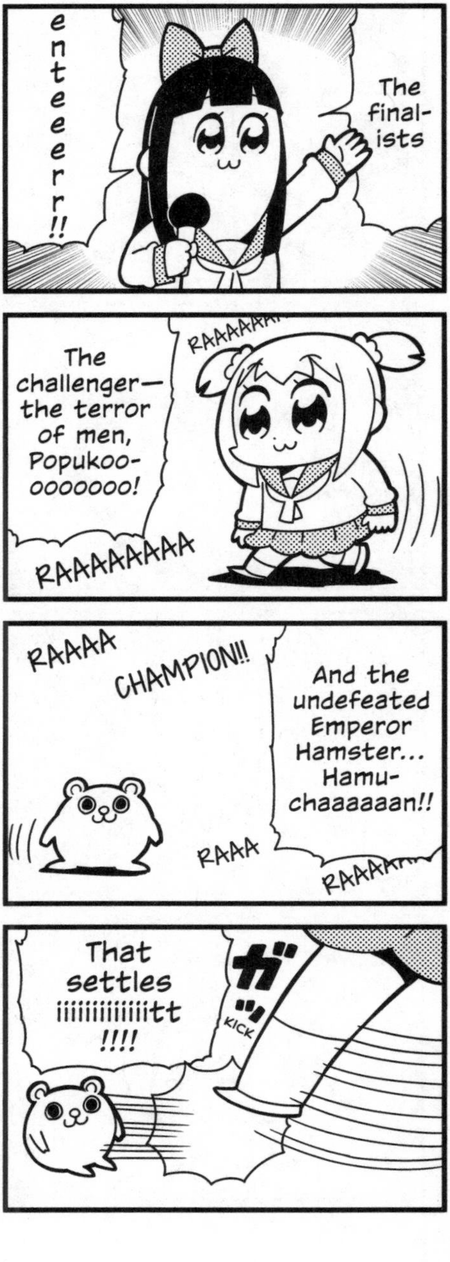
The final-
ists
enteeerr!!
The challenger—the terror of men, Popukoo-ooooooo!
RAAAAAA
RAAAAAAAA
And the undefeated Emperor Hamster... Hamu-chaaaaaan!!
RAAAA
CHAMPION!!
RAAA
That settles iiiiiiiiiiiiiitt !!!!
KICK

175

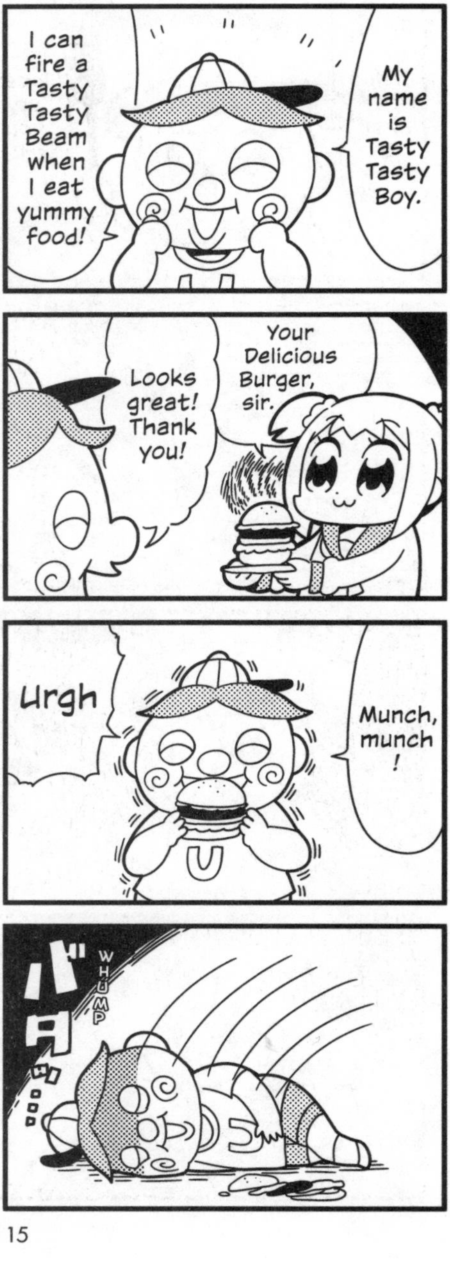
My name is Tasty Tasty Boy.
I can fire a Tasty Tasty Beam when I eat yummy food!
Your Delicious Burger, sir.
Looks great! Thank you!
Munch, munch!
Urgh
WHUMP

176

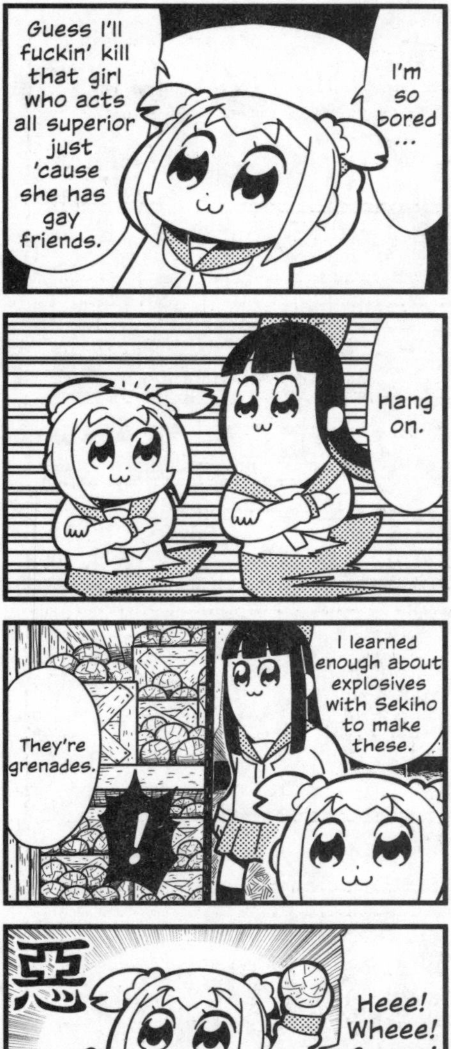
I'm so bored...
Guess I'll fuckin' kill that girl who acts all superior just 'cause she has gay friends.
Hang on.
I learned enough about explosives with Sekiho to make these.
They're grenades.
!
Heee! Wheee! Goooo!
悪
BAM

177

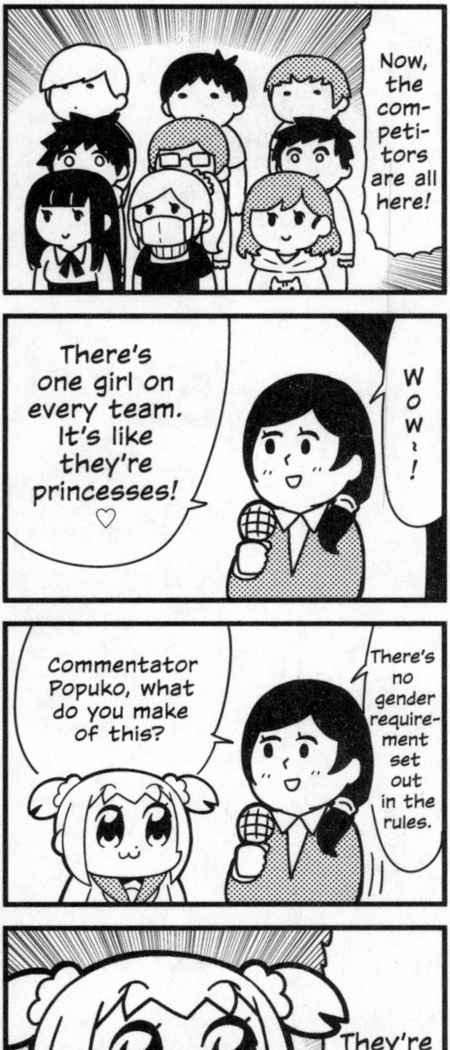
Now, the competitors are all here!
Wow~!
There's one girl on every team. It's like they're princesses! ♡
There's no gender requirement set out in the rules.
Commentator Popuko, what do you make of this?
They're trolling!

To be continued...

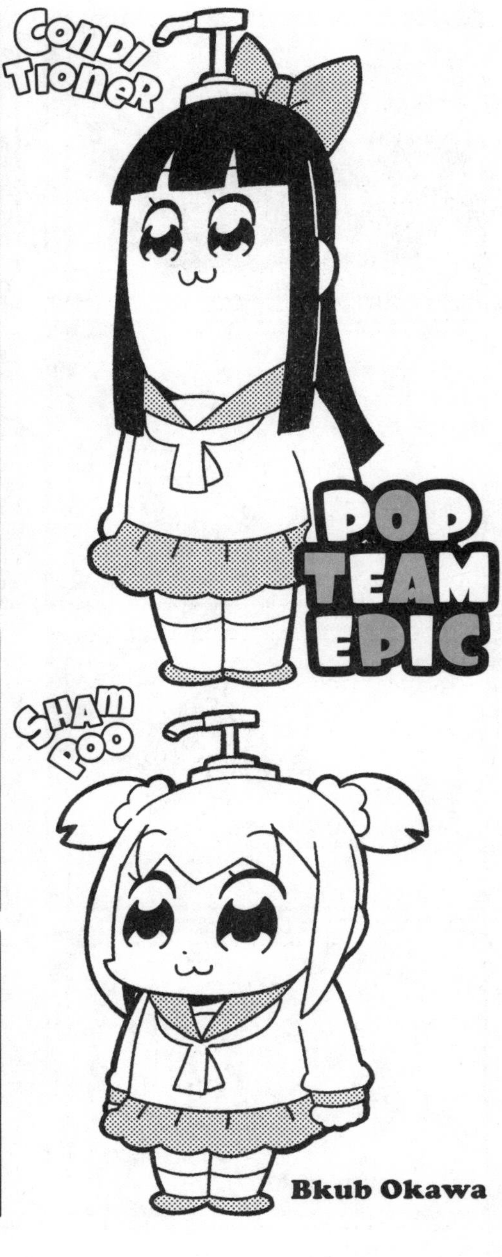
CONDITIONER
POP TEAM EPIC
SHAMPOO
Bkub Okawa

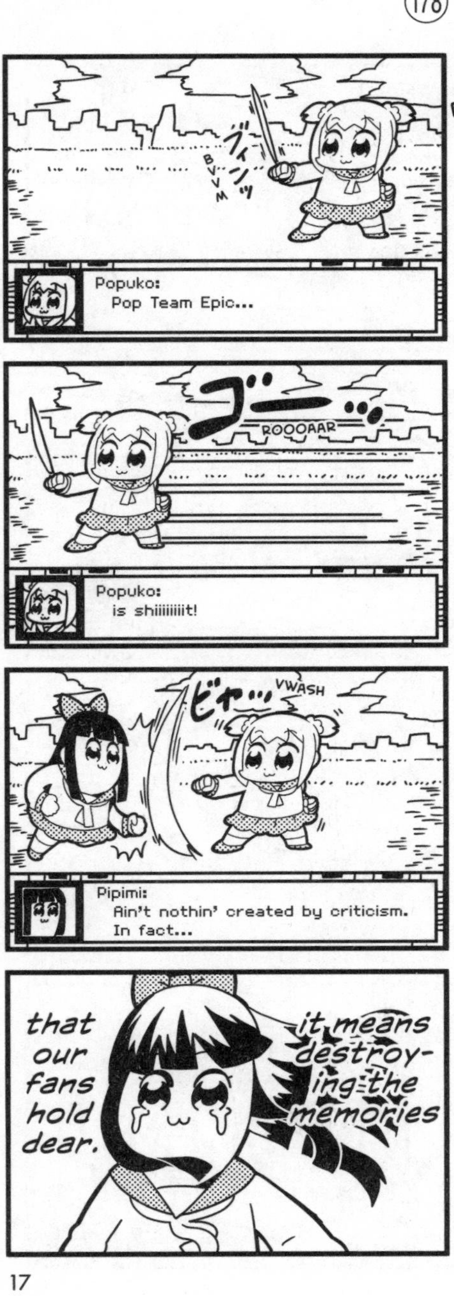
178
BVVM
Popuko:
Pop Team Epic...
ROOOAAR
Popuko:
is shiiiiiiit!
VWASH
Pipimi:
Ain't nothin' created by criticism.
In fact...
it means destroying the memories
that our fans hold dear.

179

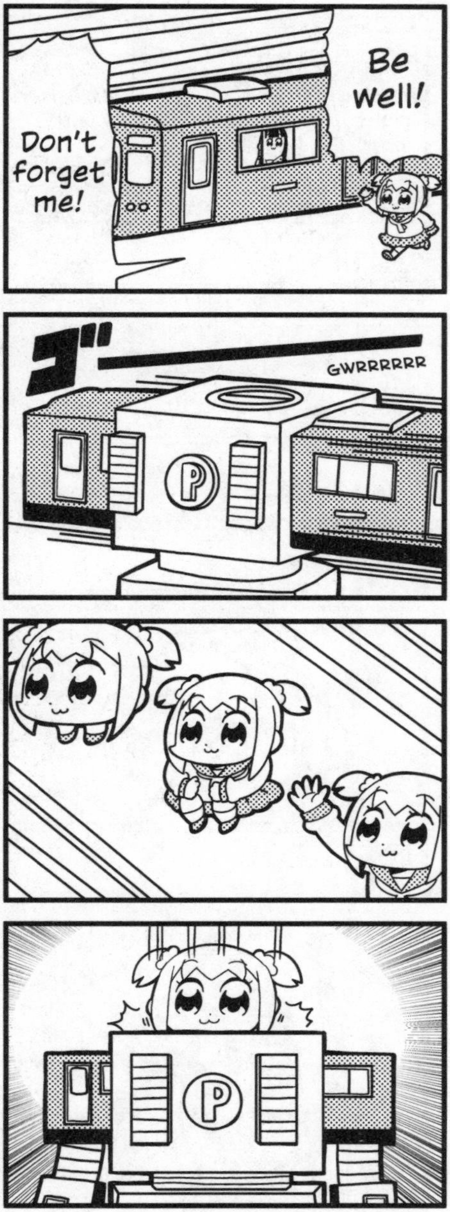
Be well!
Don't forget me!
ゴーー
GWRRRRRR

180

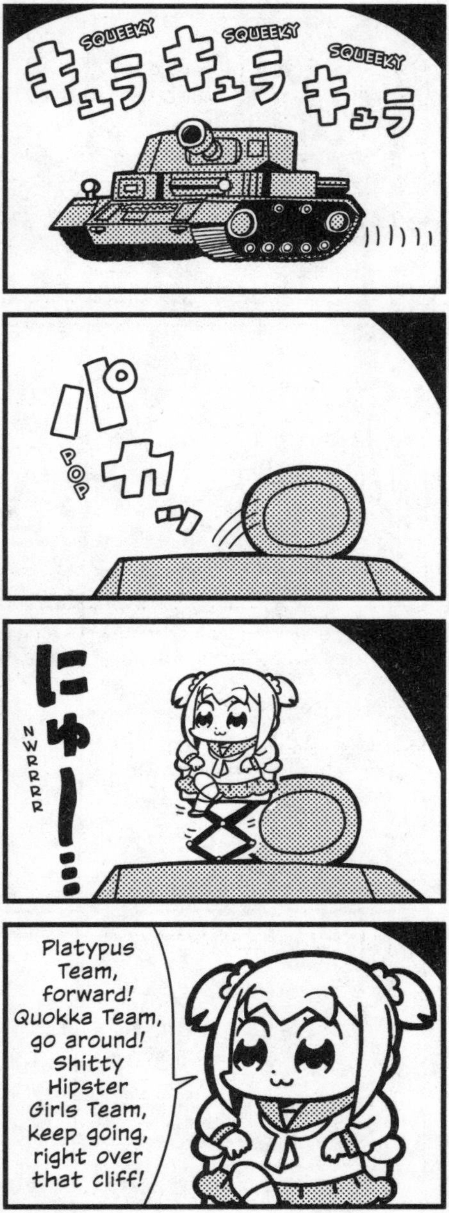
キュラ キュラ キュラ
SQUEEKY SQUEEKY SQUEEKY
パカッ
POP
にゅーー…
NWRRRR
Platypus Team, forward! Quokka Team, go around! Shitty Hipster Girls Team, keep going, right over that cliff!

181

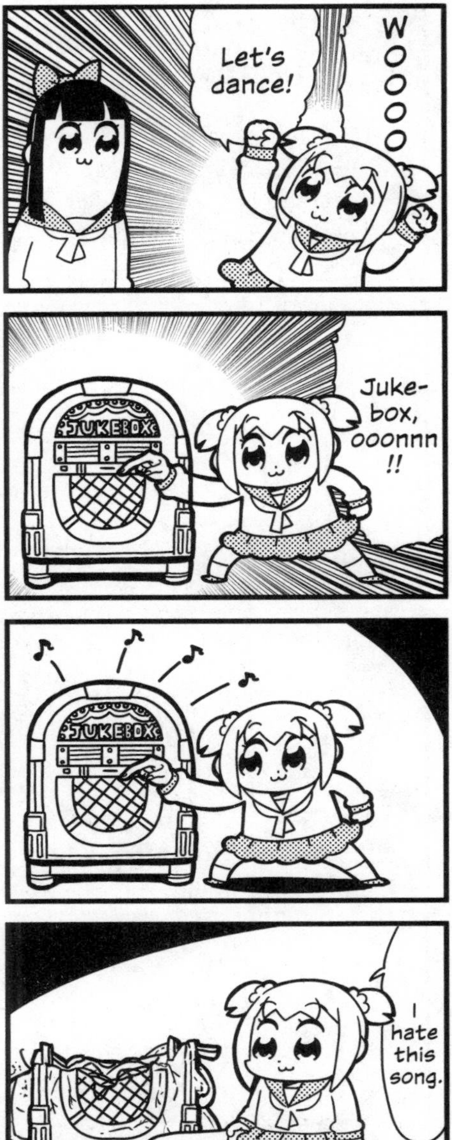

Let's dance!
WOOOOO
Juke-box, ooonnn !!
I hate this song.

182

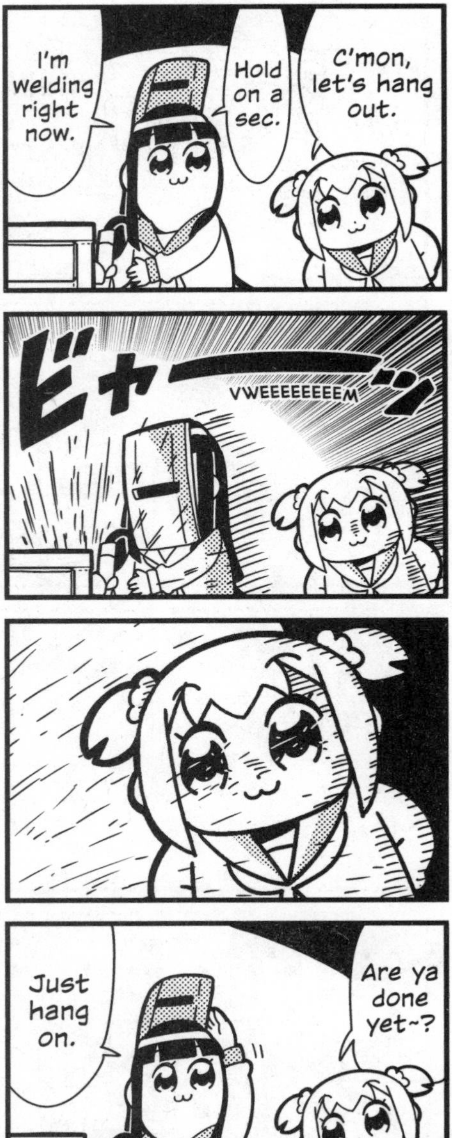

C'mon, let's hang out.
Hold on a sec.
I'm welding right now.
ビャーーッ
VWEEEEEEEEM
Are ya done yet~?
Just hang on.

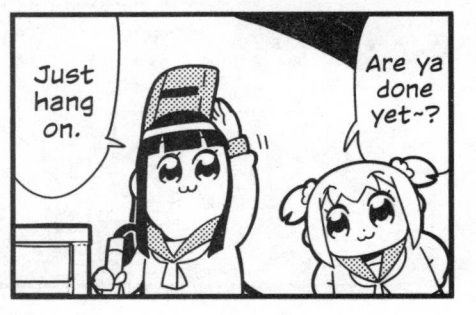

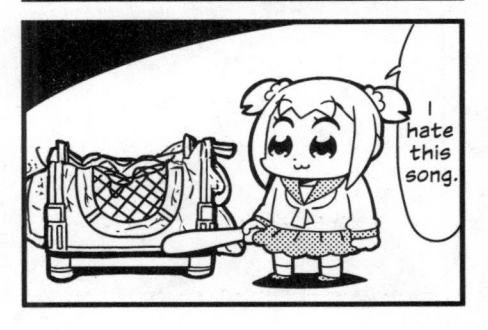

183

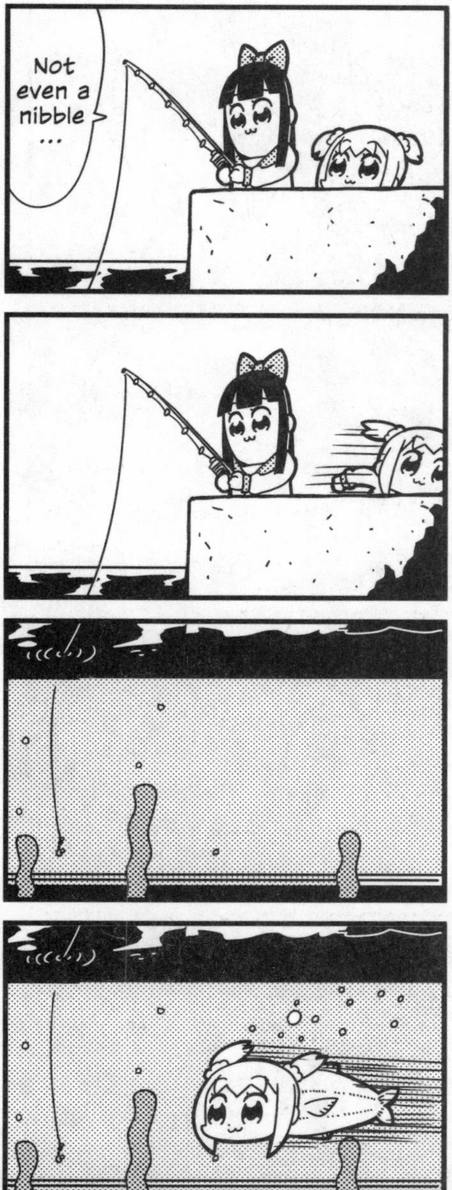
Not even a nibble …

184

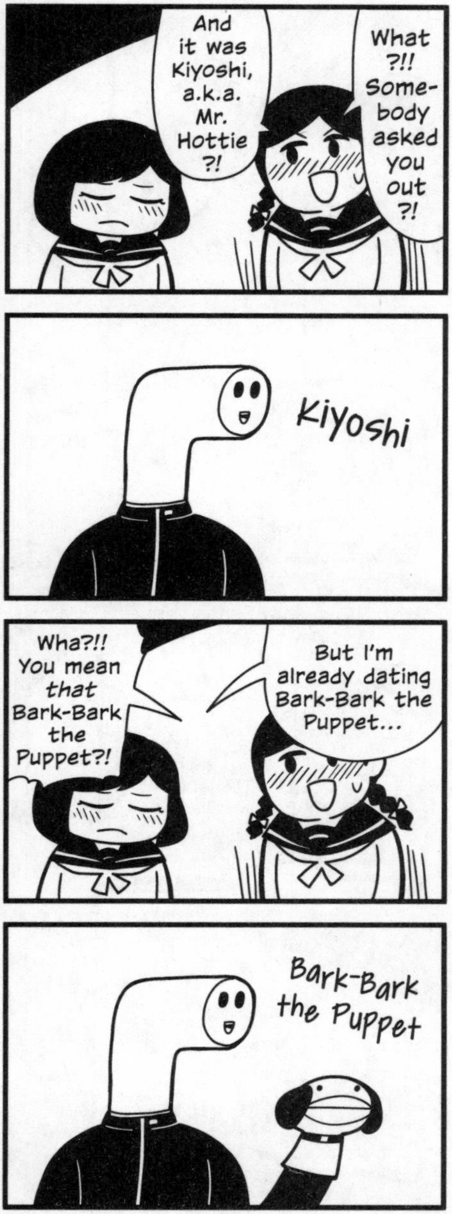
What?!! Somebody asked you out?!
And it was Kiyoshi, a.k.a. Mr. Hottie?!
Kiyoshi
But I'm already dating Bark-Bark the Puppet…
Wha?!! You mean that Bark-Bark the Puppet?!
Bark-Bark the Puppet

185

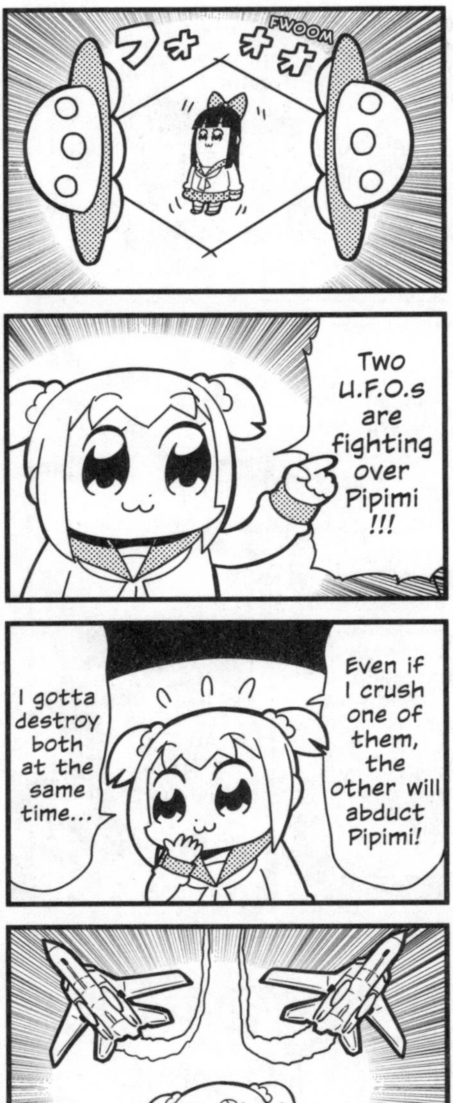
フォオオ
FWOOM
Two U.F.O.s are fighting over Pipimi !!!
Even if I crush one of them, the other will abduct Pipimi!
I gotta destroy both at the same time...
フィーン
VWEE
EEEM

186

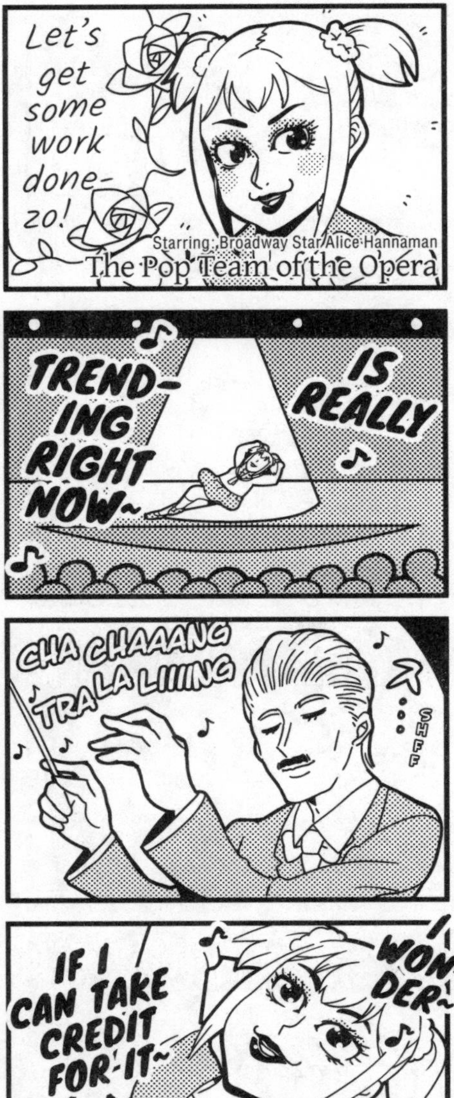
Let's get some work done-zo!
Starring: Broadway Star Alice Hannaman
The Pop Team of the Opera
IS REALLY
TRENDING RIGHT NOW~
CHA CHAAANG TRA LA LIIIING
ス…
SHFF
I WONDER~
IF I CAN TAKE CREDIT FOR IT~

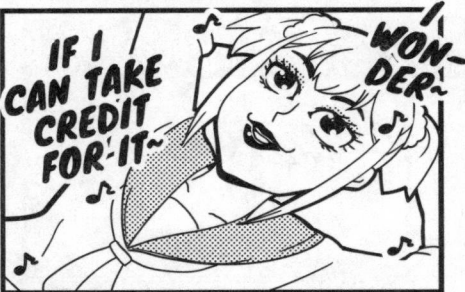

187

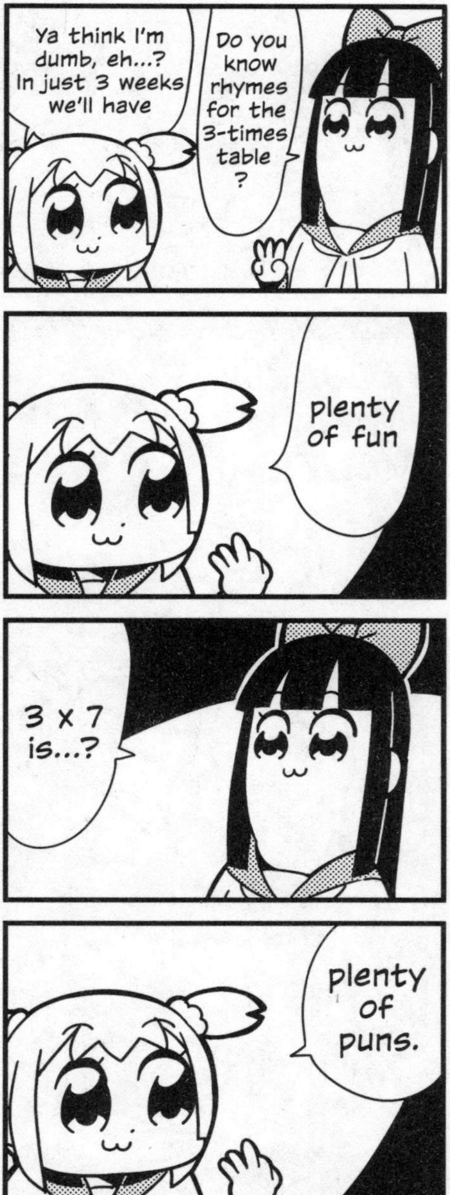
Do you know rhymes for the 3-times table ?
Ya think I'm dumb, eh...? In just 3 weeks we'll have
plenty of fun
3 x 7 is...?
plenty of puns.

●It seems we're selling merch. Awesome.

188

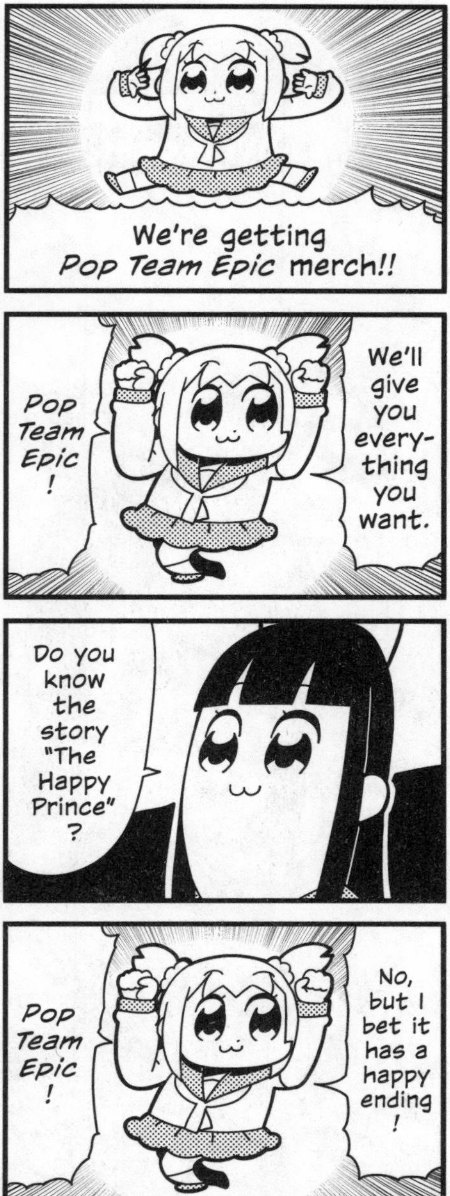
We're getting *Pop Team Epic* merch!!
We'll give you every-thing you want.
Pop Team Epic !
Do you know the story "The Happy Prince" ?
No, but I bet it has a happy ending !
Pop Team Epic !

To be continued...

Bogusevic didn't want to collaborate with us...

POP TEAM EPIC

Bkub Okawa

He might do it if you put in more work, Popuko. ♡

Cute~♡

GASP

3.

23

190

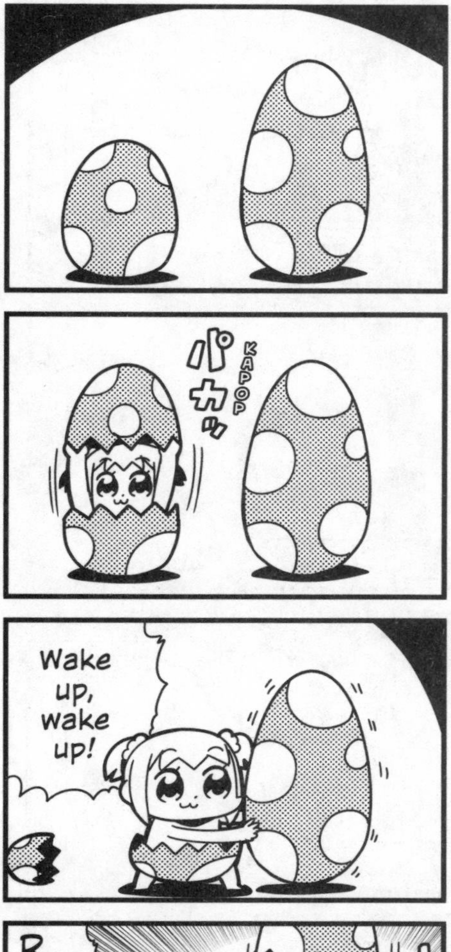
パカッ
KAPOP
Wake up, wake up!
Raaah!
パカッ
KAPOP

191

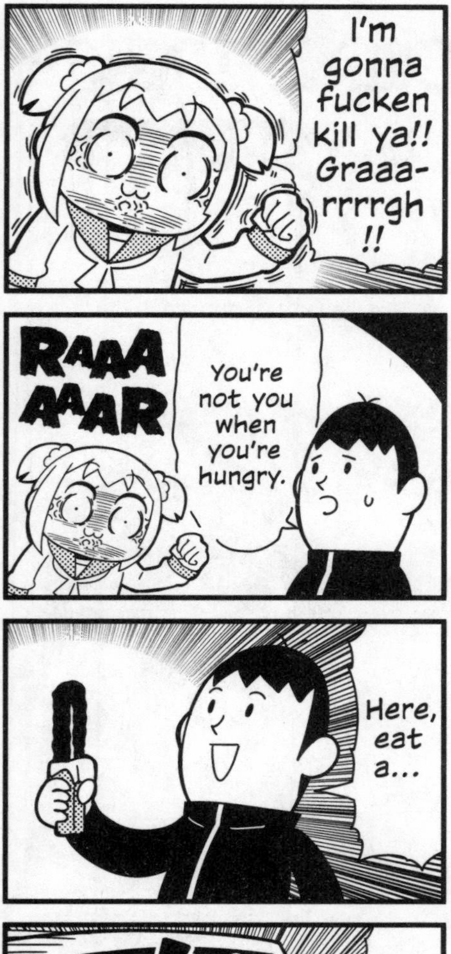
I'm gonna fucken kill ya!! Graaa-rrrrgh !!
RAAA AAAR
You're not you when you're hungry.
Here, eat a...
ドガシャ
GASMAASH
Snic —

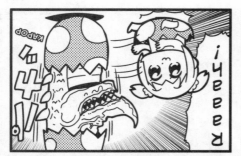

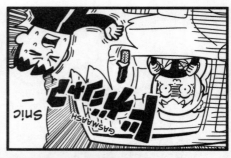

192

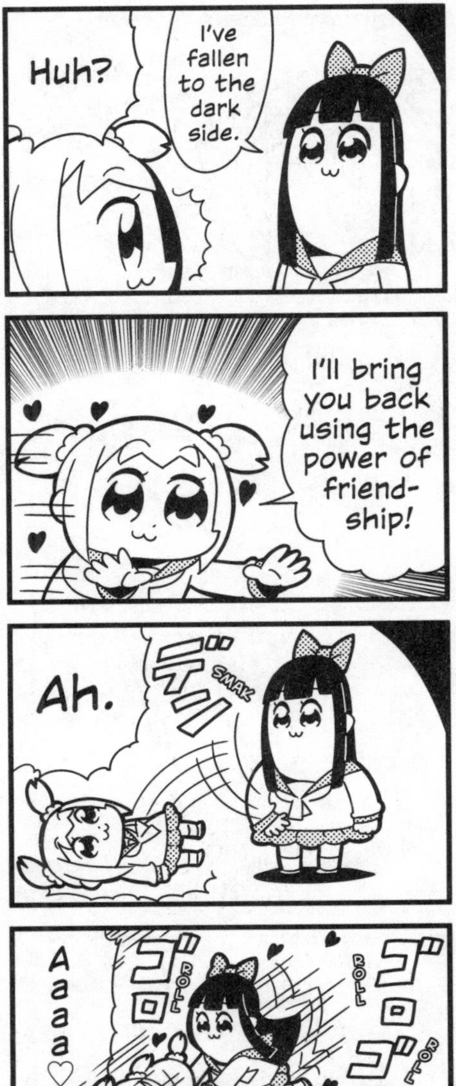
Huh?
I've fallen to the dark side.
I'll bring you back using the power of friend-ship!
Ah.
デシ
SMAK
Aaaa♡
ゴロ
ROLL
ゴロ
ROLL
ゴロ
ROLL
ゴロ
ROLL

193

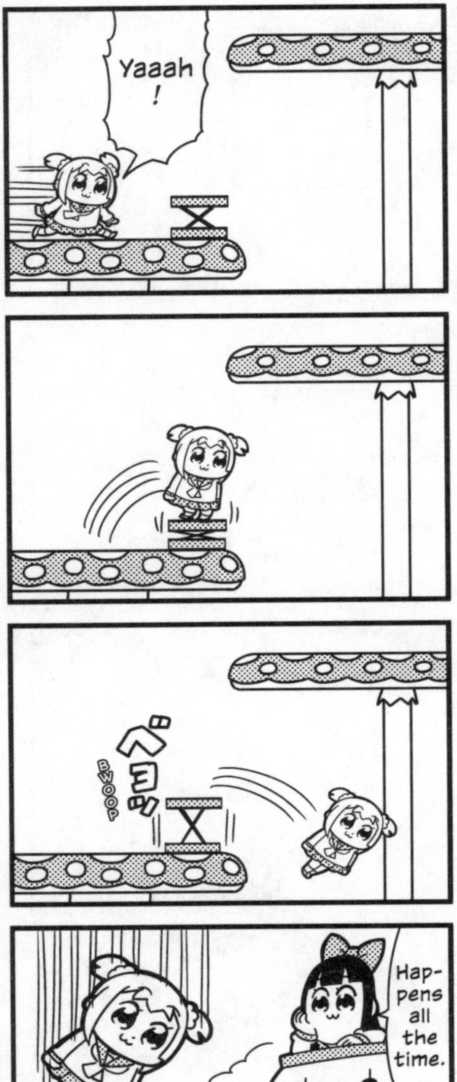
Yaaah!
べヨッ
BWOOP
Hap-pens all the time.

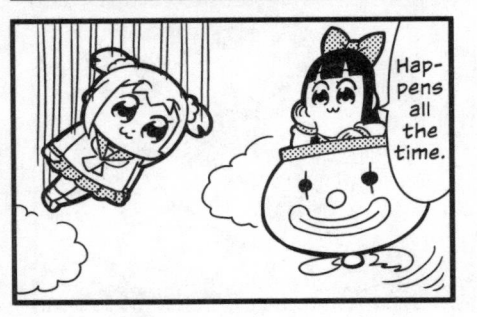

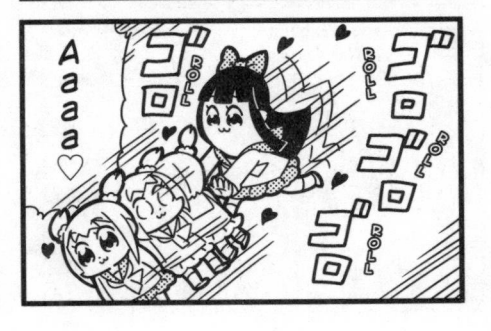

194

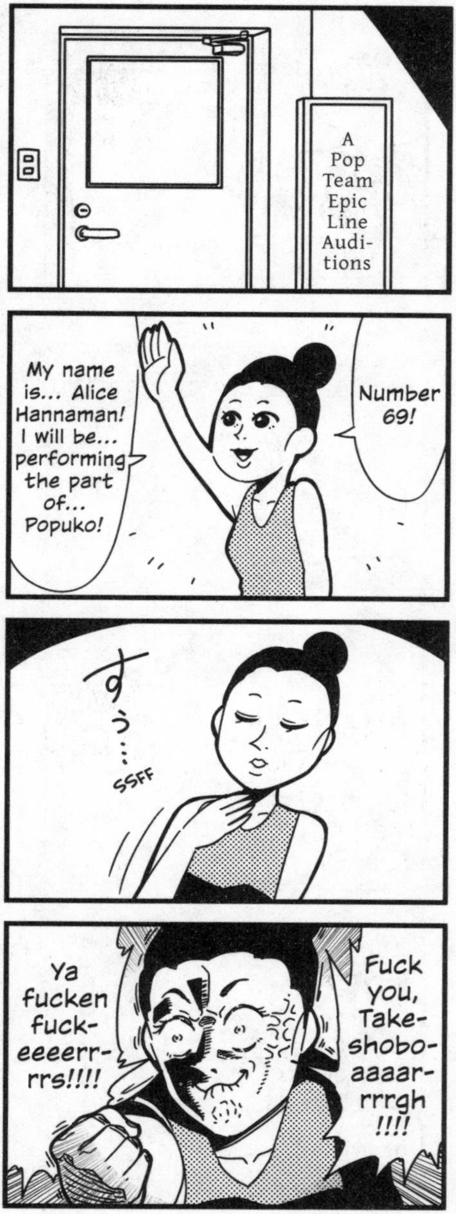
A Pop Team Epic Line Auditions
Number 69!
My name is... Alice Hannaman! I will be... performing the part of... Popuko!
すぅ…
SSFF
Fuck you, Take-shobo-aaaar-rrrgh !!!!
Ya fucken fuck-eeeerr-rrs!!!!

195

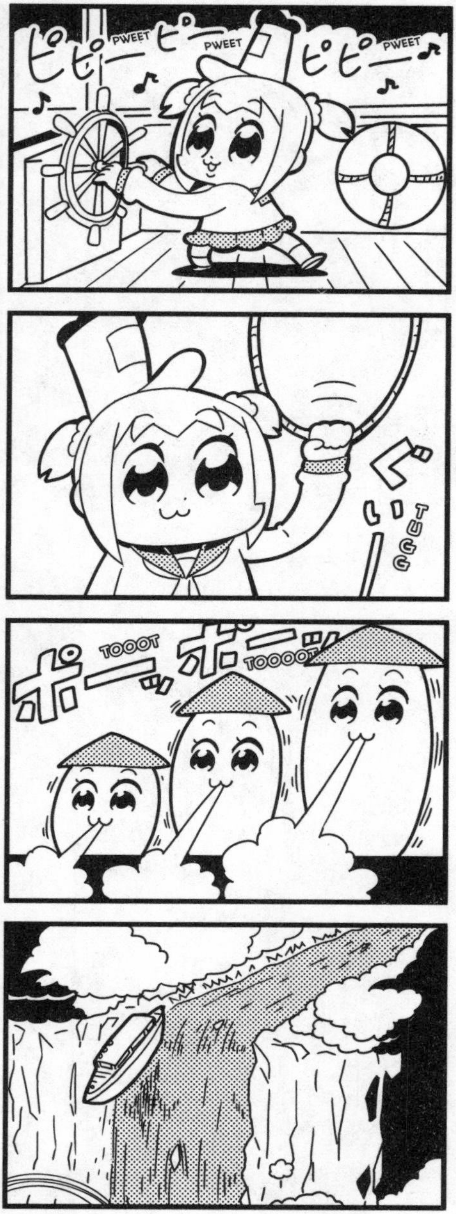
ピピー
PWEET
ピー
PWEET
ピピー
PWEET
ぐい
TUGG
ポーッ
TOOOT
ポーッ
TOOOOT

196

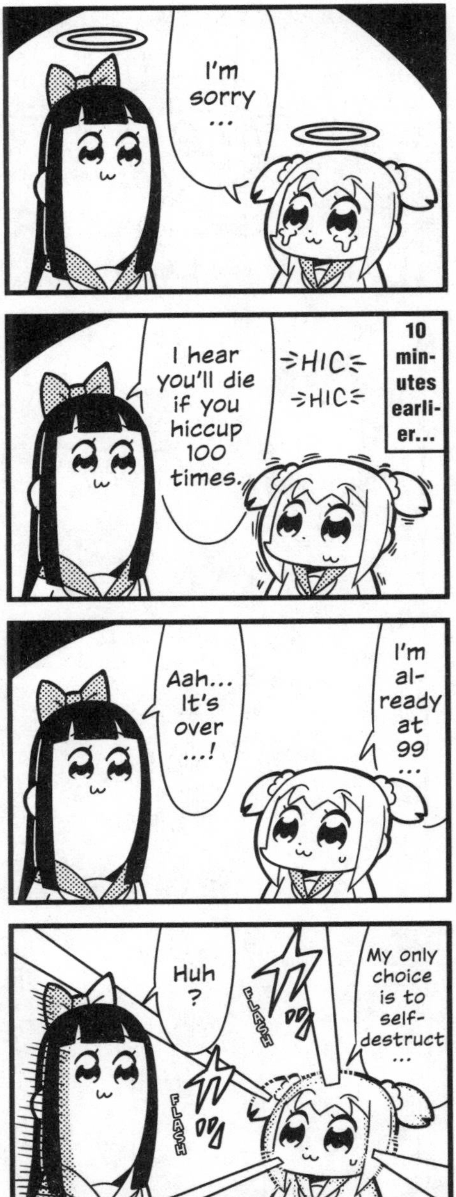
I'm sorry ...
10 min-utes earli-er...
HIC
HIC
I hear you'll die if you hiccup 100 times.
I'm al-ready at 99 ...
Aah... It's over ...!
My only choice is to self-destruct ...
FLASH
FLASH
Huh ?

197

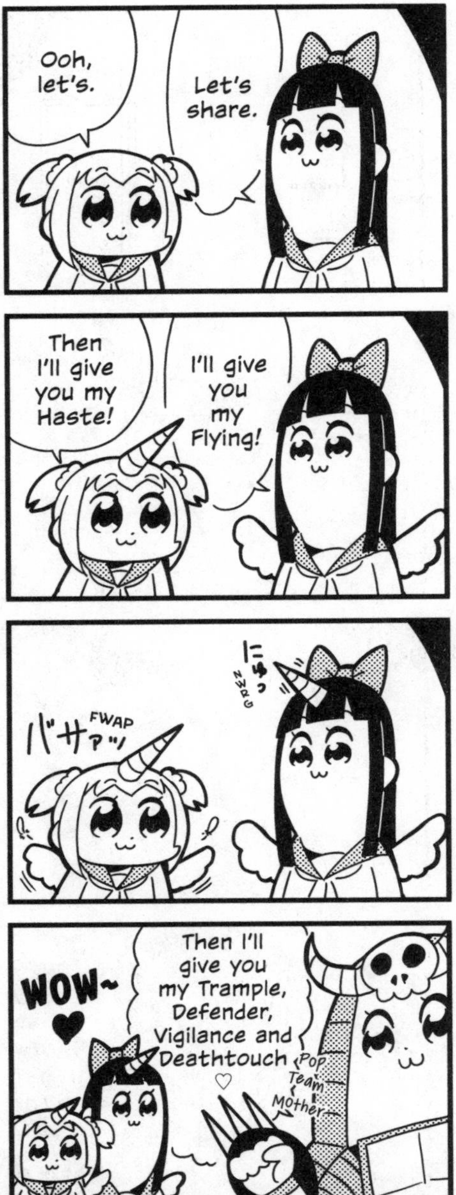
Let's share.
Ooh, let's.
I'll give you my Flying!
Then I'll give you my Haste!
にゅっ
NWRG
バサァッ
FWAP
Then I'll give you my Trample, Defender, Vigilance and Deathtouch ♡
Pop Team Mother
WOW~ ♥

198

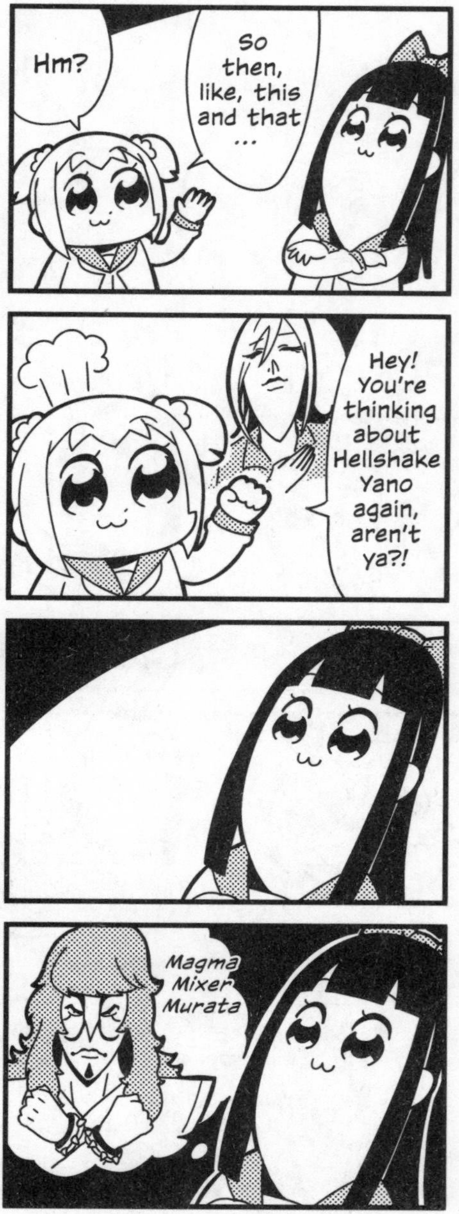
So then, like, this and that ...
Hm?
Hey! You're thinking about Hellshake Yano again, aren't ya?!
Magma Mixer Murata

199

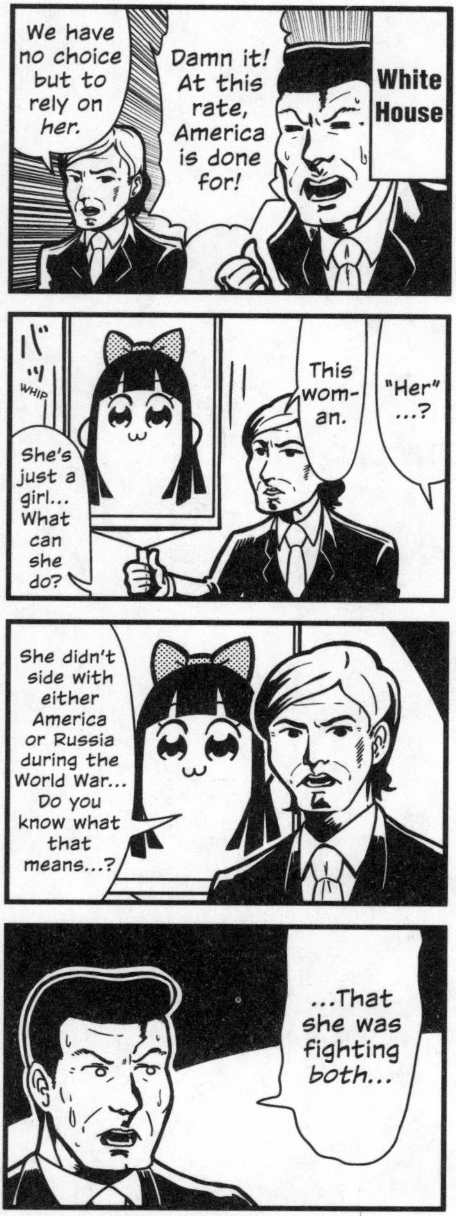
White House
Damn it! At this rate, America is done for!
We have no choice but to rely on her.
"Her" ...?
This wom-an.
WHIP
She's just a girl... What can she do?
She didn't side with either America or Russia during the World War... Do you know what that means...?
...That she was fighting both...

To be continued...

Are you as dumb as a door-nail?
Ya think I'm dumb, eh...?
Leg Ba-zoo-ka!
KICK

パカラッ
CLOPPITY
パカラッ
CLOPPITY
In the whirlpool we'll go deeper In this world that's getting cheaper
I wanna ride on a white horse~ I want to ride on a white horse~!
パカラッ
CLOPPITY
パカラッ
CLOPPITY
Awright, we're starting up the shit manga again.
Huh? What're ya lookin' at? This ain't a show! Beat it! Scram !!

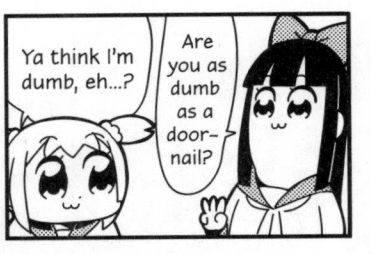

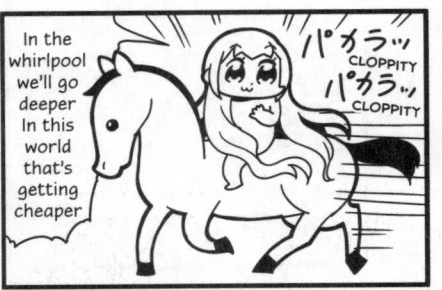

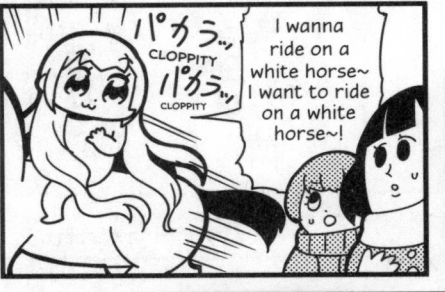

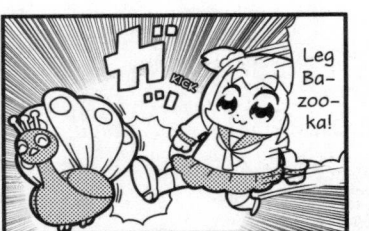

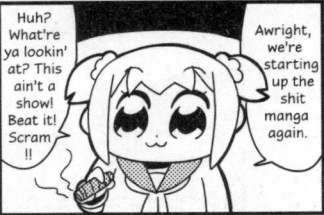

Heey.
チャキッ CHAK
サ SHFF サ SHFF サ SHFF サ SHFF サ
She's totally Z-targeted and getting closer.
チャキッ CHAK
Want love~? Get closer ~♪
Hold her hand, be forward ~♪
You want love? Get closer~♪

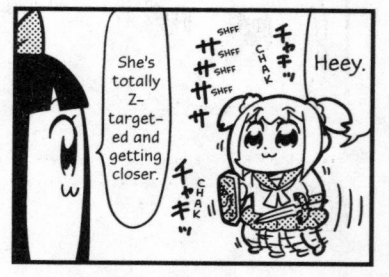

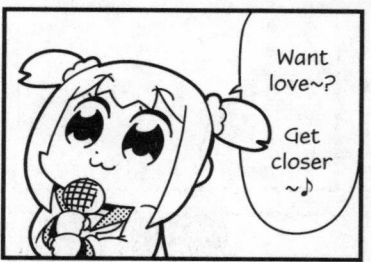

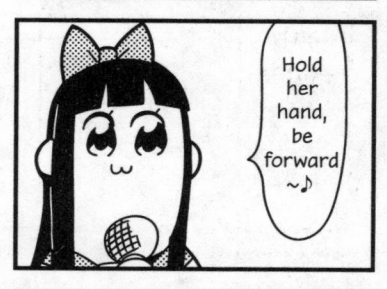

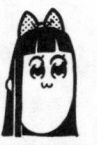

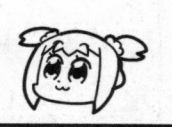

POP TEAM EPIC

Bkub Okawa

Would you have any Grey Poupon ?!
?
Cthulhu hasn't got any Grey Poupon.
Your only option is to fight him.
← ALLY
← ALLY
VS

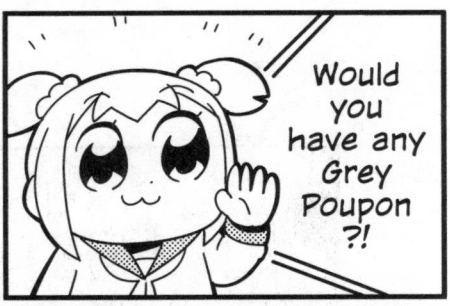

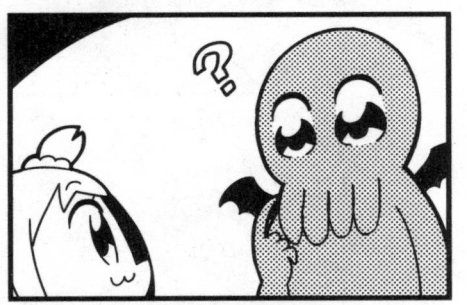

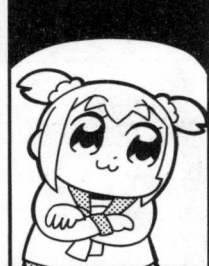

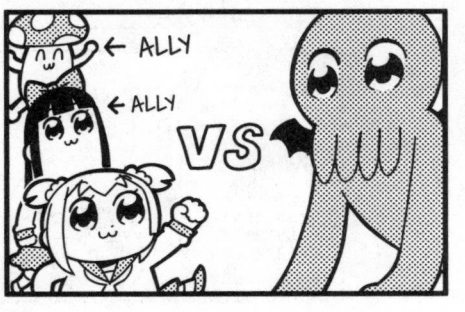

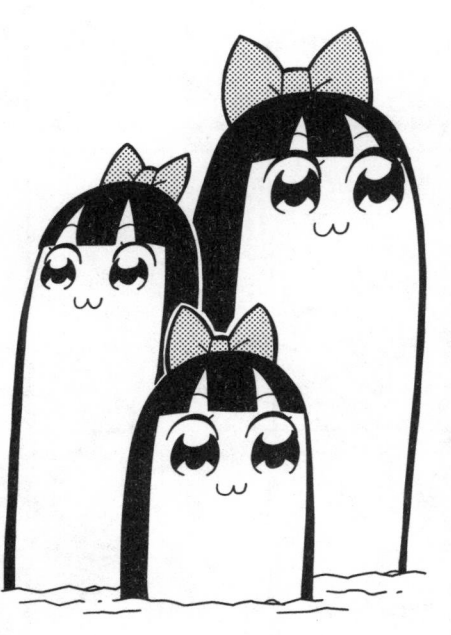

201

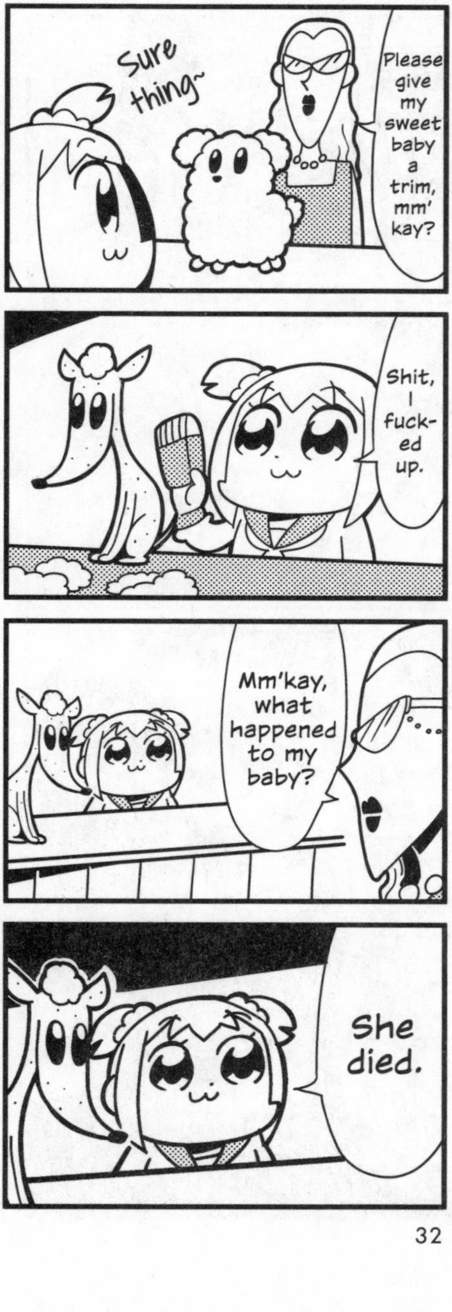
Please give my sweet baby a trim, mm' kay?
Sure thing~
Shit, I fuck-ed up.
Mm'kay, what happened to my baby?
She died.

202

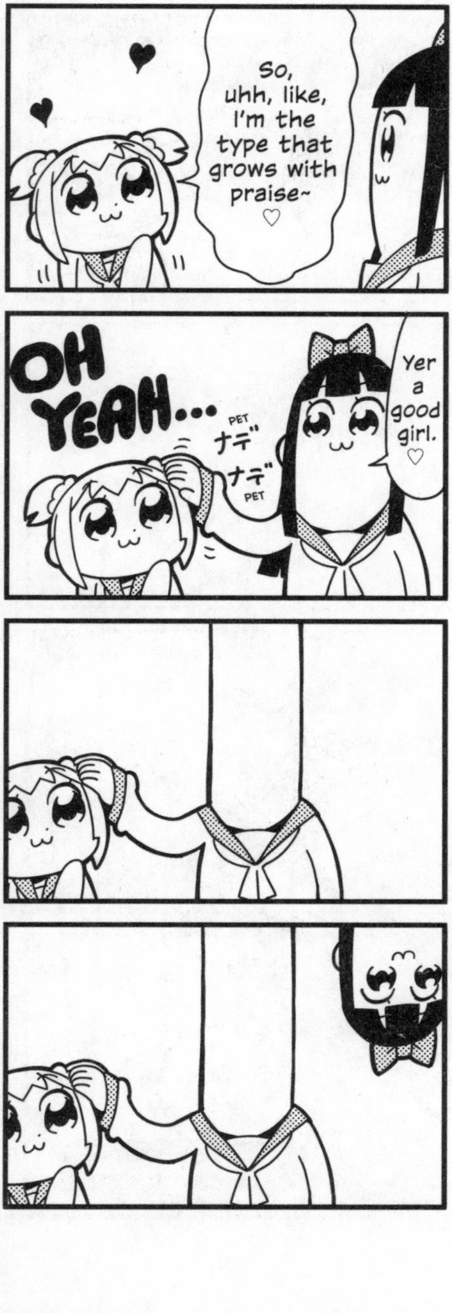
So, uhh, like, I'm the type that grows with praise~ ♡
Yer a good girl. ♡
OH YEAH...
ナデ PET
ナデ PET

203

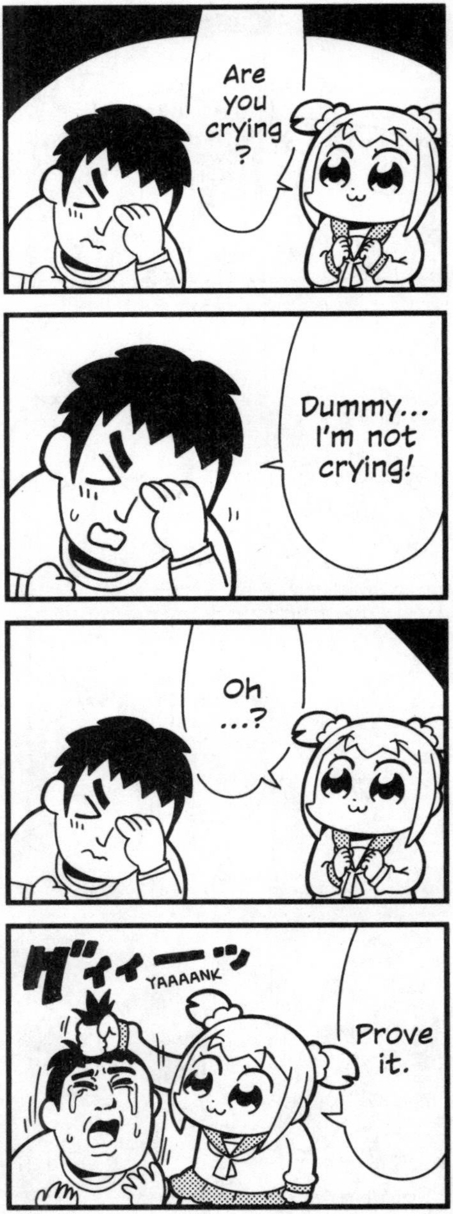

Are you crying ?
Dummy... I'm not crying!
Oh ...?
YAAAANK
Prove it.

204

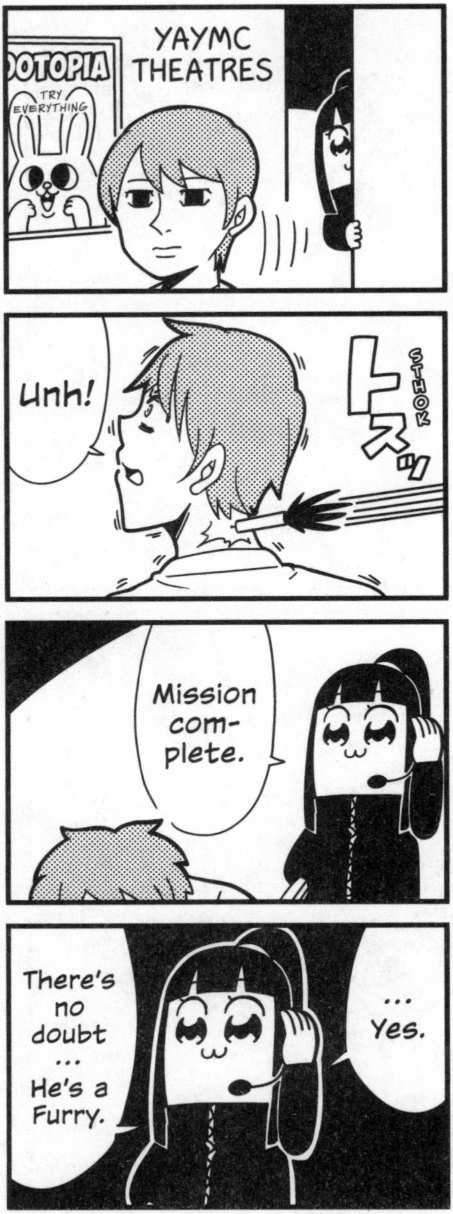

YAYMC THEATRES
OOTOPIA
TRY EVERYTHING
トスッ
STHOK
Unh!
Mission com- plete.
There's no doubt ... He's a Furry.
... Yes.

205

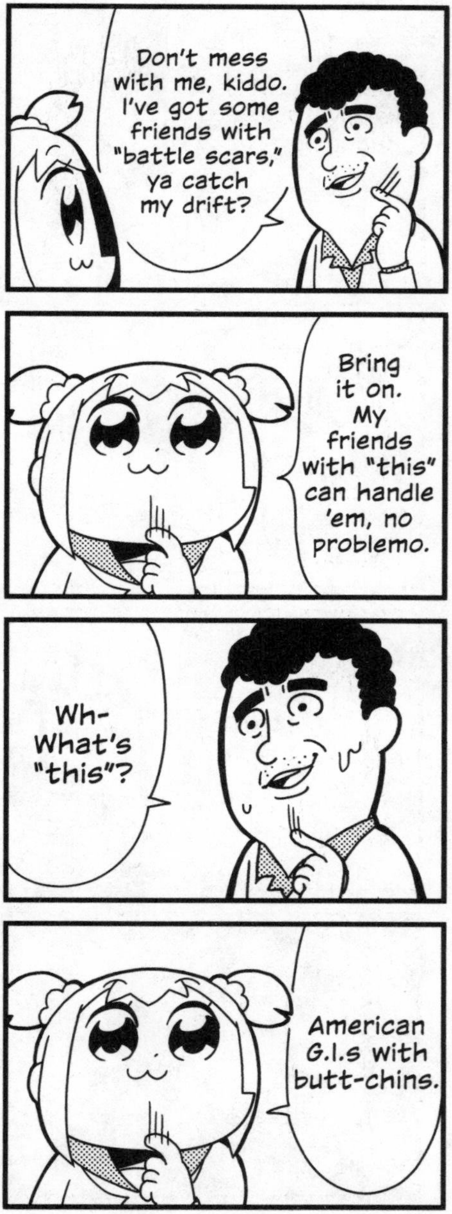
Don't mess with me, kiddo. I've got some friends with "battle scars," ya catch my drift?
Bring it on. My friends with "this" can handle 'em, no problemo.
Wh- What's "this"?
American G.I.s with butt-chins.

206

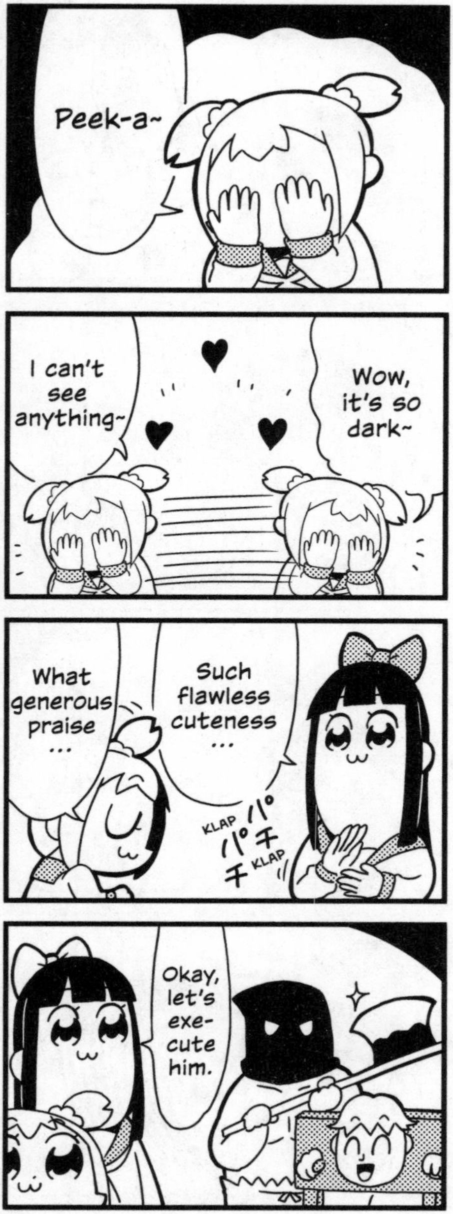
Peek-a~
Wow, it's so dark~
I can't see anything~
Such flawless cuteness ...
What generous praise ...
パチ KLAP
パチ KLAP
Okay, let's exe-cute him.

207

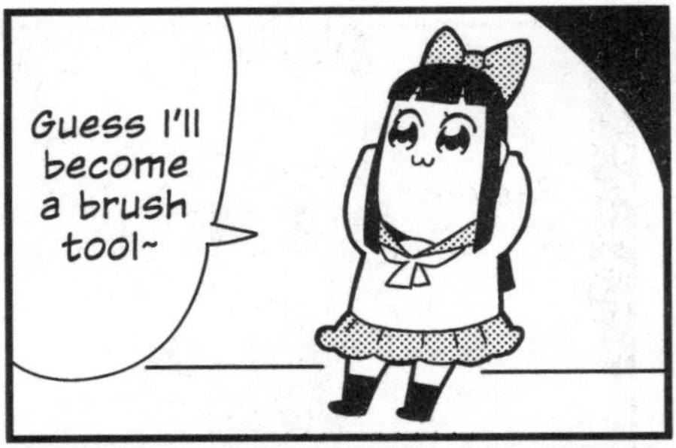
Guess I'll become a brush tool~

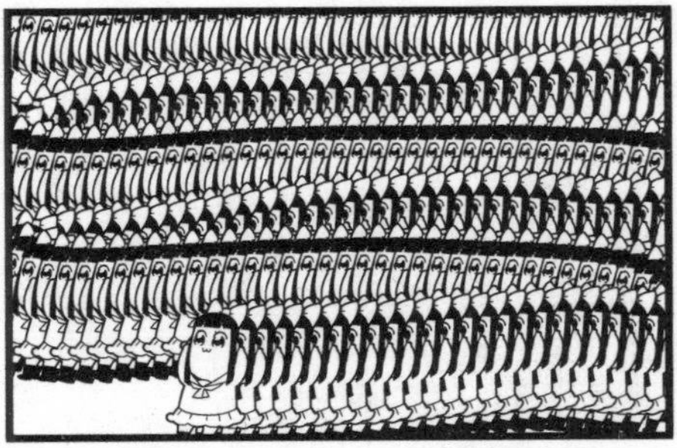

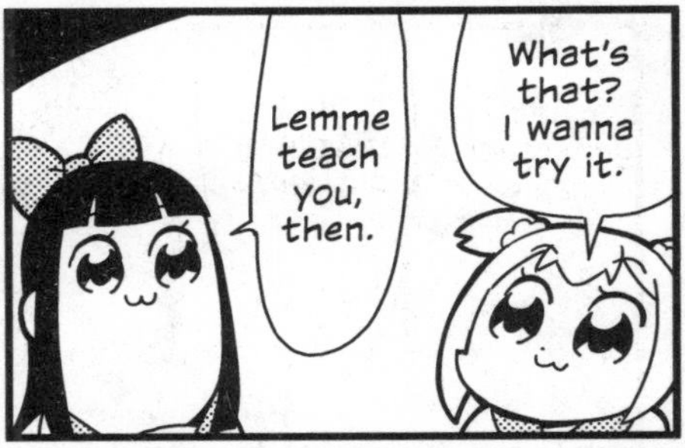
What's that? I wanna try it.
Lemme teach you, then.

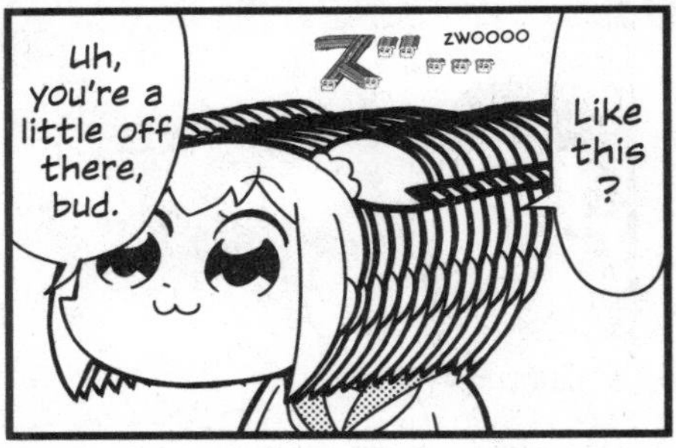
ZWOOOO
Like this ?
Uh, you're a little off there, bud.

208

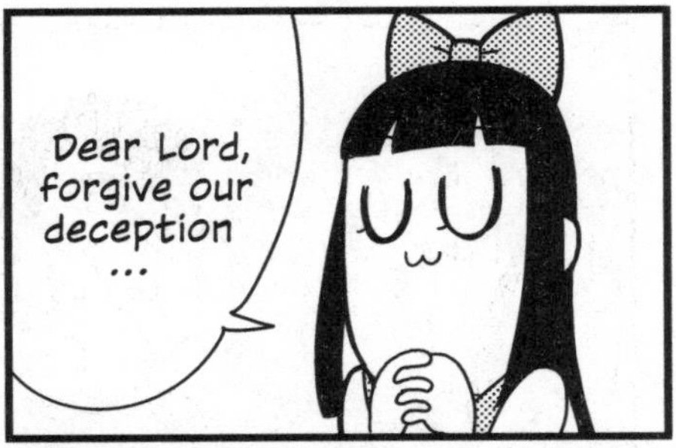
Dear Lord, forgive our deception ...

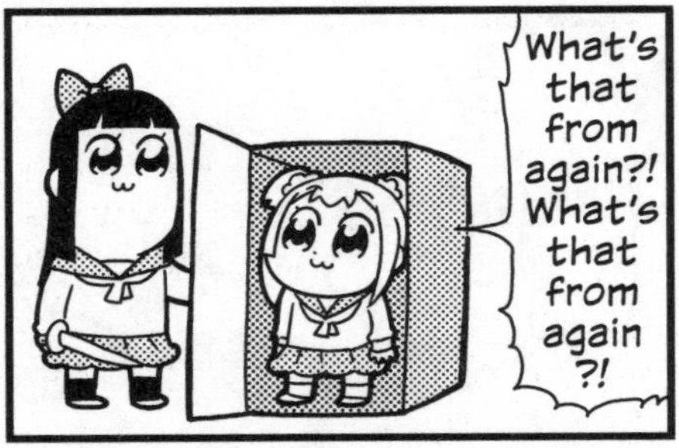
What's that from again?! What's that from again ?!

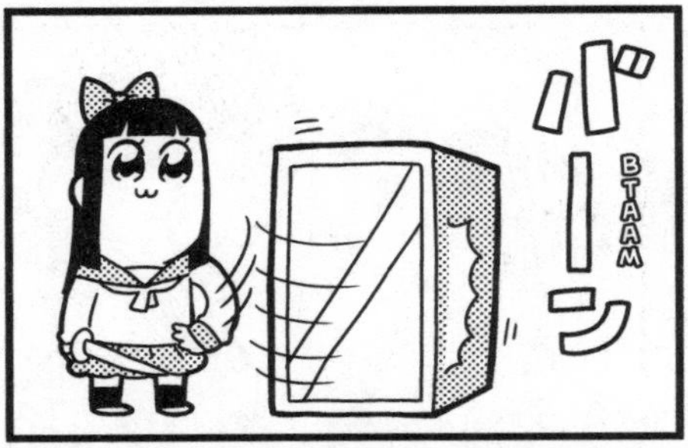
BTAAM

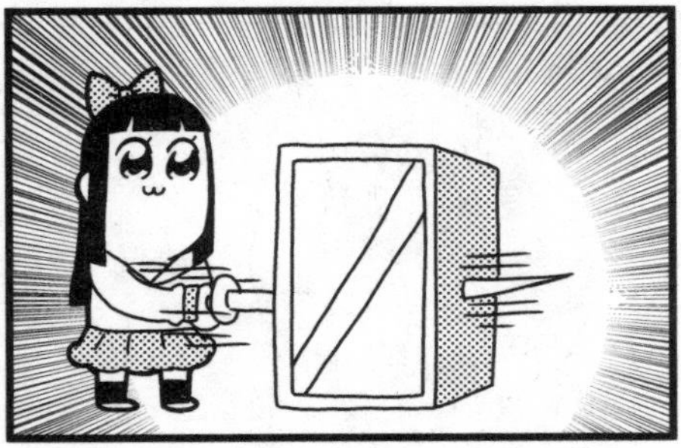

209

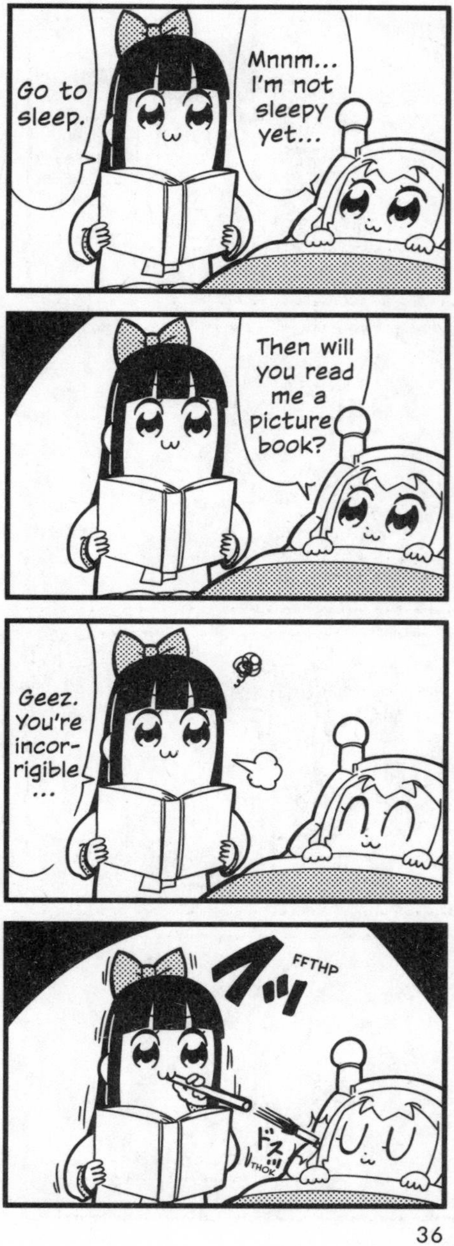
Mnnm... I'm not sleepy yet...
Go to sleep.
Then will you read me a picture book?
Geez. You're incorrigible...
FFTHP
ドス THOK

210

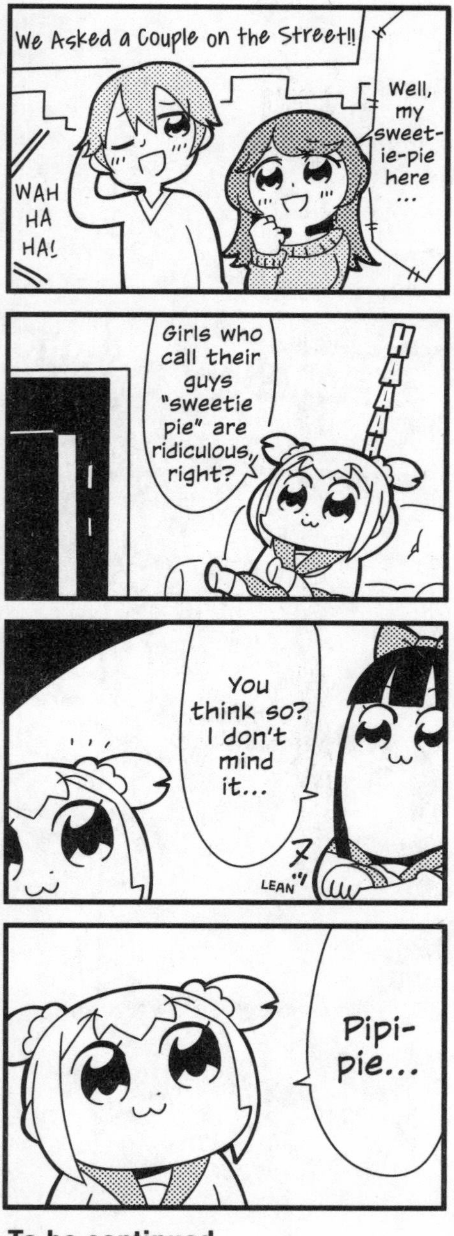
We Asked a Couple on the Street!!
Well, my sweetie-pie here...
WAH HA HA!
Girls who call their guys "sweetie pie" are ridiculous, right?
You think so? I don't mind it...
LEAN
Pipi-pie...

To be continued...

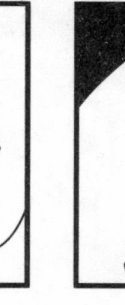

211

POP TEAM EPIC

Bkub Okawa

Is it true that you embezzled political funds to buy *Pop Team Epic* for yourself?!
Don't use the citizens' taxes as your own piggy bank!!

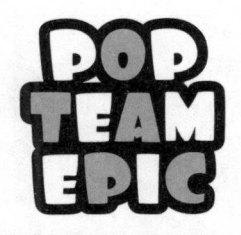

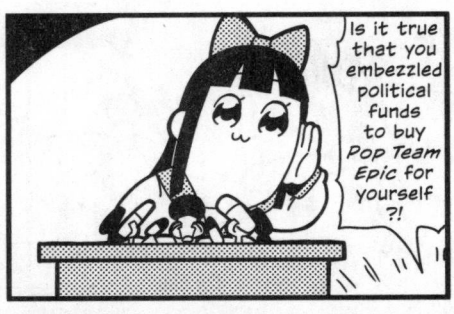

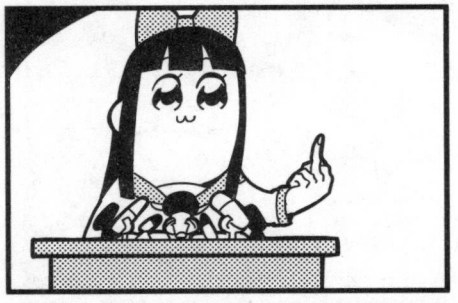

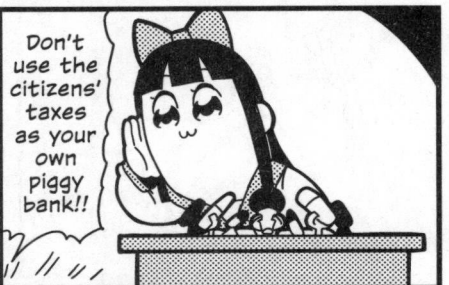

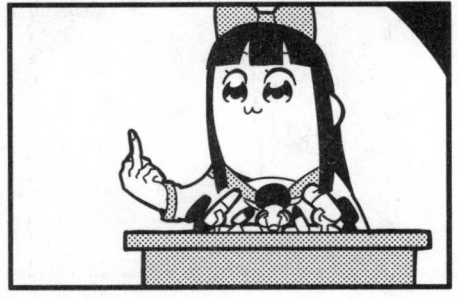

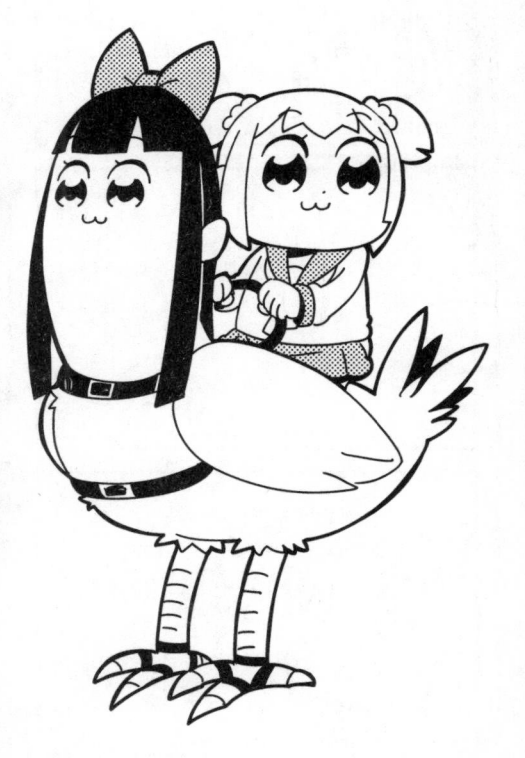

212

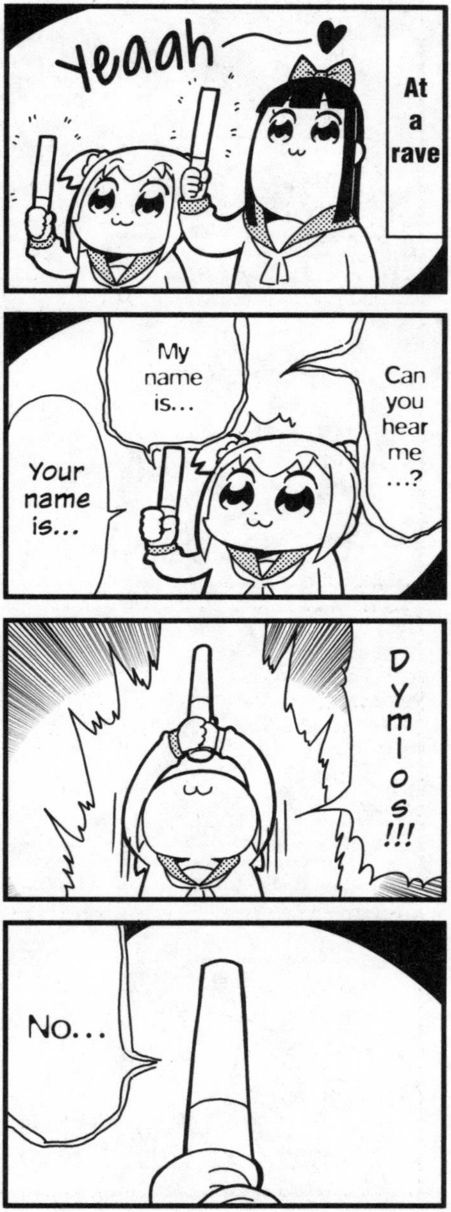
At a rave
Yeaah—♥
Can you hear me …?
My name is…
Your name is…
DYmIoS!!!
No…

213

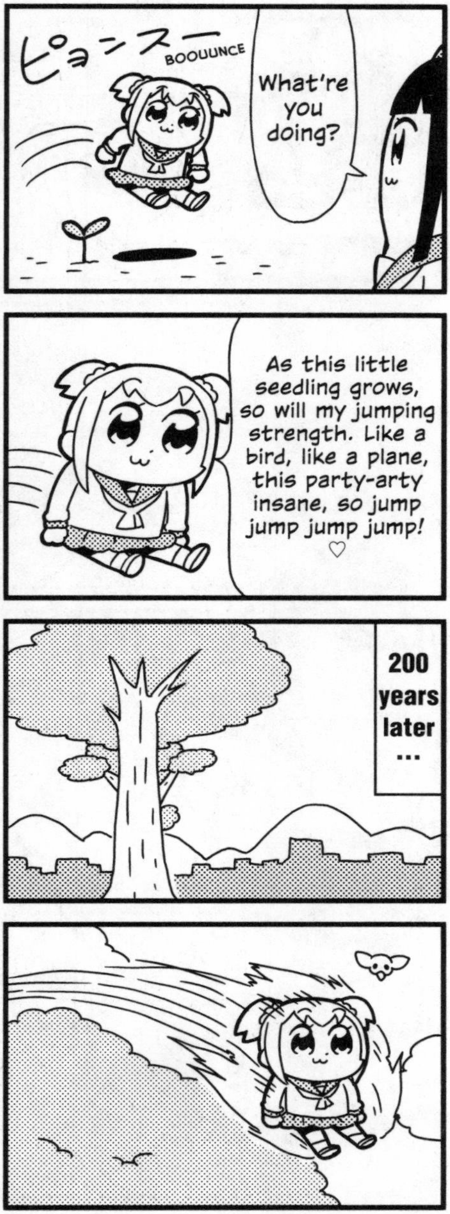
ピョンスー
BOOUUNCE
What're you doing?
As this little seedling grows, so will my jumping strength. Like a bird, like a plane, this party-arty insane, so jump jump jump jump! ♡
200 years later …

214

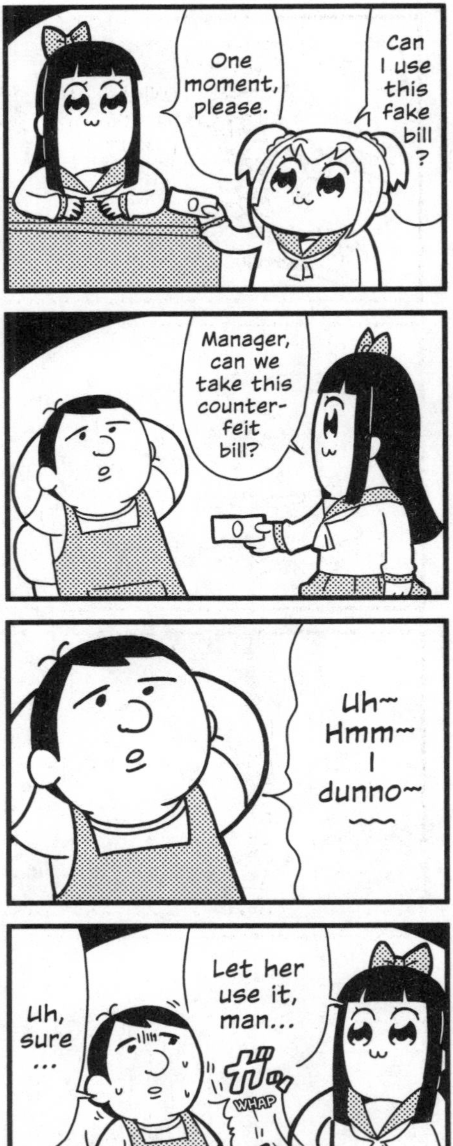
Can I use this fake bill?
One moment, please.
Manager, can we take this counter-feit bill?
Uh~ Hmm~ I dunno~
Let her use it, man...
ガッ
WHAP
Uh, sure ...

215

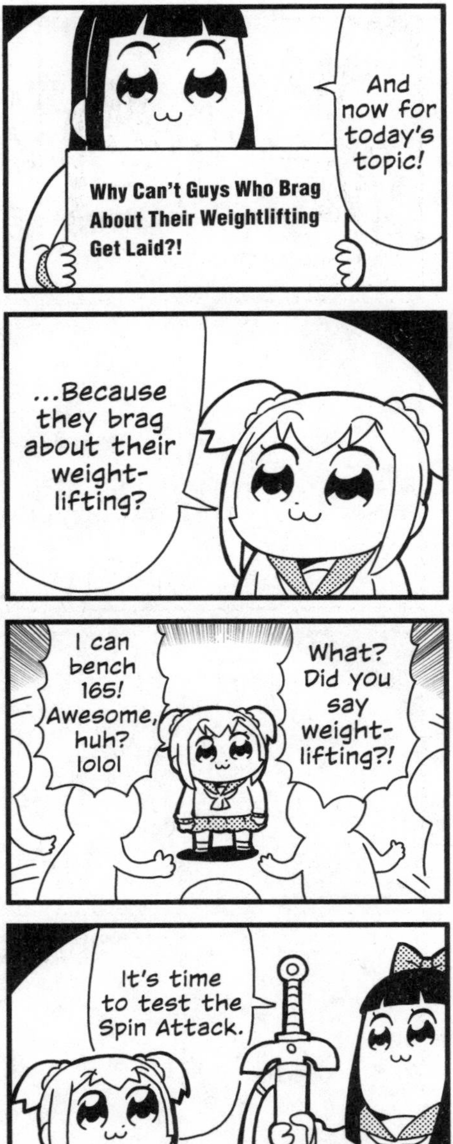
And now for today's topic!
Why Can't Guys Who Brag About Their Weightlifting Get Laid?!
...Because they brag about their weight-lifting?
What? Did you say weight-lifting?!
I can bench 165! Awesome, huh? lolol
It's time to test the Spin Attack.

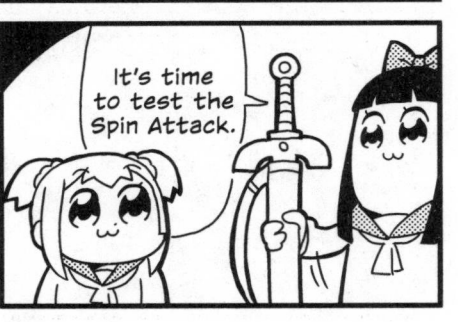

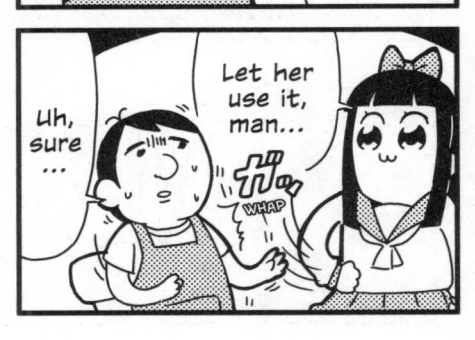

216

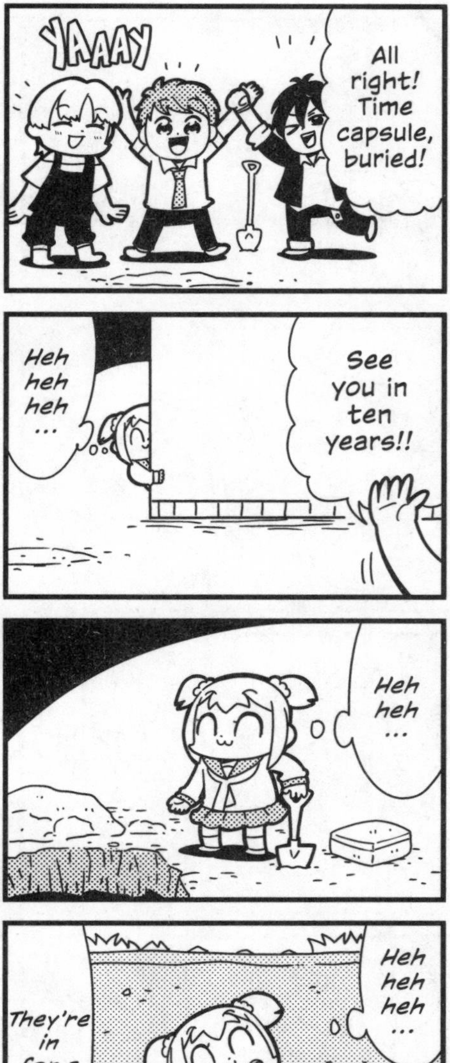
All right! Time capsule, buried!
YAAAY
See you in ten years!!
Heh heh heh ...
Heh heh ...
Heh heh heh ...
They're in for a shock ~!

217

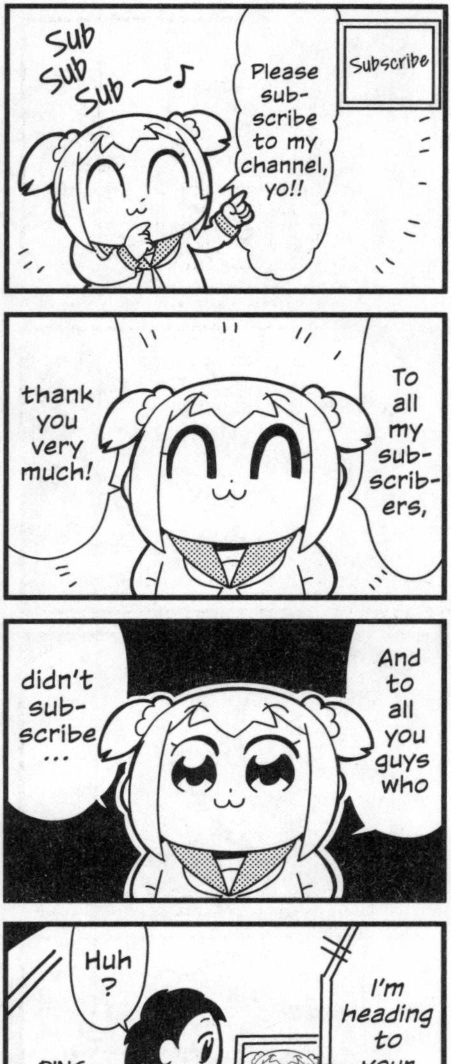
Sub Sub Sub ~♪
Please sub-scribe to my channel, yo!!
Subscribe
To all my sub-scrib-ers,
thank you very much!
And to all you guys who
didn't sub-scribe ...
I'm heading to your house right now.
Huh ?
DING-DONG~ ♪

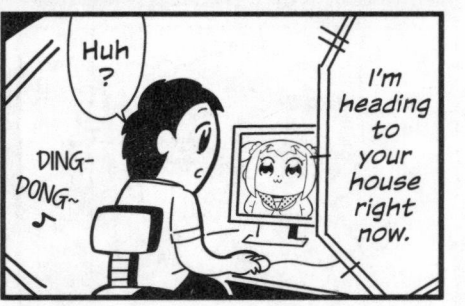

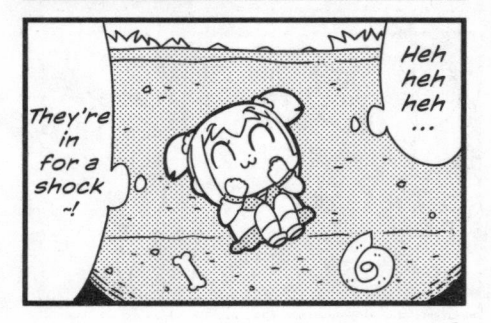

218

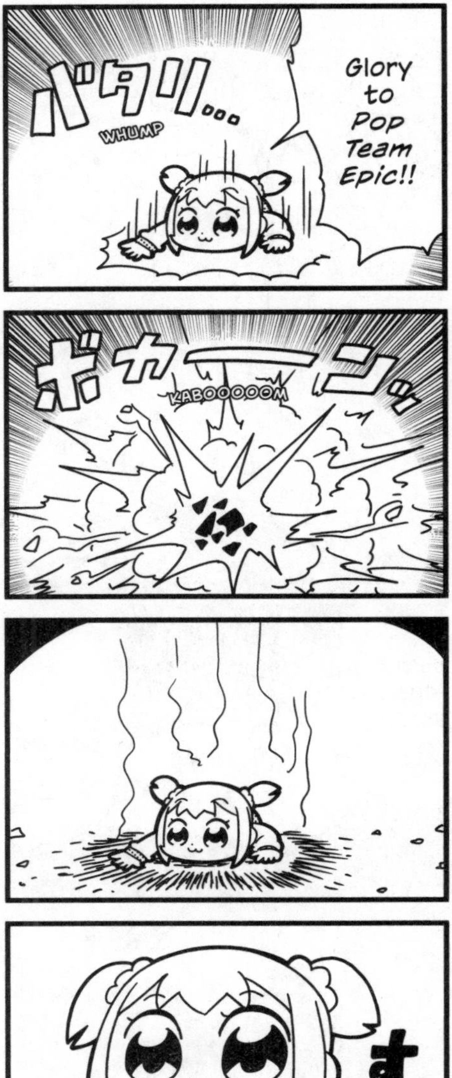
Glory to Pop Team Epic!!
バタリ…
WHUMP
ボカーーン
KABOOOOOOM
すっく
RISE

219

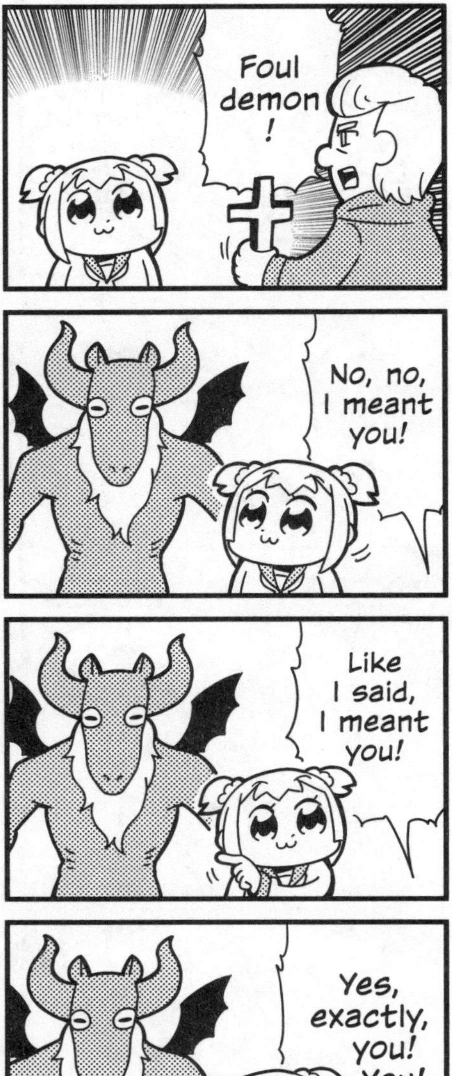
Foul demon!
No, no, I meant you!
Like I said, I meant you!
Yes, exactly, you! You!

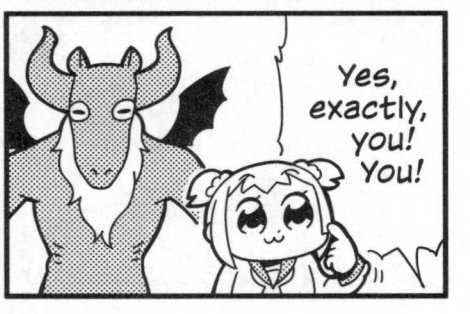

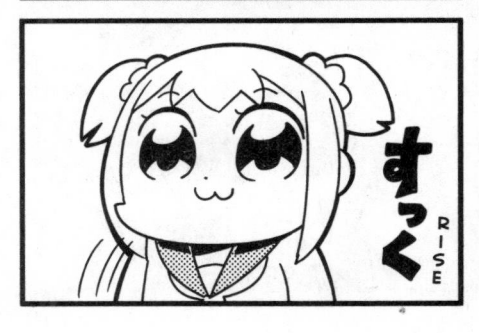

220

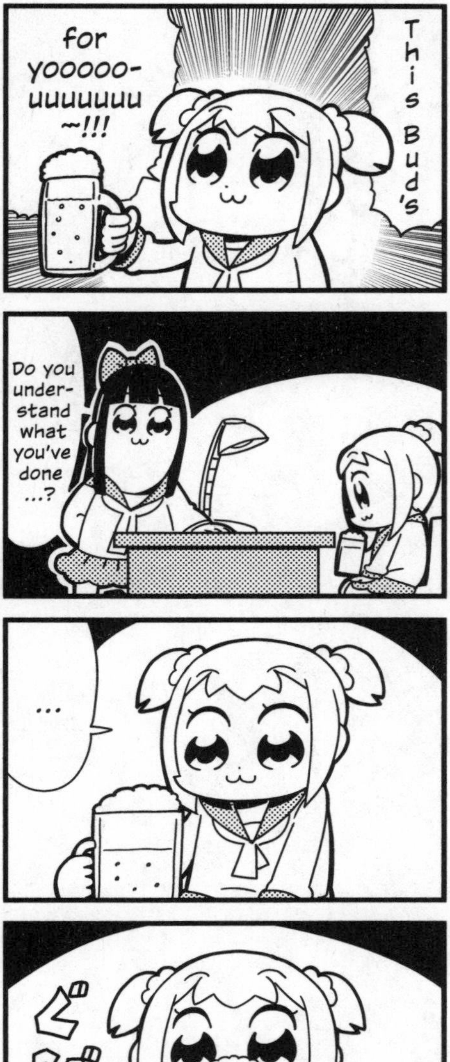
This Bud's
for yooooo-uuuuuuu~!!!
Do you under-stand what you've done ...?
...
ぐびっ
GLUG

221

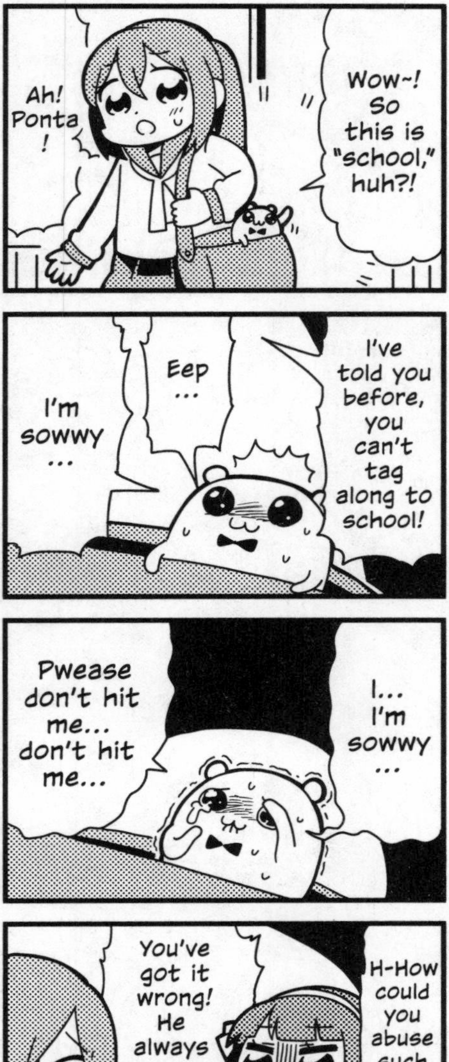
Wow~! So this is "school," huh?!
Ah! Ponta!
I've told you before, you can't tag along to school!
Eep ...
I'm sowwy ...
I... I'm sowwy ...
Pwease don't hit me... don't hit me...
H-How could you abuse such a poor little soul ...
You've got it wrong! He always plays the victim card!

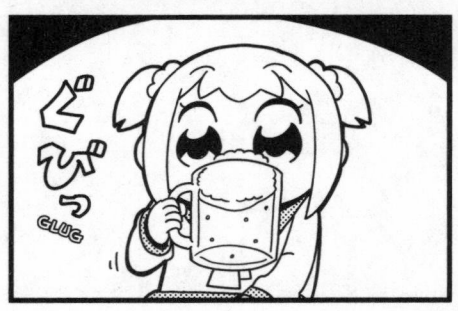

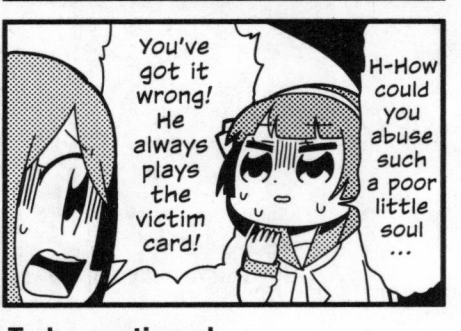

To be continued...

222

POP TEAM EPIC

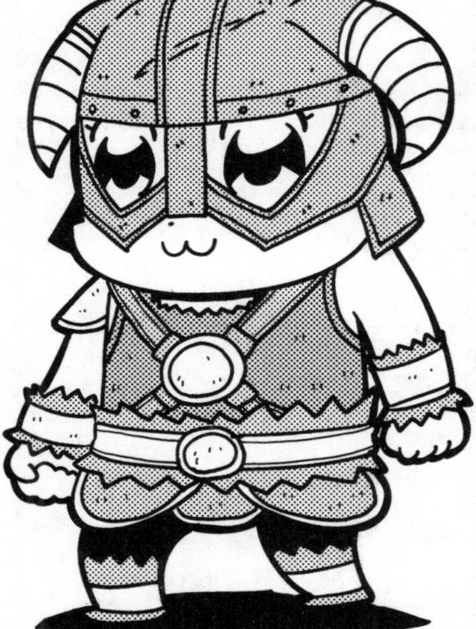

Bkub Okawa

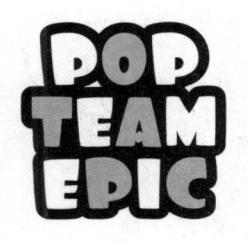

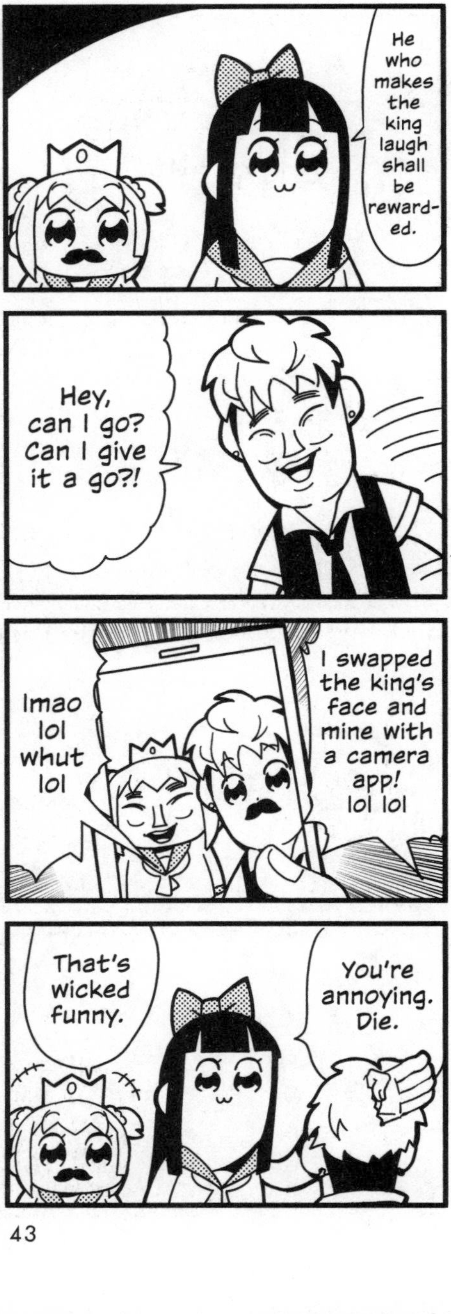
He who makes the king laugh shall be reward-ed.
Hey, can I go? Can I give it a go?!
I swapped the king's face and mine with a camera app! lol lol
lmao lol whut lol
You're annoying. Die.
That's wicked funny.

223

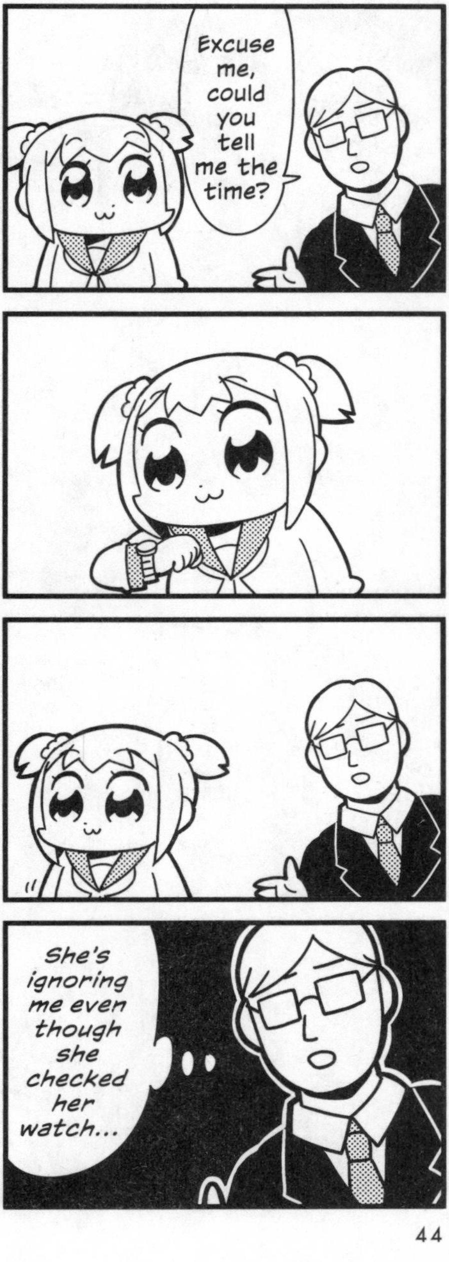
Excuse me, could you tell me the time?
She's ignoring me even though she checked her watch...

224

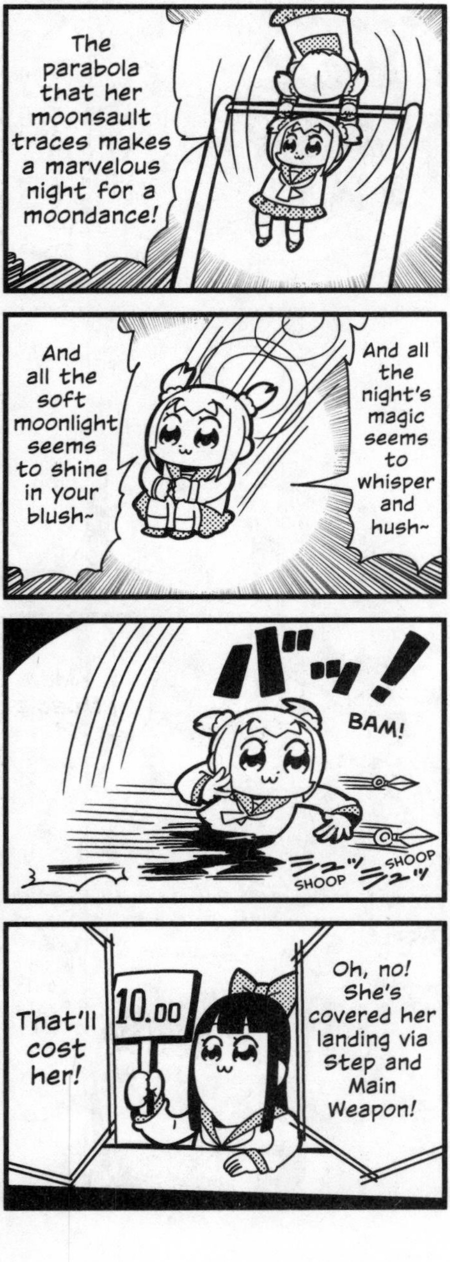
The parabola that her moonsault traces makes a marvelous night for a moondance!
And all the soft moonlight seems to shine in your blush~
And all the night's magic seems to whisper and hush~
バッ!
BAM!
シュッ
SHOOP
シュッ
SHOOP
Oh, no! She's covered her landing via Step and Main Weapon!
10.00
That'll cost her!

225

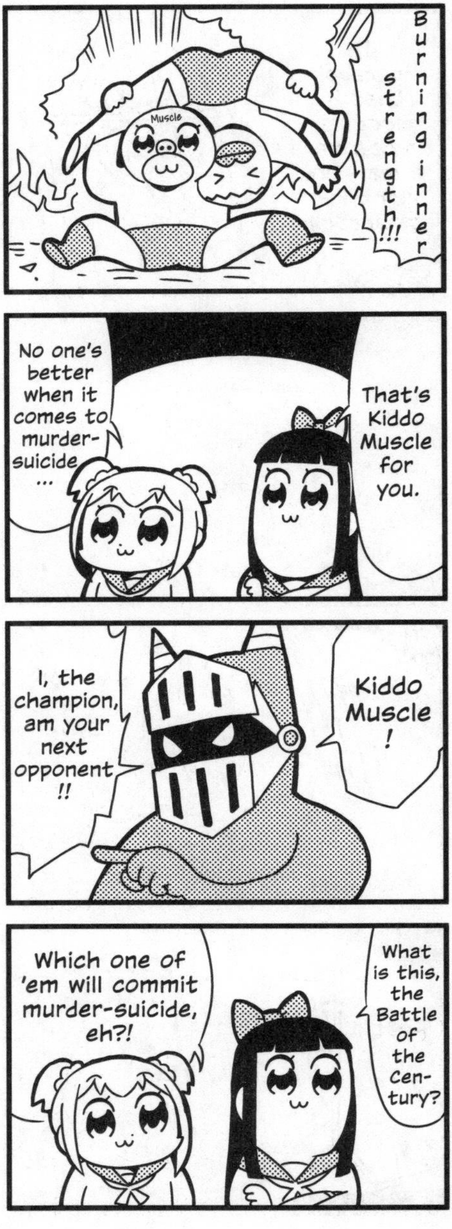
Burning inner strength!!!
Muscle
That's Kiddo Muscle for you.
No one's better when it comes to murder-suicide...
Kiddo Muscle!
I, the champion, am your next opponent!!
What is this, the Battle of the Cen-tury?
Which one of 'em will commit murder-suicide, eh?!

226

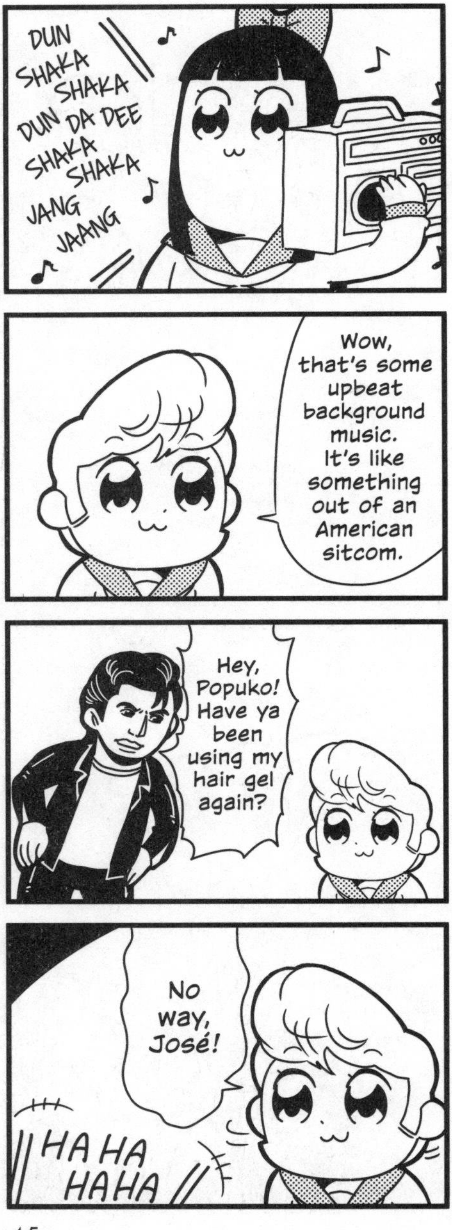
DUN SHAKA SHAKA DUN DA DEE SHAKA SHAKA JANG JAANG
Wow, that's some upbeat background music. It's like something out of an American sitcom.
Hey, Popuko! Have ya been using my hair gel again?
No way, José!
HA HA HAHA

227

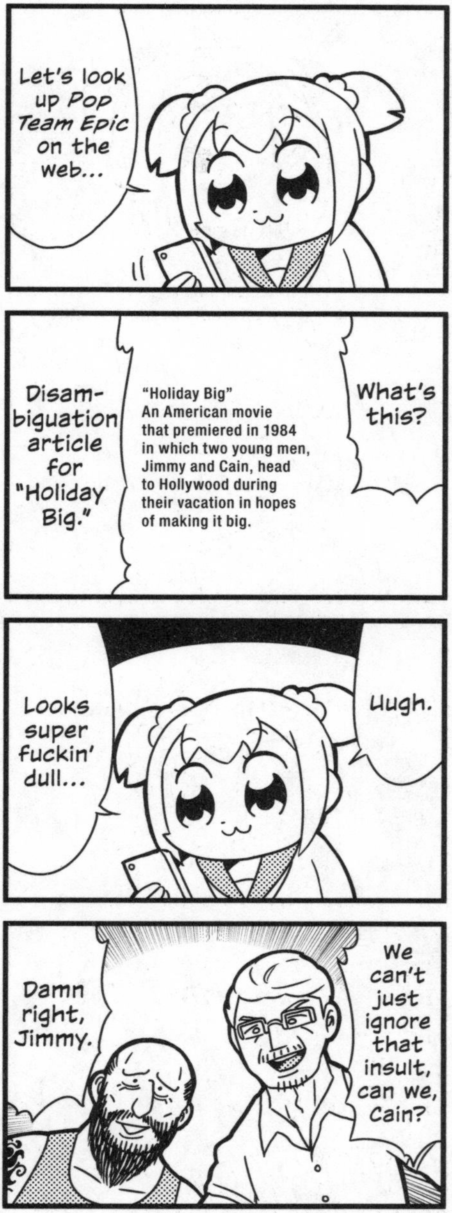
Let's look up *Pop Team Epic* on the web...
What's this?
Disam-biguation article for "Holiday Big."
"Holiday Big"
An American movie that premiered in 1984 in which two young men, Jimmy and Cain, head to Hollywood during their vacation in hopes of making it big.
Uugh.
Looks super fuckin' dull...
We can't just ignore that insult, can we, Cain?
Damn right, Jimmy.

228

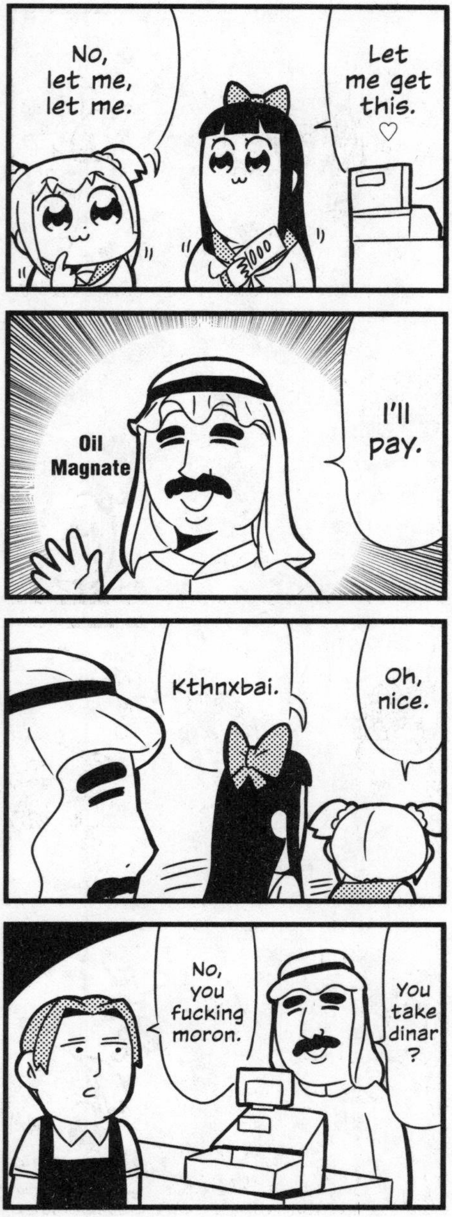
Let me get this. ♡
No, let me, let me.
I'll pay.
Oil Magnate
Oh, nice.
Kthnxbai.
You take dinar?
No, you fucking moron.

229

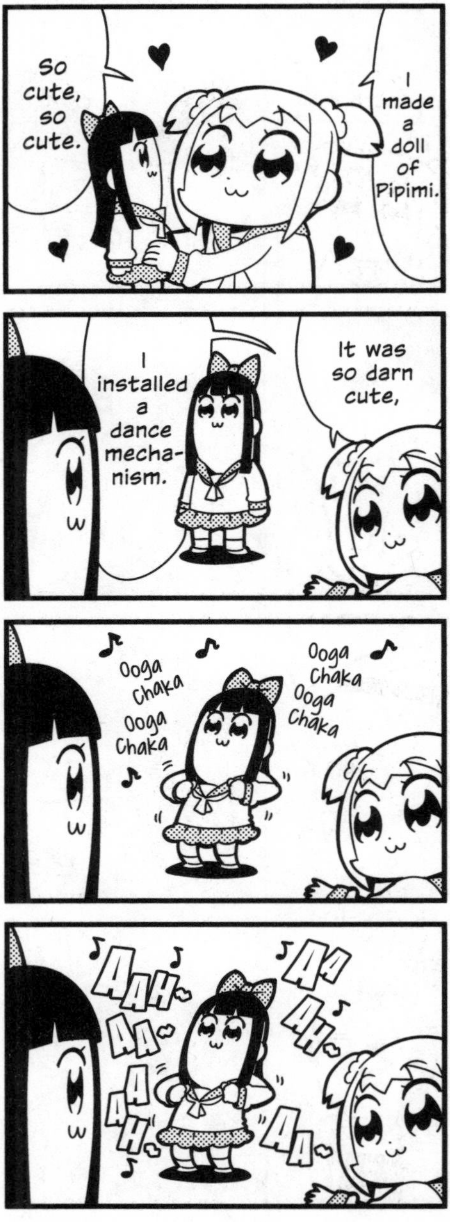
I made a doll of Pipimi.
So cute, so cute.
It was so darn cute,
I installed a dance mechanism.
Ooga Chaka Ooga Chaka
Ooga Chaka Ooga Chaka
AAH~ AA~ AAAH~
AA AH~ AA~

230

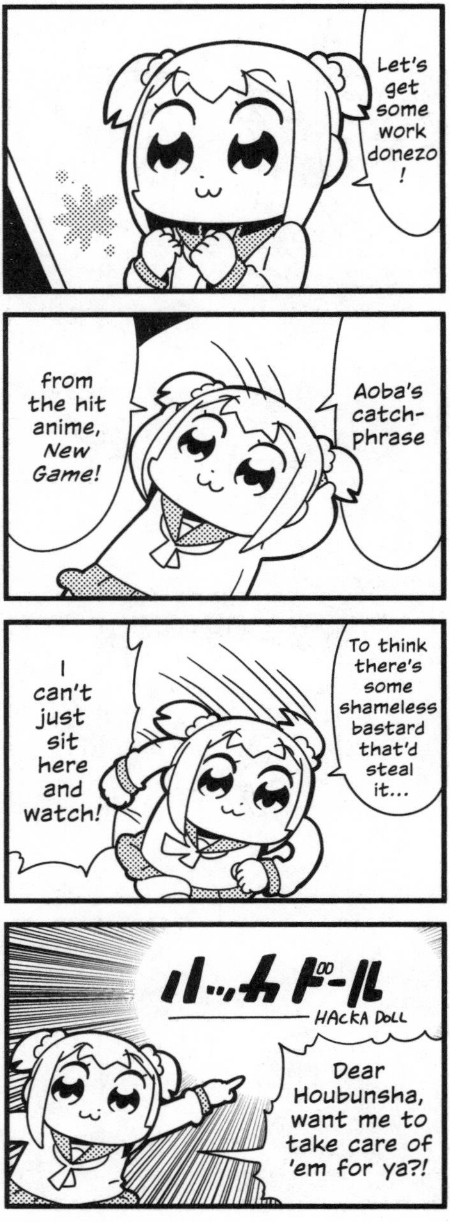
Let's get some work donezo!
Aoba's catchphrase
from the hit anime, New Game!
To think there's some shameless bastard that'd steal it...
I can't just sit here and watch!
ハッカドール
HACKA DOLL
Dear Houbunsha, want me to take care of 'em for ya?!

231

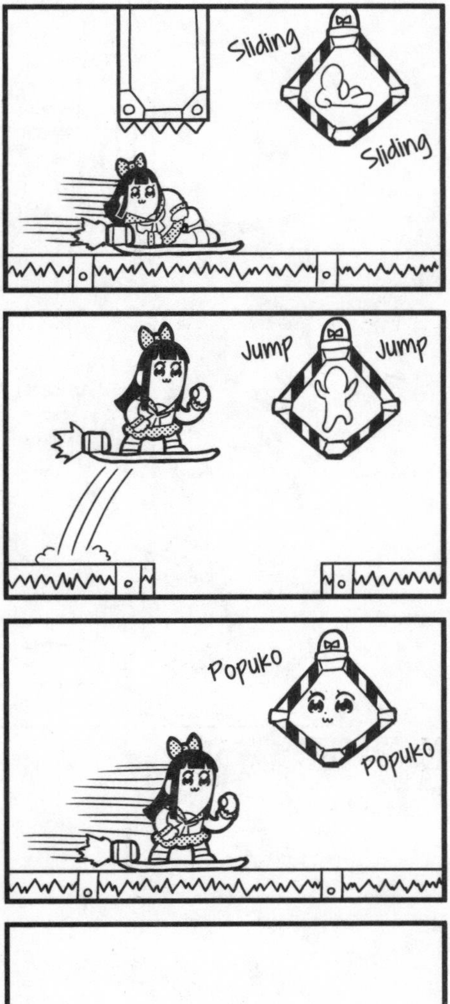
Sliding
Sliding
Jump
Jump
Popuko
Popuko
LA

232

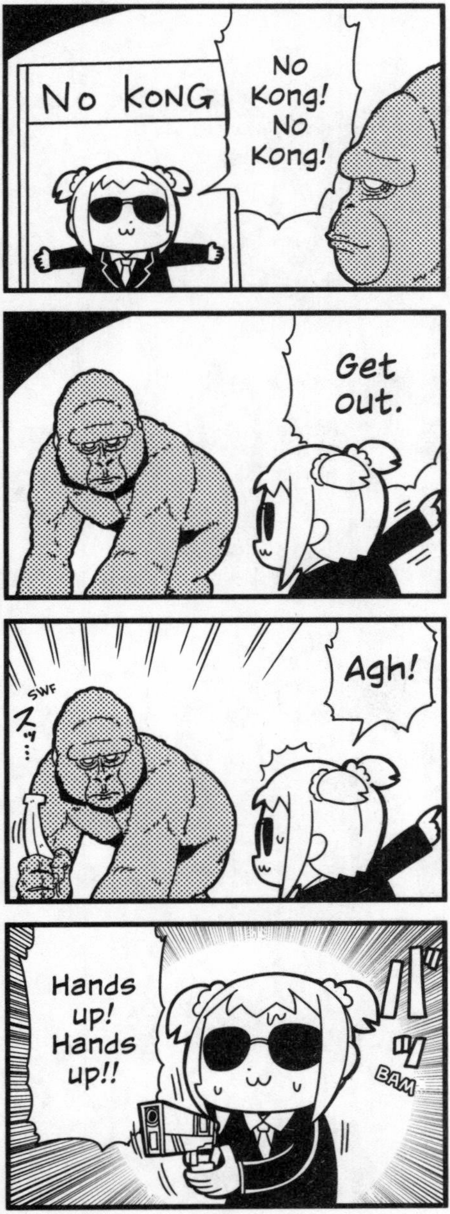
No KONG
No Kong! No Kong!
Get out.
Agh!
SWF
Hands up! Hands up!!
BAM

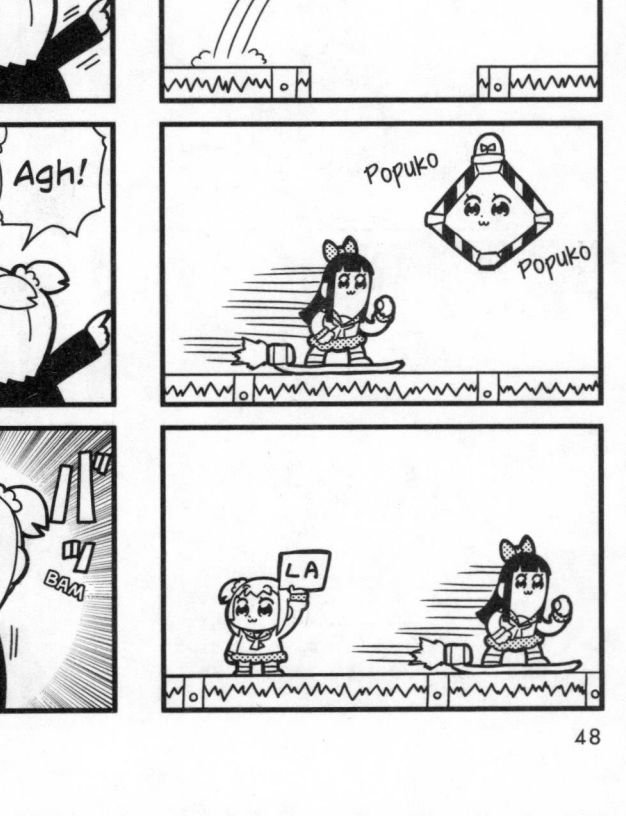

To be continued...

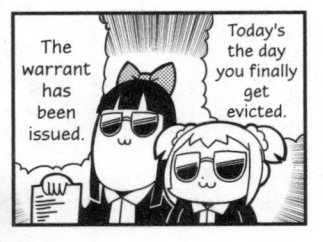

Let's Visit the **Pop Team Epic Café!**

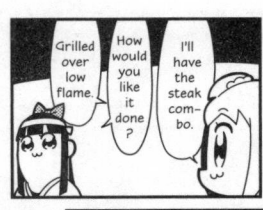

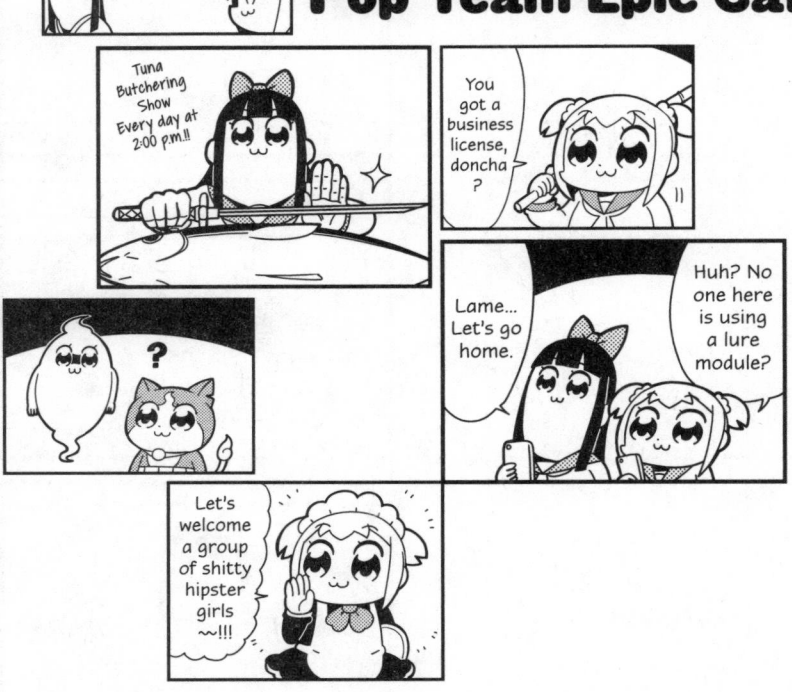

Today's the day you finally get evicted.
The warrant has been issued.

I'll have the steak com- bo.
How would you like it done ?
Grilled over low flame.

You got a business license, doncha ?
Tuna Butchering Show Every day at 2:00 p.m.!!
Huh? No one here is using a lure module?
Lame... Let's go home.
?
Let's welcome a group of shitty hipster girls ~!!!

*The Pop Team Epic Café closed in 2016.

POP TEAM EPIC SURPRISE JAPAN VISIT
Hold on, ya shitty jour-nal-ist.
Huh?
We're 100% native Japanese, ya hear?
I-I'll fix it right away!
POP TEAM SUSHI
P

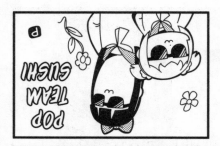

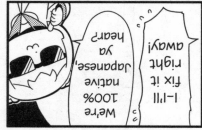

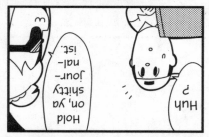

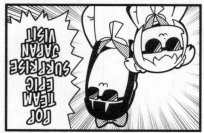

POP TEAM EPIC

Bkub Okawa

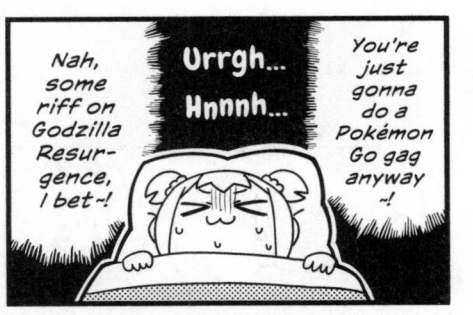

233

You're just gonna do a Pokémon Go gag anyway ~!
Urrgh... Hnnnh...
Nah, some riff on Godzilla Resurgence, I bet~!
Whassa matter, Popuchin?
I can't sleep 'cause of the pressure.
That's why I, Popuchin, have decided...
I won't make any more trendy pop culture references! I'll blaze my own trail!
But... donezo...
Let me at least keep donezo...

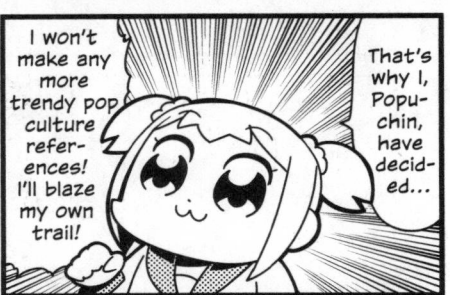

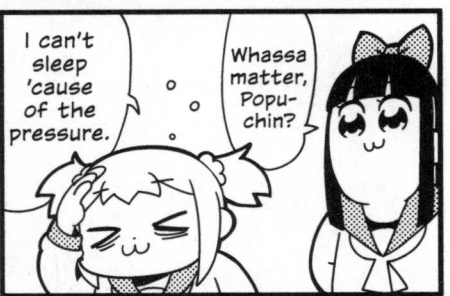

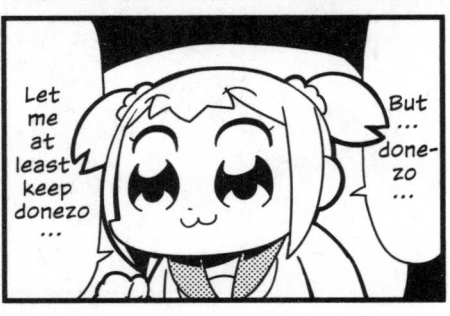

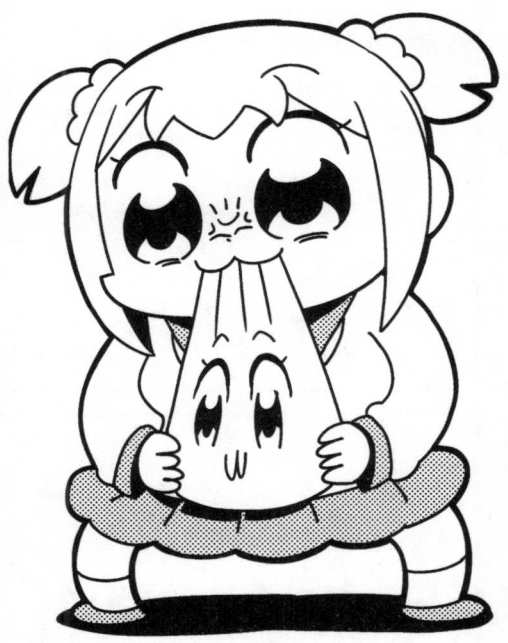

(234)

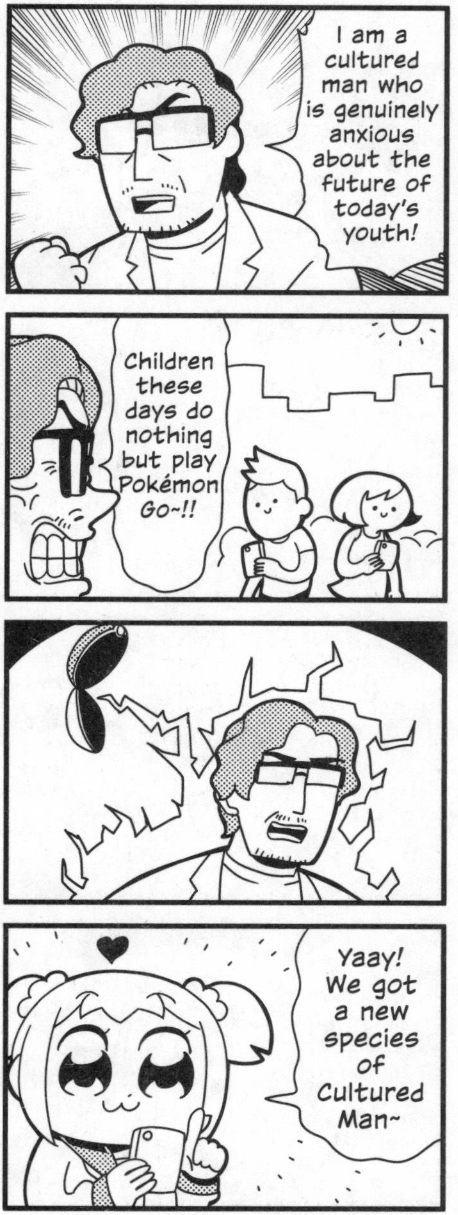
I am a cultured man who is genuinely anxious about the future of today's youth!
Children these days do nothing but play Pokémon Go~!!
Yaay! We got a new species of Cultured Man~

(235)

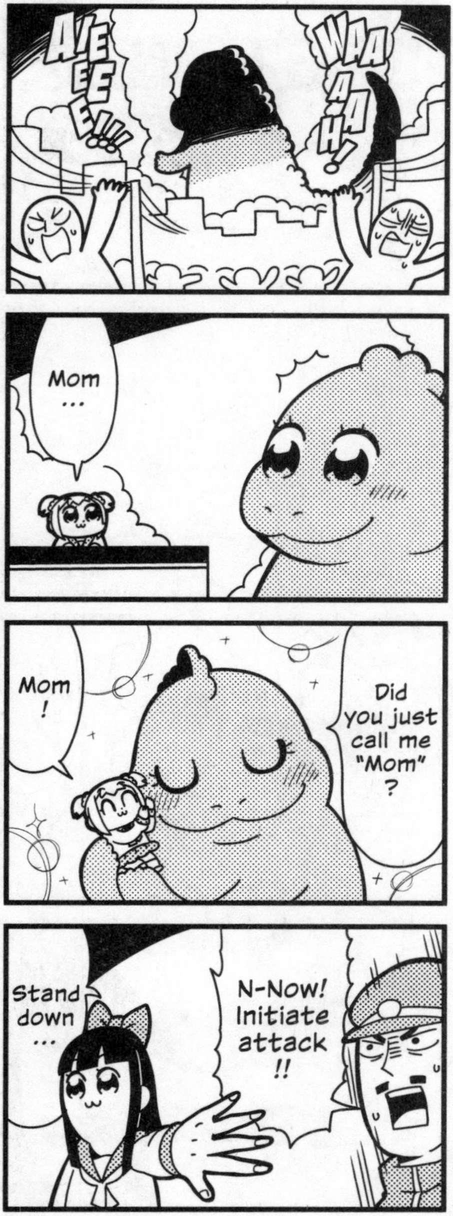
WAAAAH!
AIEEEE!!!
Mom ...
Did you just call me "Mom" ?
Mom !
N-Now! Initiate attack !!
Stand down ...

236

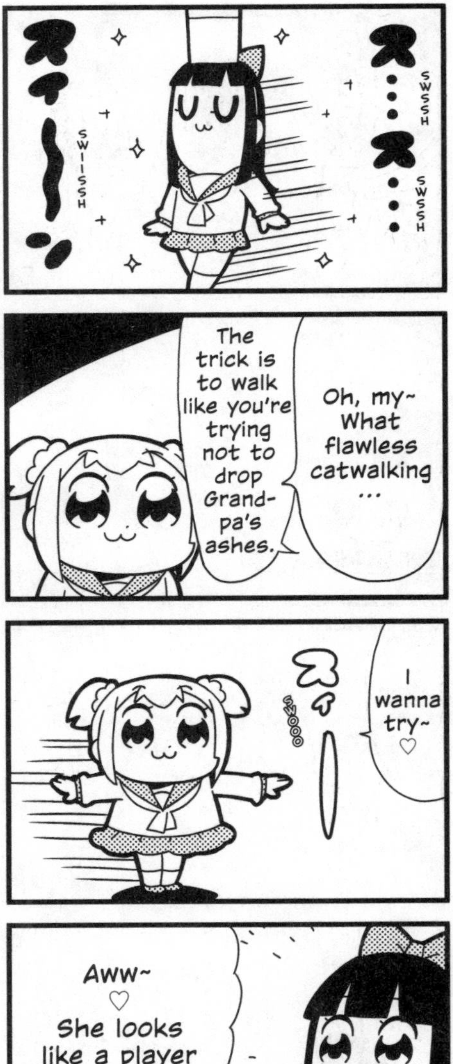
SWSSH
SWSSH
SWIISSH
The trick is to walk like you're trying not to drop Grand-pa's ashes.
Oh, my~ What flawless catwalking ...
SWOOO
I wanna try~ ♡
Aww~ ♡ She looks like a player model bug. So cute ♡

237

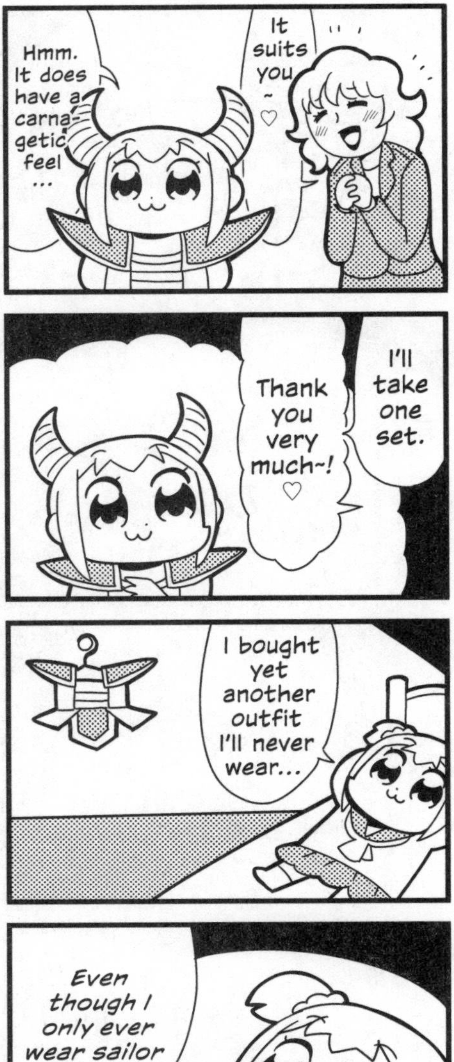
It suits you ~ ♡
Hmm. It does have a carna-getic feel ...
I'll take one set.
Thank you very much~! ♡
I bought yet another outfit I'll never wear...
Even though I only ever wear sailor uniforms ...

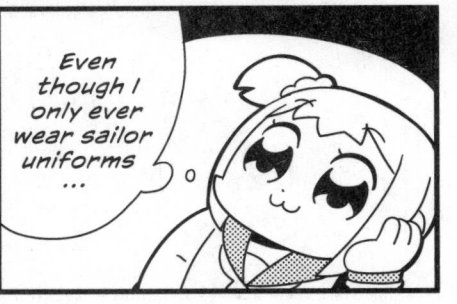

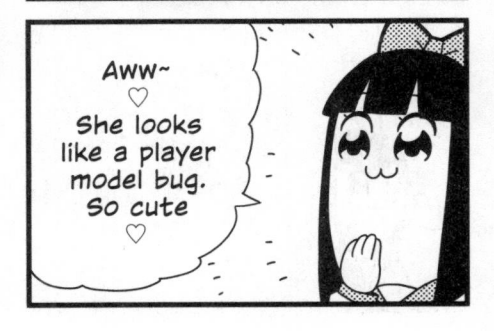

238

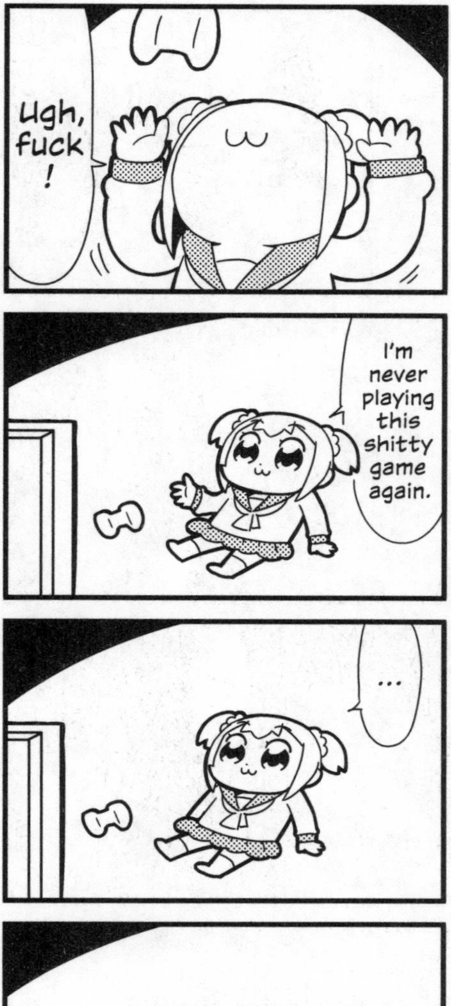
Ugh, fuck!
I'm never playing this shitty game again.
...

239

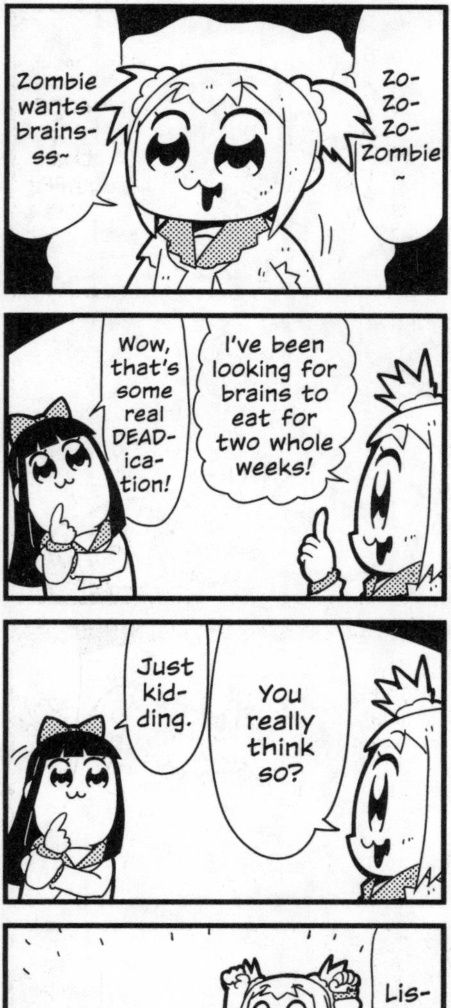
Zo-Zo-Zo-Zombie~
Zombie wants brainss~
I've been looking for brains to eat for two whole weeks!
Wow, that's some real DEAD-ica-tion!
You really think so?
Just kid-ding.
Lis-ten, you~♡

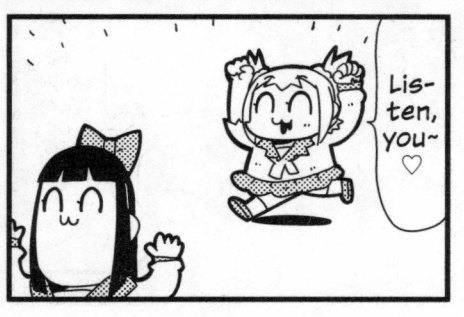

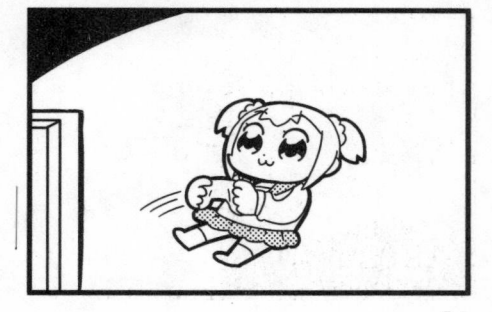

240

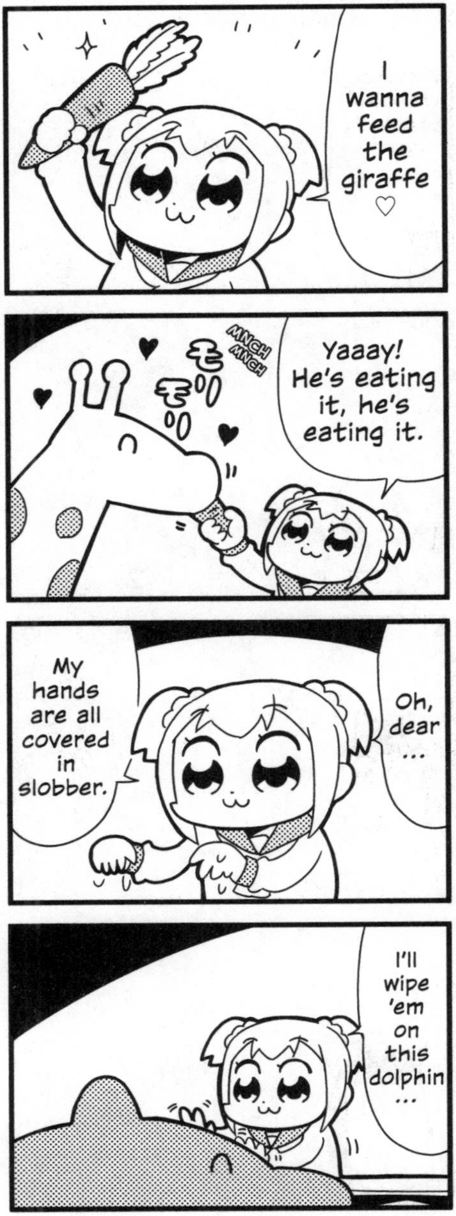
I wanna feed the giraffe ♡
Yaaay! He's eating it, he's eating it.
MNCH MNCH
Oh, dear ...
My hands are all covered in slobber.
I'll wipe 'em on this dolphin ...

241

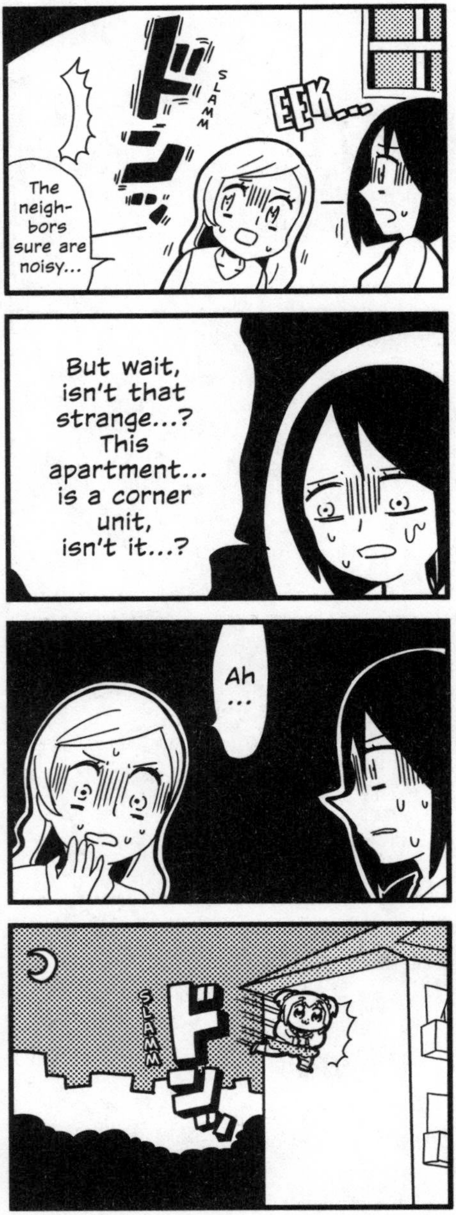
SLAMM
EEK...
The neighbors sure are noisy...
But wait, isn't that strange...? This apartment... is a corner unit, isn't it...?
Ah ...
SLAMM

242

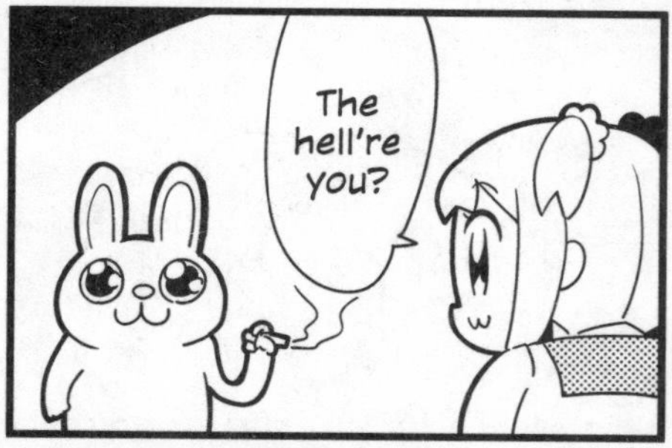
The hell're you?

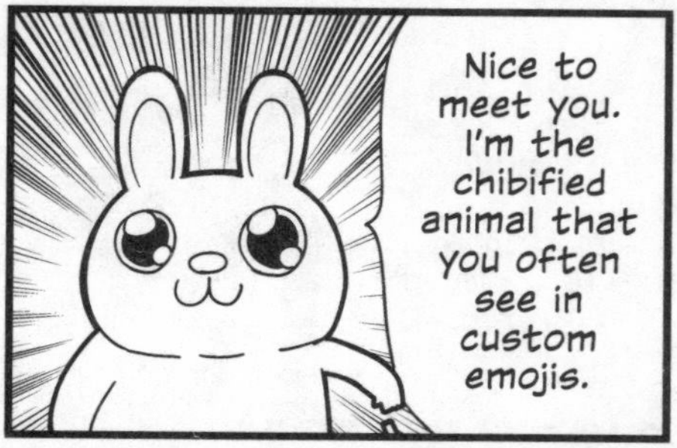
Nice to meet you. I'm the chibified animal that you often see in custom emojis.

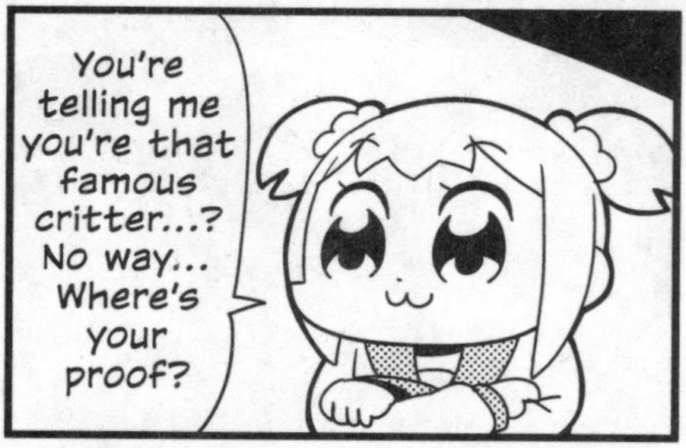
You're telling me you're that famous critter...? No way... Where's your proof?

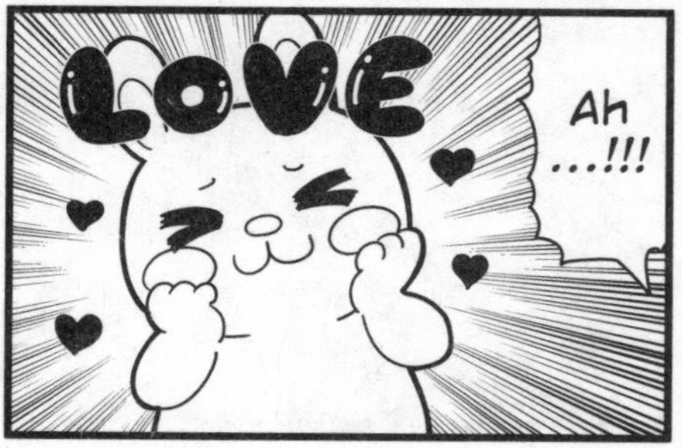
LOVE
Ah ...!!!

243

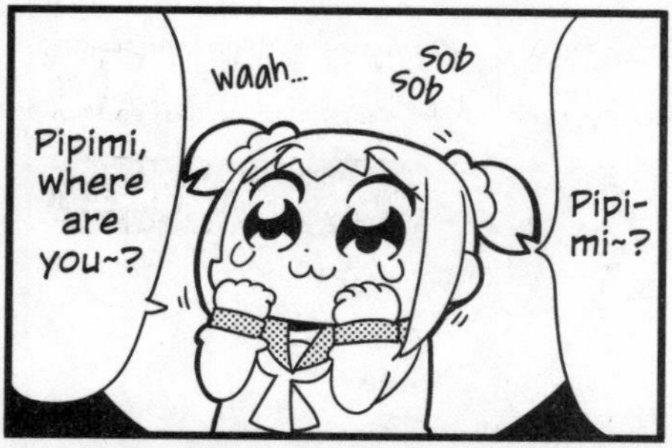
Pipimi, where are you~?
waah...
sob sob
Pipi-mi~?

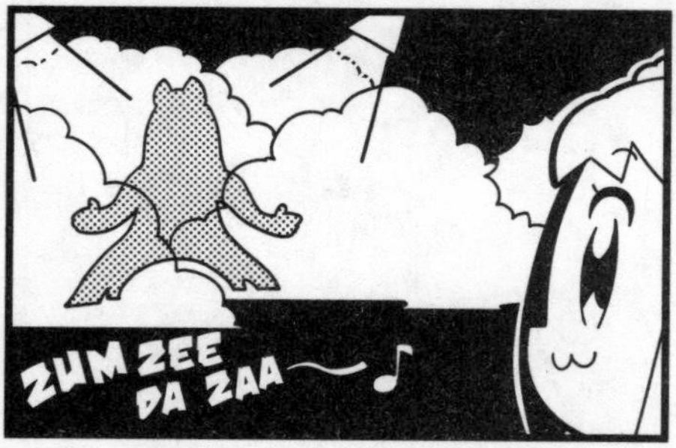
ZUM ZEE DA ZAA~

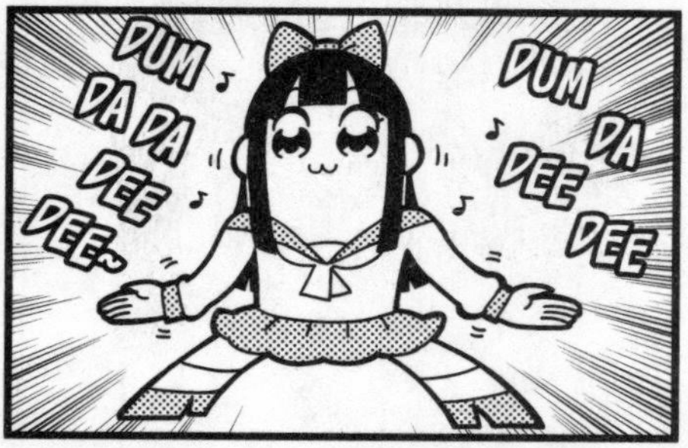
DUM DA DEE DEE
DUM DA DA DEE DEE~

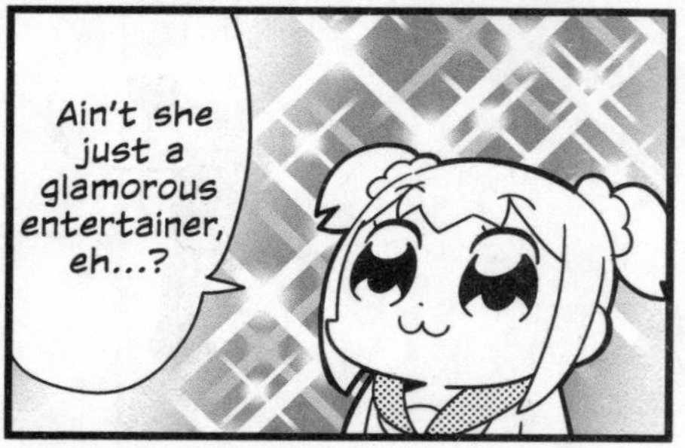
Ain't she just a glamorous entertainer, eh...?

To be continued...

POP TEAM EPIC

Bkub Okawa

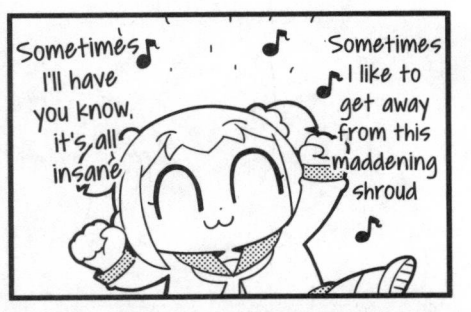

244

Sometimes I like to get away from this maddening shroud
Sometimes I'll have you know, it's all insane
TAKE SHO BO
Disciplinary Action Notification
Violation
You have publicly disgraced the company
Penalty
Reduced compensation for manuscripts
Submit Apology Letter
Apology Letter
Oh, I've got a good mind to throw it all away
Throw it all away

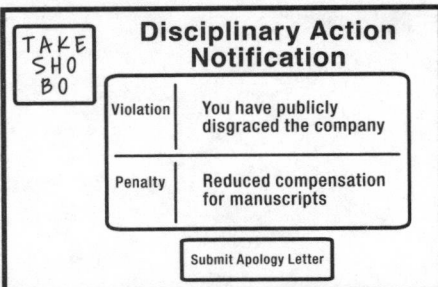

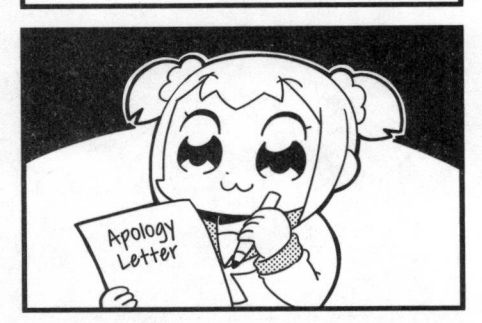

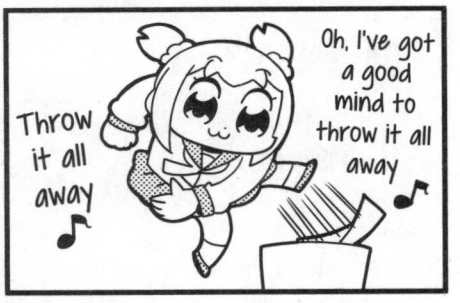

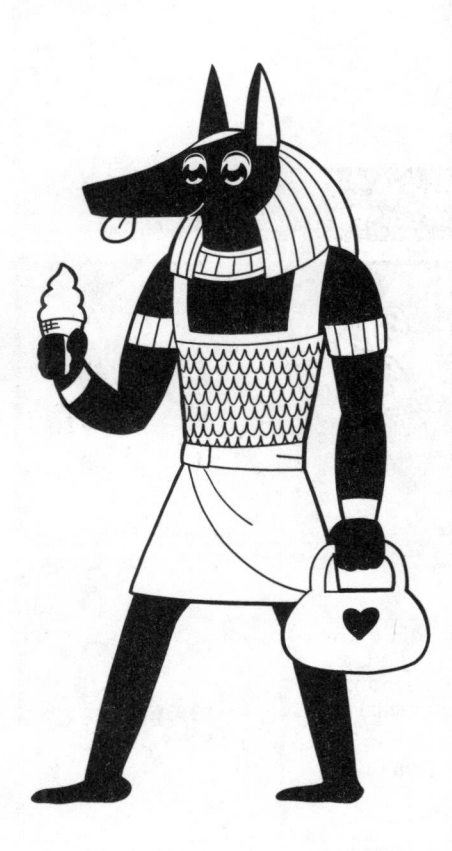

245

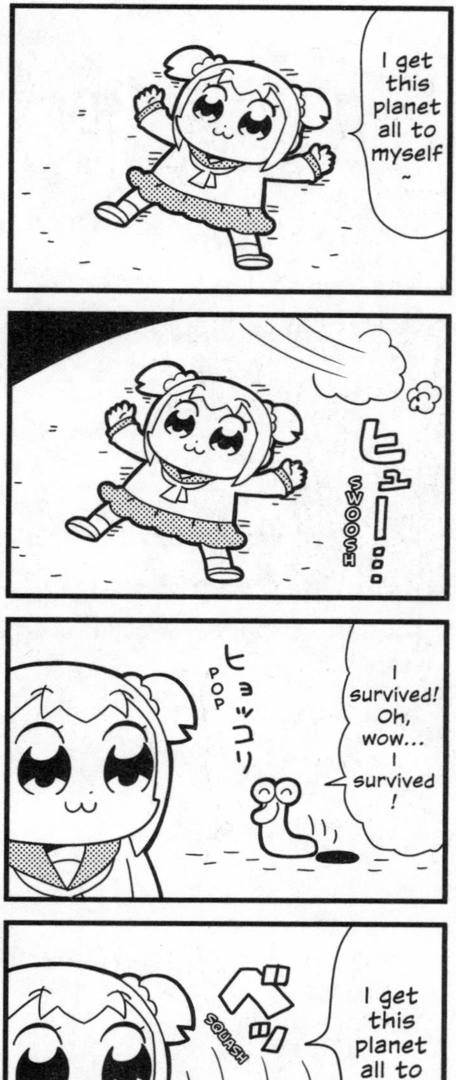
I get this planet all to myself ~
ヒューー…
SWOOSH
ヒョッコリ
POP
I survived! Oh, wow... I survived!
ベシッ
SQUASH
I get this planet all to myself.

246

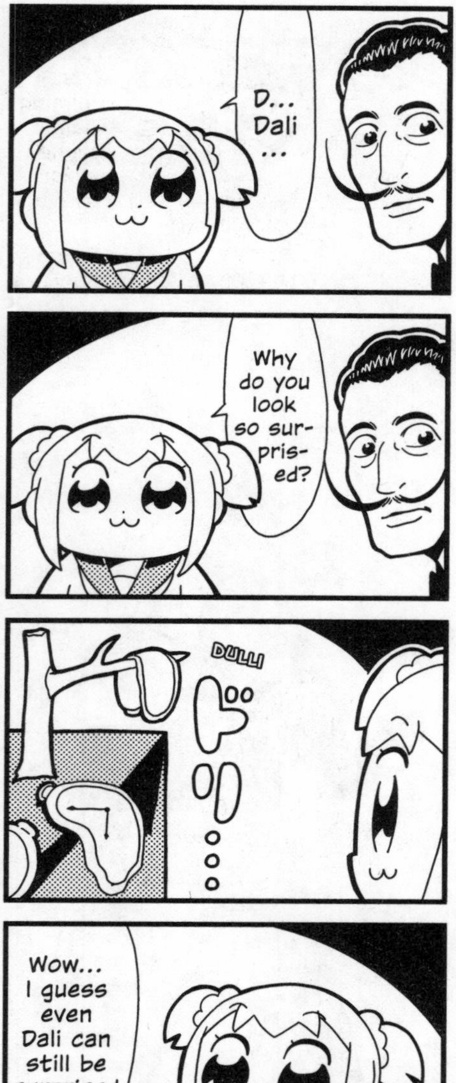
D... Dali ...
Why do you look so sur-pris-ed?
DULLI
oo
ooo
Wow... I guess even Dali can still be surprised some-times!

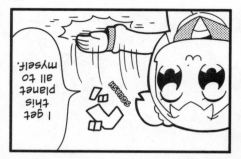

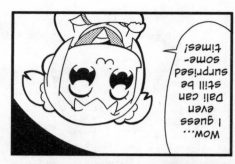

247

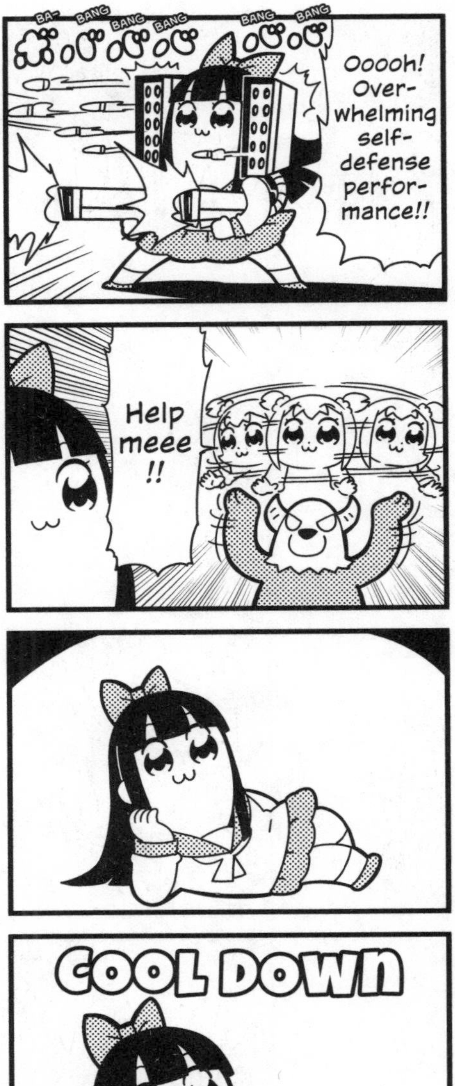
BA-BANG BANG BANG BANG BANG
Ooooh! Over-whelming self-defense perfor-mance!!
Help meee !!
COOL DOWN

248

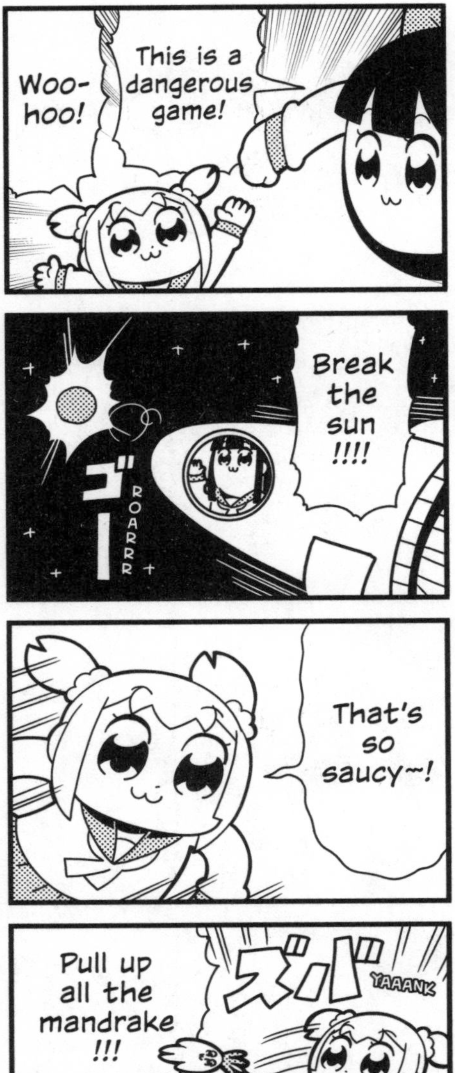
This is a dangerous game!
Woo-hoo!
Break the sun !!!!
ROARRR
That's so saucy~!
YAAANK
Pull up all the mandrake !!!

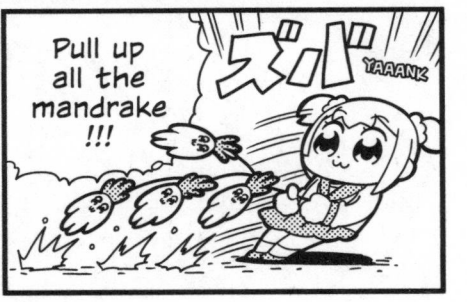

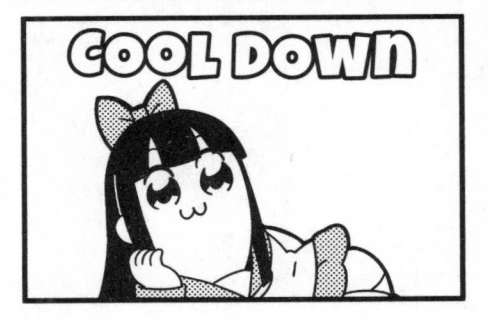

249

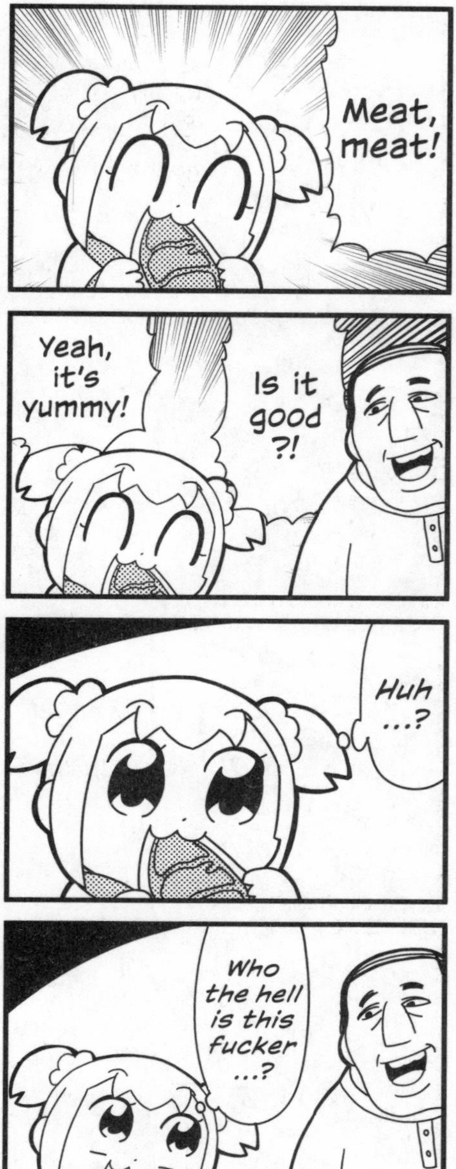
Meat, meat!
Is it good ?!
Yeah, it's yummy!
Huh ...?
Who the hell is this fucker ...?

250

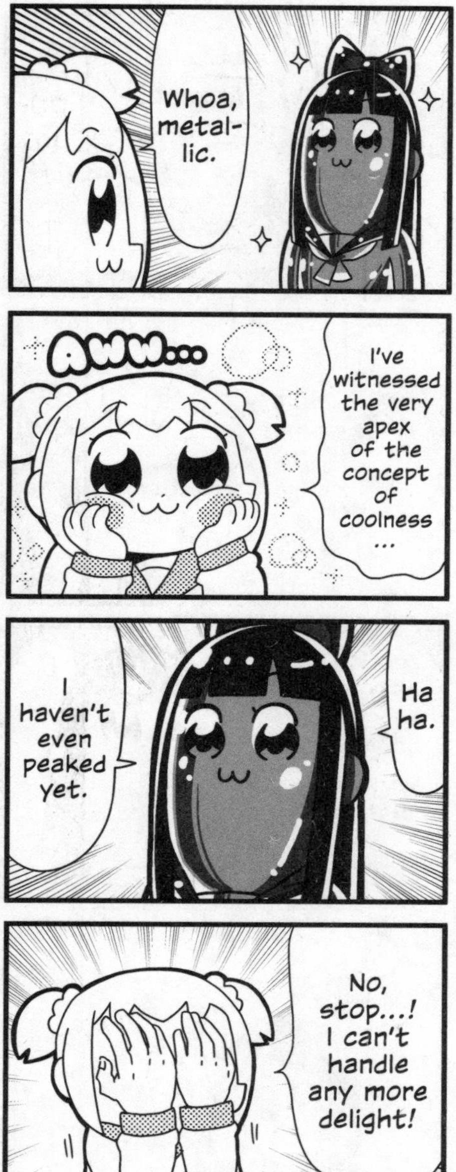
Whoa, metal-lic.
AWW...
I've witnessed the very apex of the concept of coolness ...
Ha ha.
I haven't even peaked yet.
No, stop...! I can't handle any more delight!

251

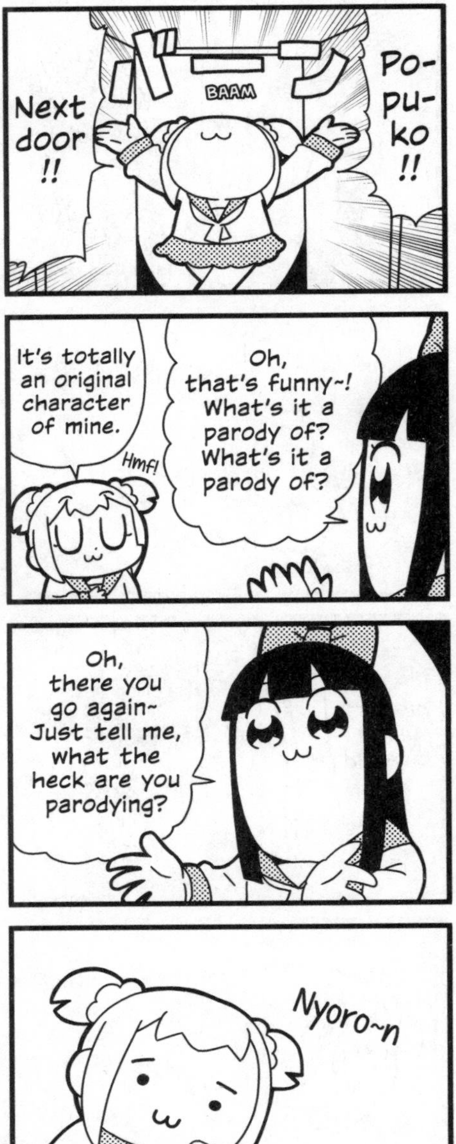
Po-pu-ko!!
BAAM
Next door!!
Oh, that's funny~! What's it a parody of? What's it a parody of?
It's totally an original character of mine.
Hmf!
Oh, there you go again~ Just tell me, what the heck are you parodying?
Nyoro~n

252

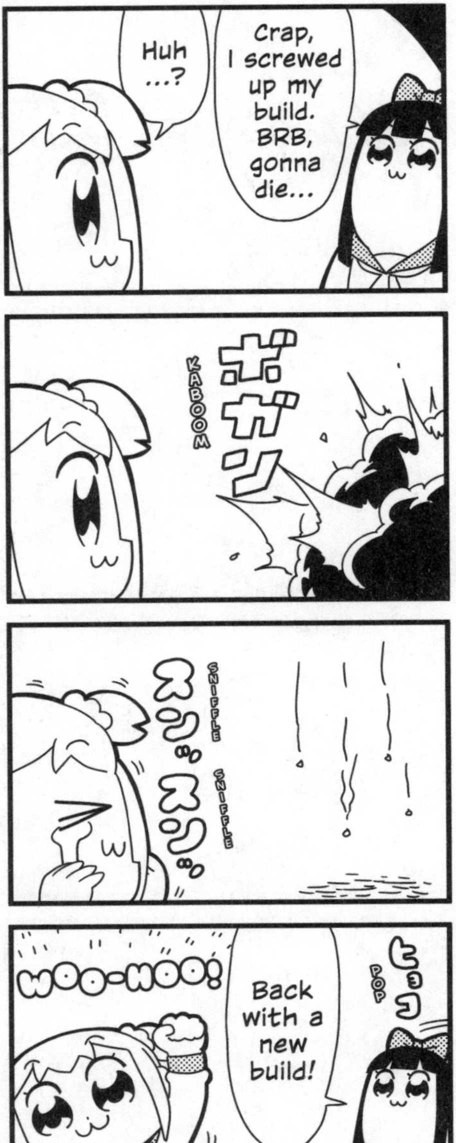
Crap, I screwed up my build. BRB, gonna die...
Huh ...?
KABOOM
SNIFFLE
SNIFFLE
POP
Back with a new build!
WOO-HOO!

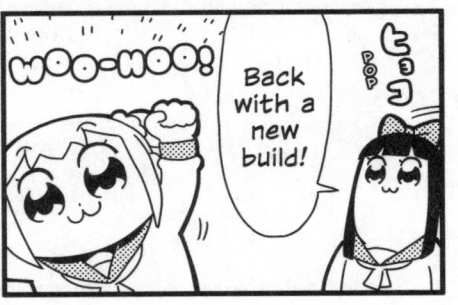

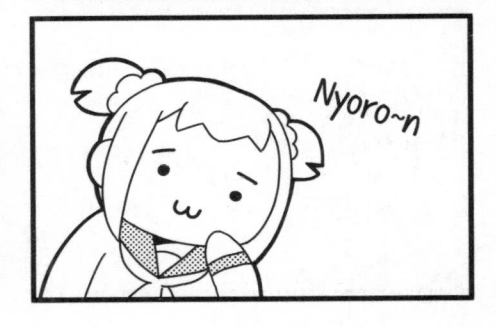

253

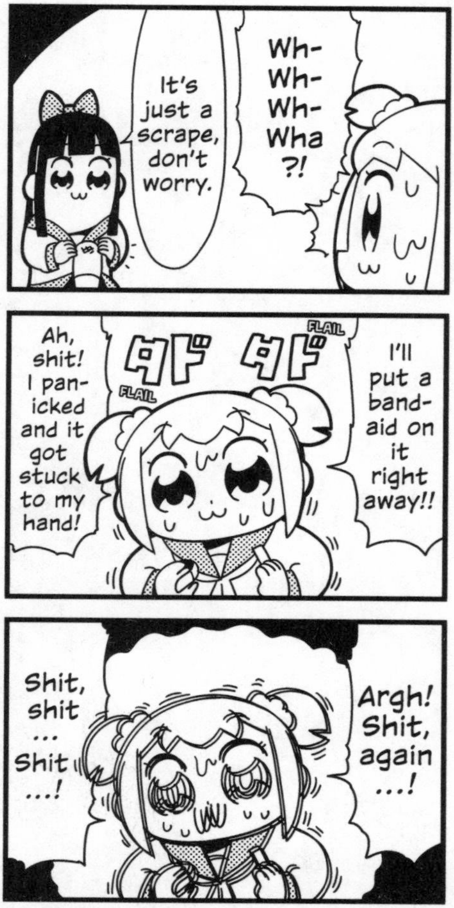
Wh-
Wh-
Wh-
Wha ?!
It's just a scrape, don't worry.
I'll put a band-aid on it right away!!
FLAIL
タド タド
FLAIL
Ah, shit! I panicked and it got stuck to my hand!
Argh! Shit, again ...!
Shit, shit ... Shit ...!
Shiiiiiiiiiiiiiiiiiiiiiiiiittt!!!

254

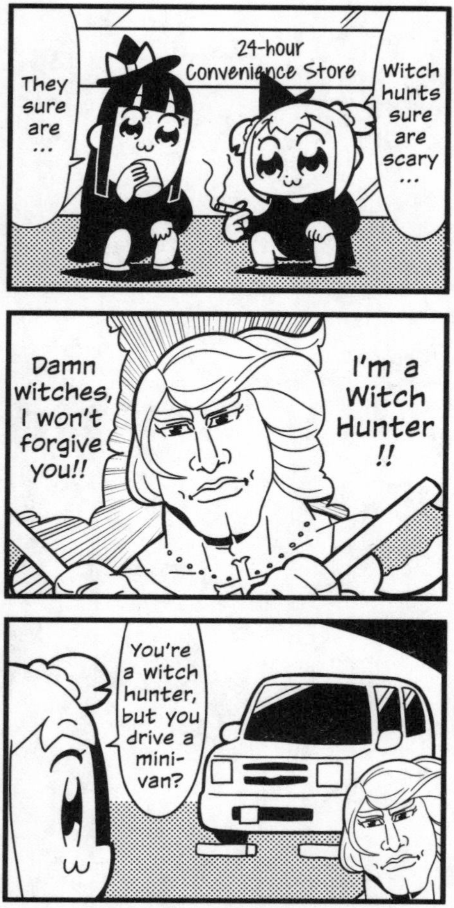
24-hour Convenience Store
Witch hunts sure are scary ...
They sure are ...
I'm a Witch Hunter !!
Damn witches, I won't forgive you!!
You're a witch hunter, but you drive a mini-van?
Did you just make fun of minivans ?
Damn witches, I won't forgive you!!!

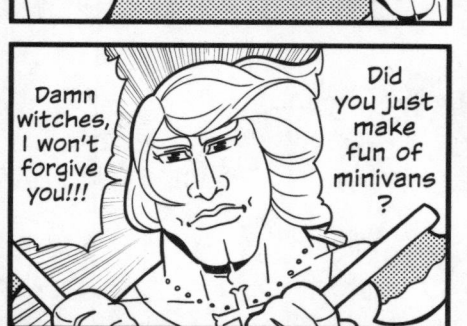

To be continued...

Waaaa
ヒィーン
WHIIIINE
Oh, poor girl. Can't tie your kimono?
I'll give you a hand!
You are my every-thing...
?

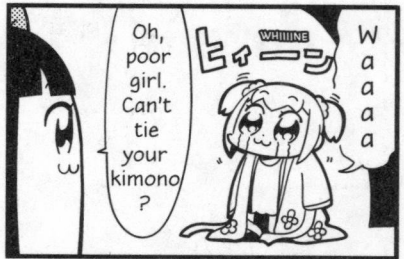

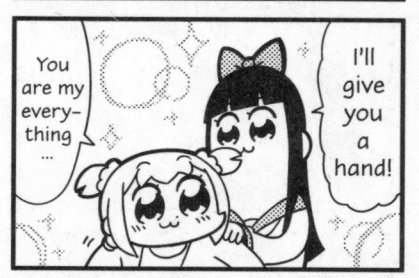

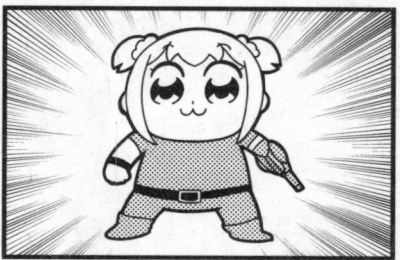

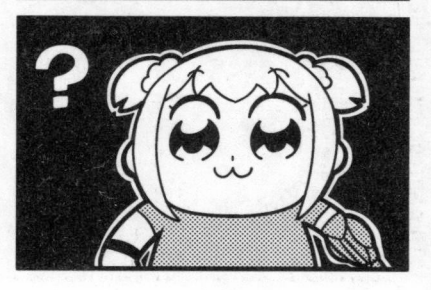

255

POP TEAM EPIC

Bkub Okawa

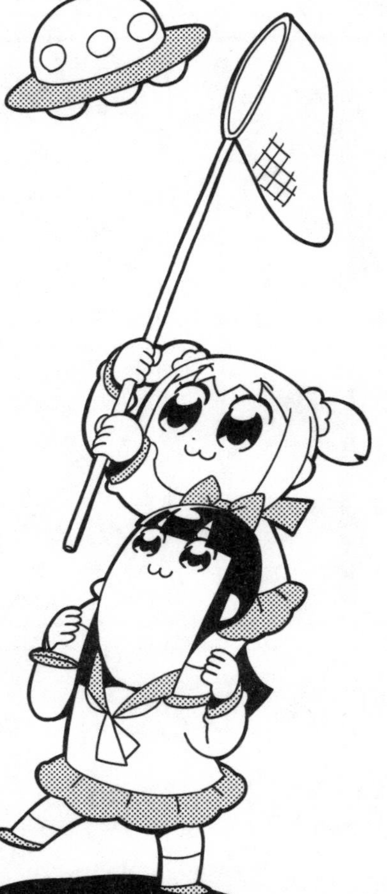

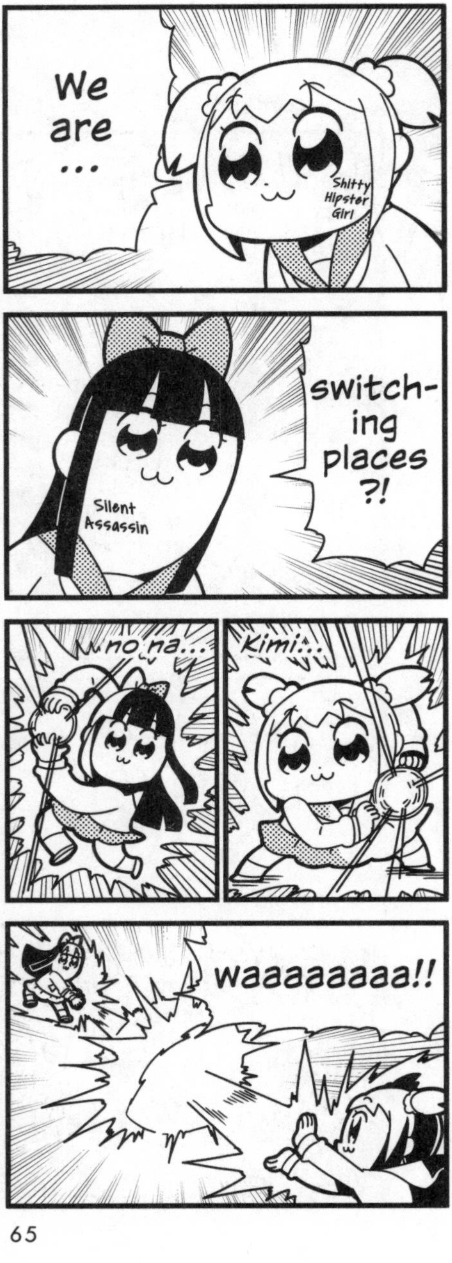

We are ...
Shitty Hipster Girl
switch-ing places ?!
Silent Assassin
Kimi...
...no na...
waaaaaaaa!!

☆This author must not have watched the film.

256

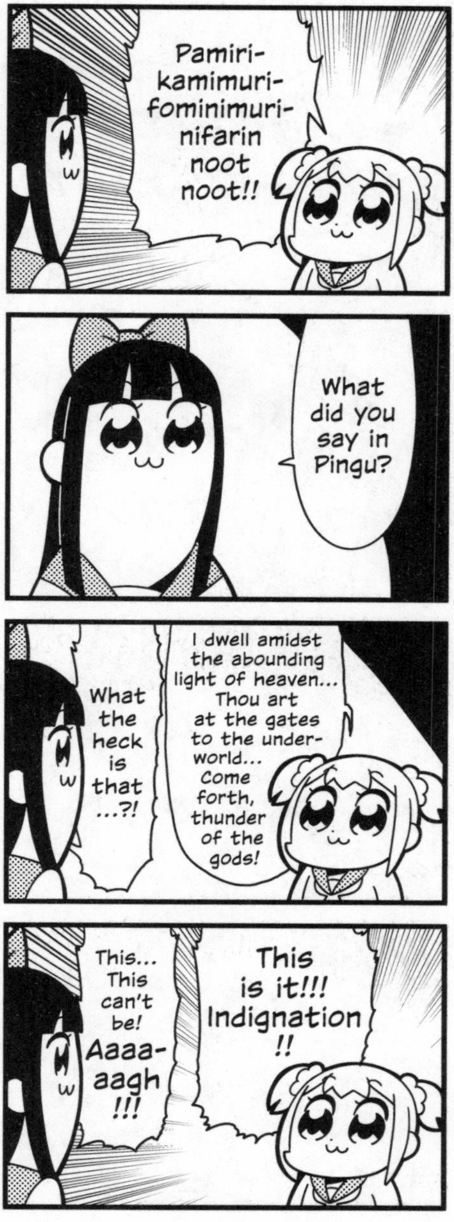
Pamiri-kamimuri-fominimuri-nifarin noot noot!!
What did you say in Pingu?
I dwell amidst the abounding light of heaven... Thou art at the gates to the under-world... Come forth, thunder of the gods!
What the heck is that ...?!
This is it!!! Indignation !!
This... This can't be! Aaaa-aagh !!!

257

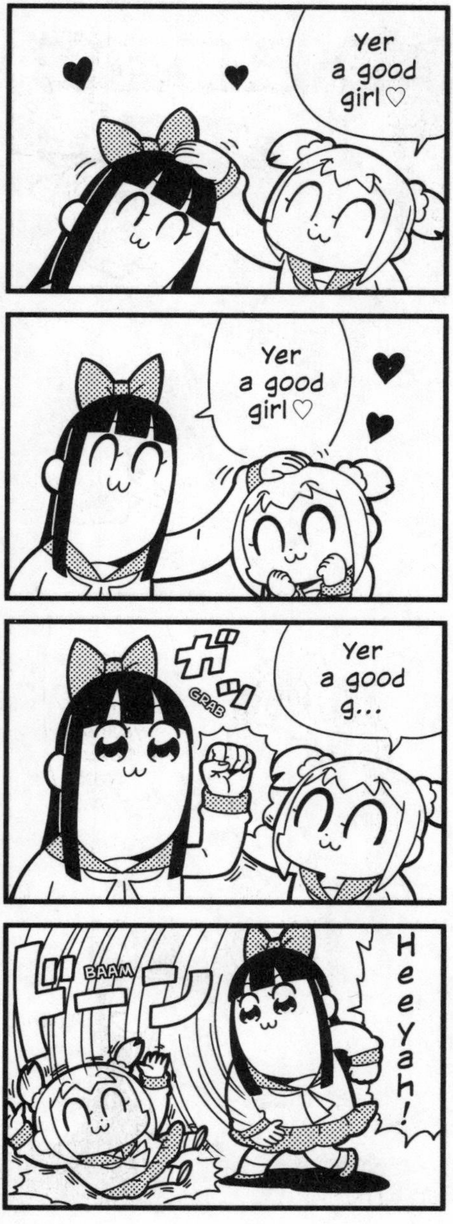
Yer a good girl♡
Yer a good girl♡
Yer a good g...
GRAB
Heeyah!
BAAM

258

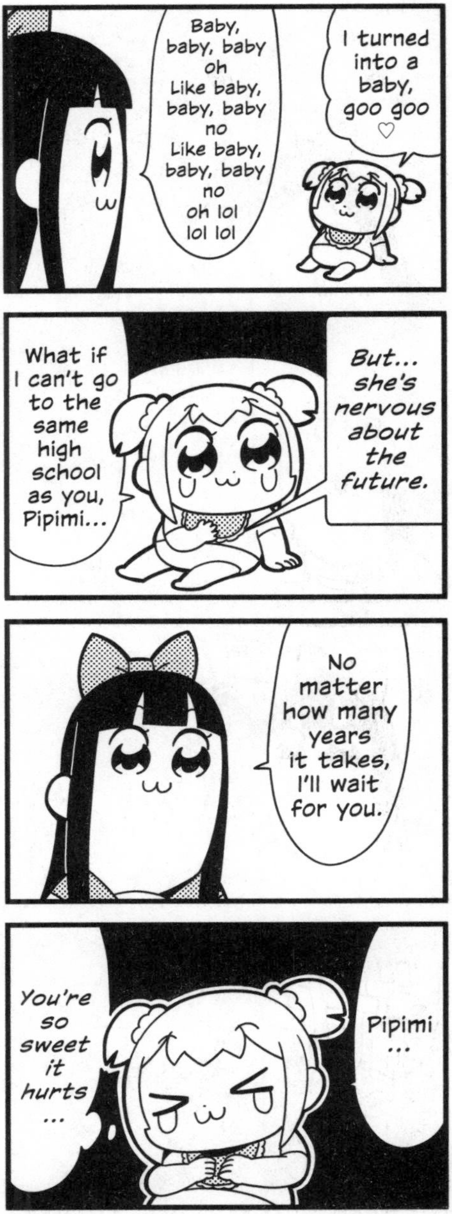
I turned into a baby, goo goo ♡
Baby, baby, baby oh Like baby, baby, baby no Like baby, baby, baby no oh lol lol lol
But... she's nervous about the future.
What if I can't go to the same high school as you, Pipimi...
No matter how many years it takes, I'll wait for you.
Pipimi ...
You're so sweet it hurts ...

259

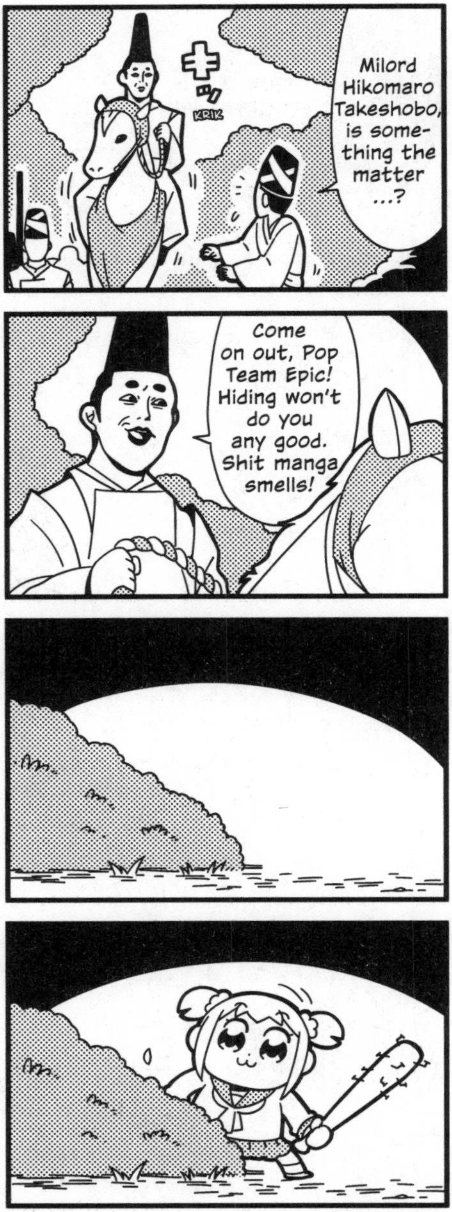
Milord Hikomaro Takeshobo, is something the matter ...?
KRIK
Come on out, Pop Team Epic! Hiding won't do you any good. Shit manga smells!

260

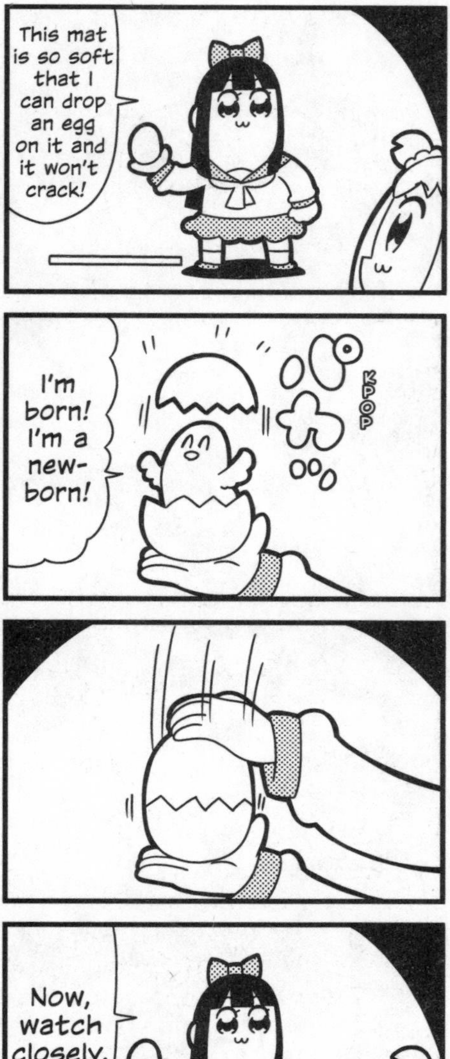
This mat is so soft that I can drop an egg on it and it won't crack!
I'm born! I'm a new-born!
KPOP
Now, watch closely.

261

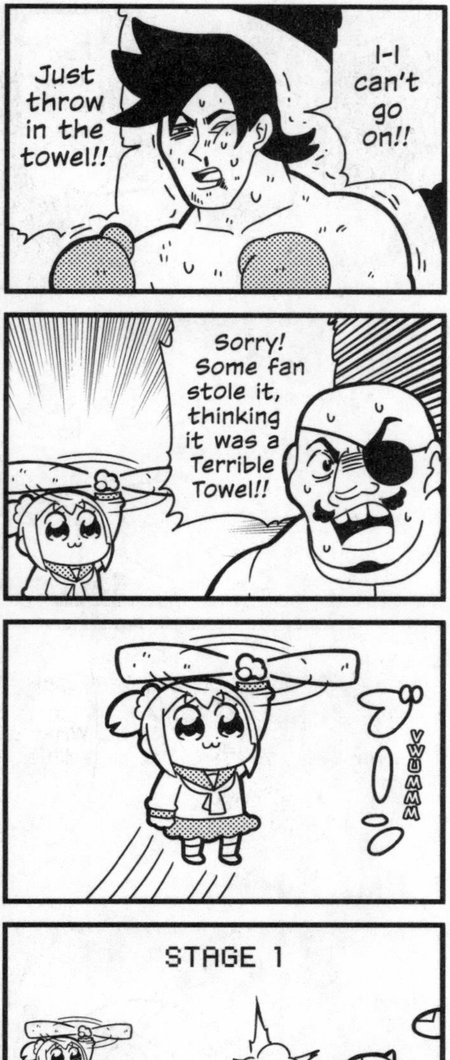
I-I can't go on!!
Just throw in the towel!!
Sorry! Some fan stole it, thinking it was a Terrible Towel!!
VWUMMM
STAGE 1

262

I am the Demon King ...
Demon King! Since your throne was destroyed, I have prepared a beanbag chair instead!
Ooh ... What's this ...?
This is awe-some ♡ I don't even want to move...
Hells yeah. Demon King has been sealed away.

263

Just gonna ...
go win the world.
Okay, I won it ...
Seri-ously ?!
She's seri-ous.
Wait, seriously ?!
Super serious ...
Yet an-other lie was told that day ...

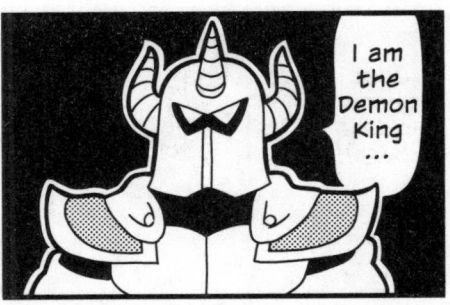

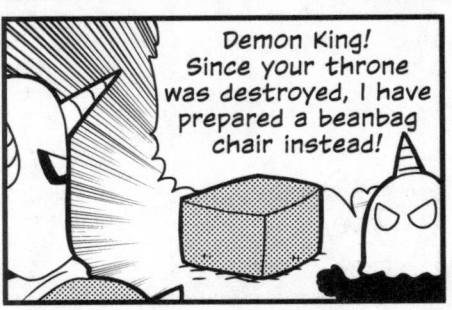

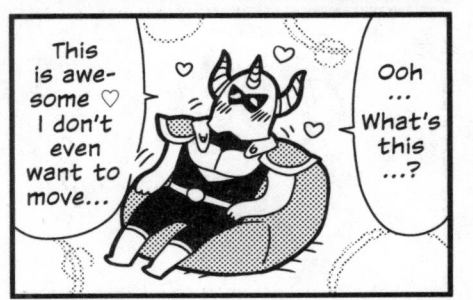

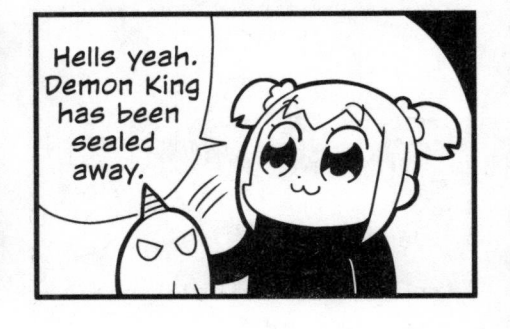

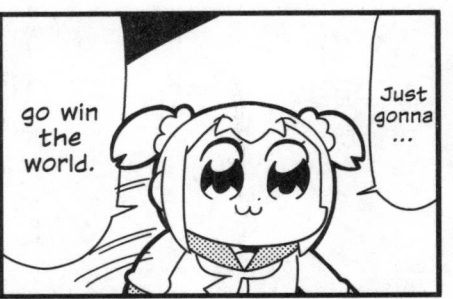

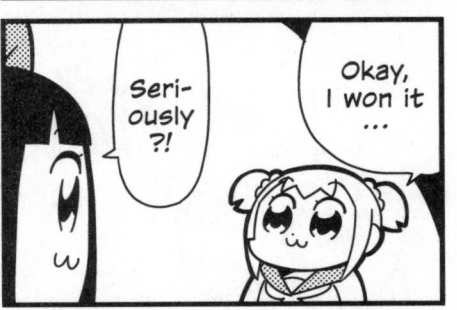

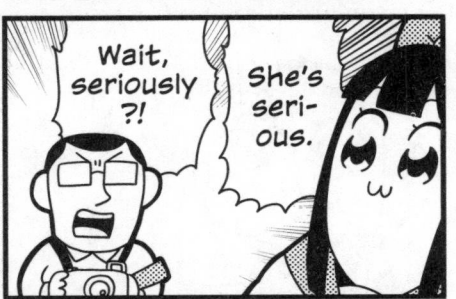

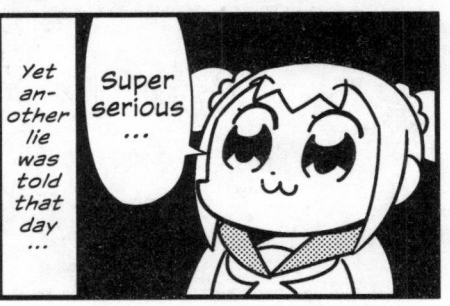

264

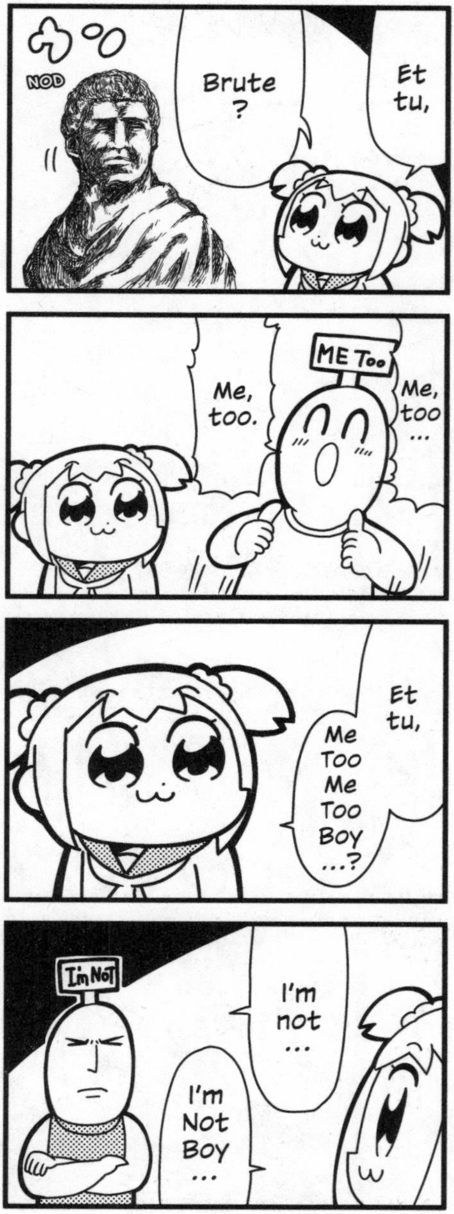
Et tu,
Brute ?
NOD
Me, too ...
ME Too
Me, too.
Et tu,
Me Too Me Too Boy ...?
I'm Not
I'm not ...
I'm Not Boy ...

265

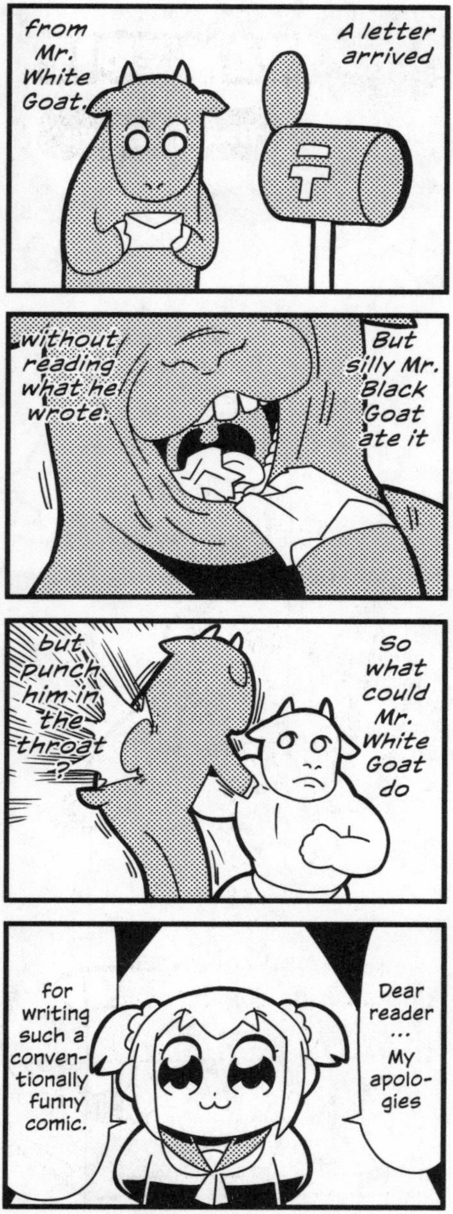
A letter arrived
from Mr. White Goat.
But silly Mr. Black Goat ate it
without reading what he wrote.
So what could Mr. White Goat do
but punch him in the throat ?
Dear reader ... My apologies
for writing such a conventionally funny comic.

To be continued...

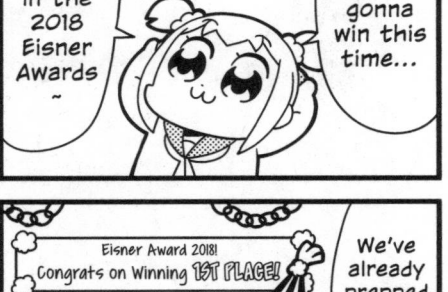

POP TEAM EPIC

Bkub Okawa

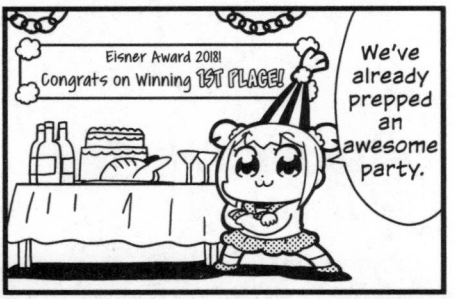

266

Yeah! We're gonna win this time...
First place in the 2018 Eisner Awards ~
Eisner Award 2018! Congrats on Winning 1ST PLACE!
We've already prepped an awesome party.
These seats are for the fanboys ♡
And these seats are for the haters and Takeshobo employees ♡

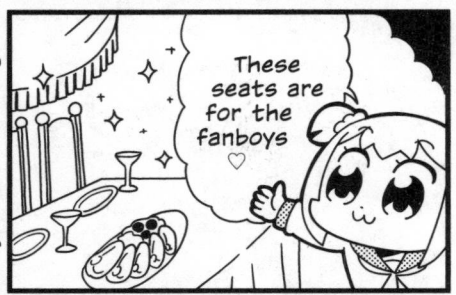

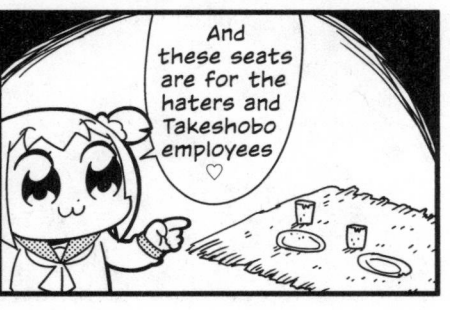

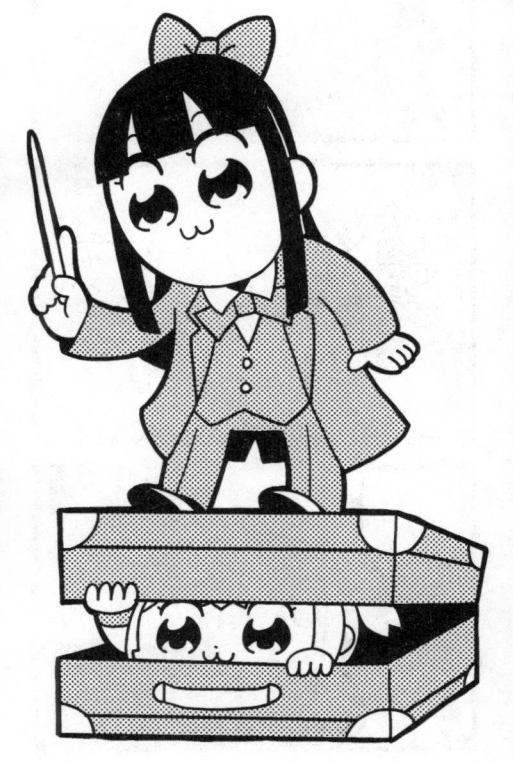

☆This manga ain't award-worthy! It ain't amazing! It's shit!!

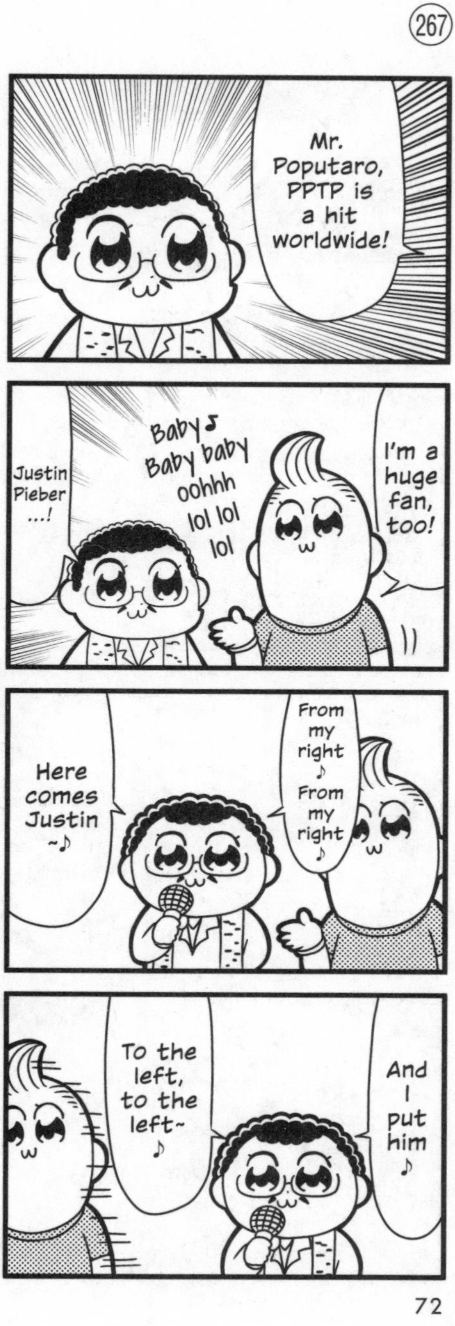
267
Mr. Poputaro, PPTP is a hit worldwide!
I'm a huge fan, too!
Baby♪ Baby baby oohhh lol lol lol
Justin Pieber ...!
From my right ♪ From my right ♪
Here comes Justin ~♪
And I put him ♪
To the left, to the left~ ♪

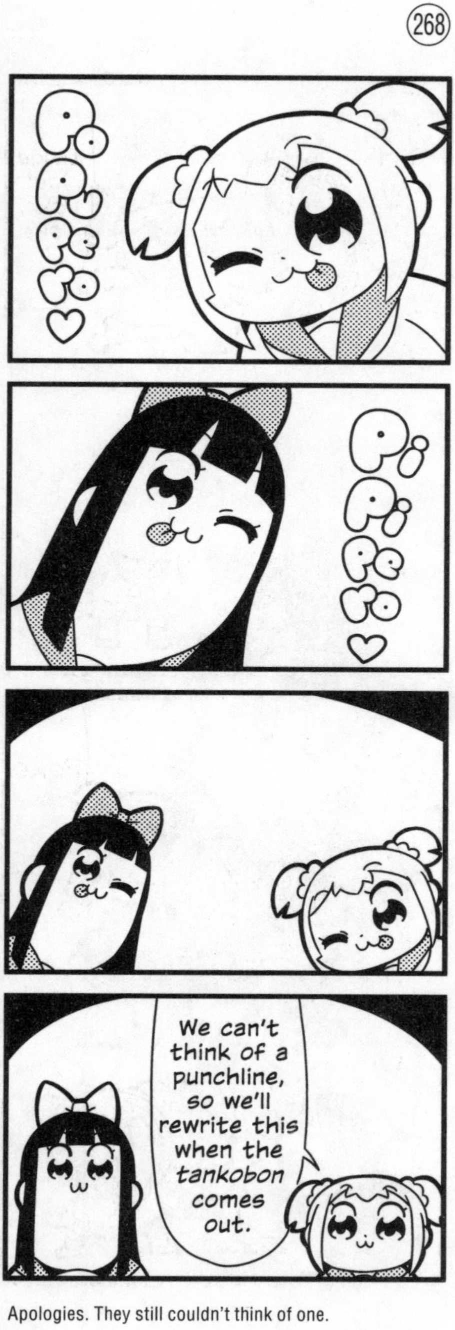
268
Po Pu Pe ro ♡
Pi Pi Pe ro ♡
We can't think of a punchline, so we'll rewrite this when the tankobon comes out.

Apologies. They still couldn't think of one.

269

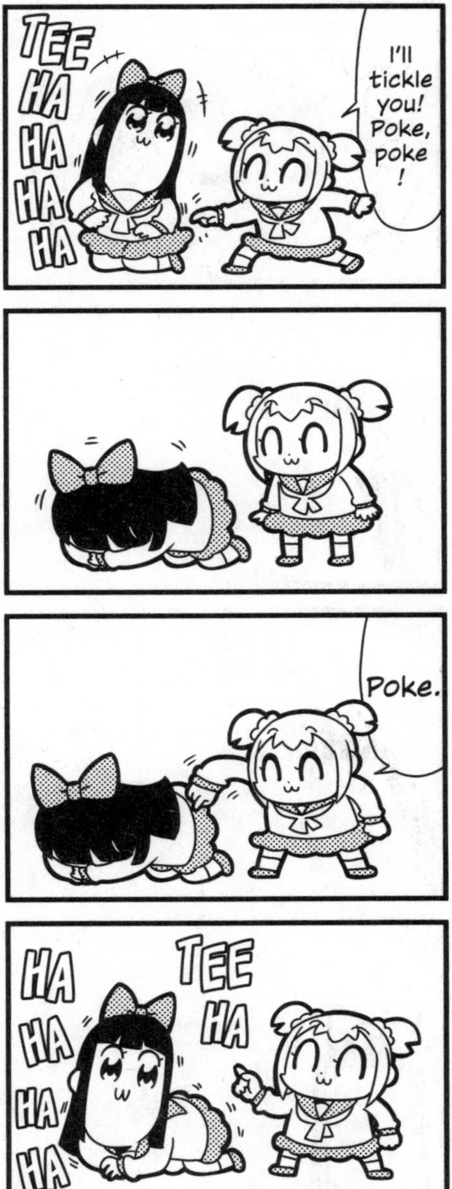
I'll tickle you! Poke, poke!
TEE HA HA HA HA
Poke.
TEE HA
HA HA HA HA

270

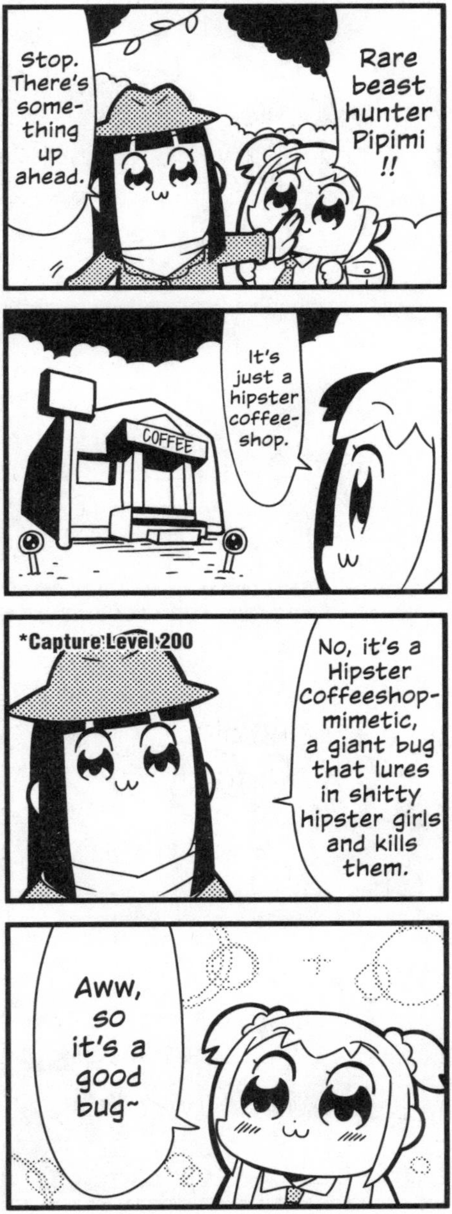
Rare beast hunter Pipimi !!
Stop. There's something up ahead.
It's just a hipster coffee-shop.
COFFEE
No, it's a Hipster Coffeeshop-mimetic, a giant bug that lures in shitty hipster girls and kills them.
*Capture Level 200
Aww, so it's a good bug~

271

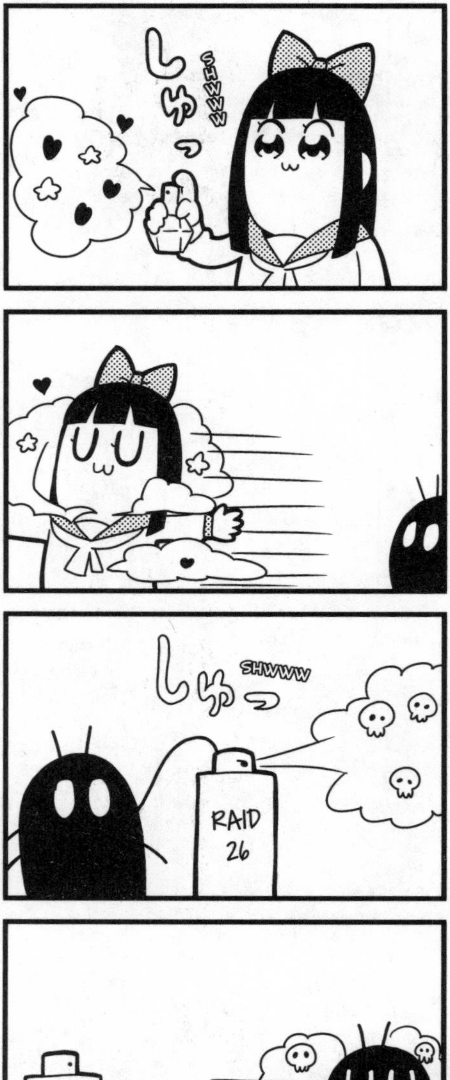
しゅっ
SHWWW
しゅっ
SHWWW
RAID 26
RAID 26

272

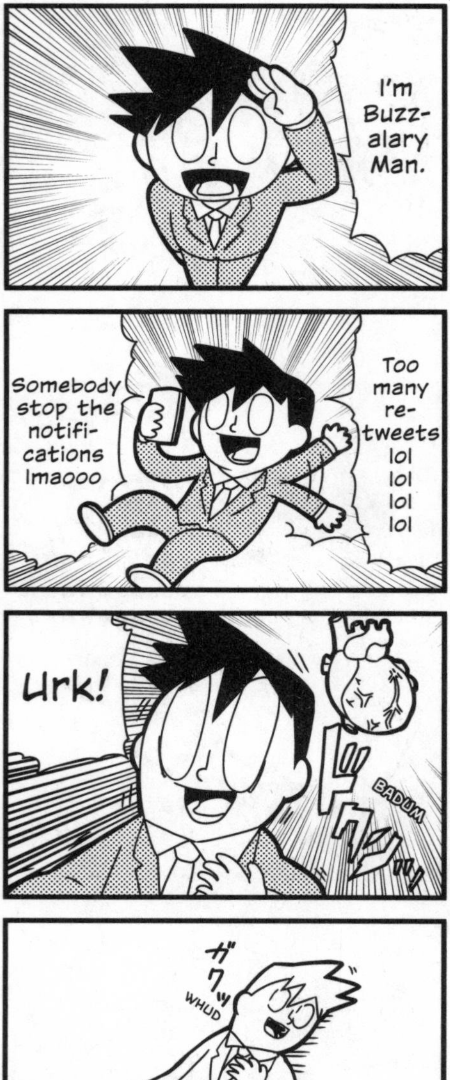
I'm Buzz-alary Man.
Too many re-tweets lol lol lol lol
Somebody stop the notifi-cations lmaooo
Urk!
BADUM
WHUD

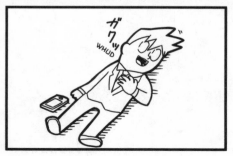

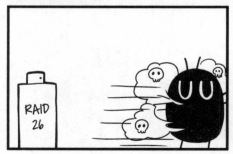

273

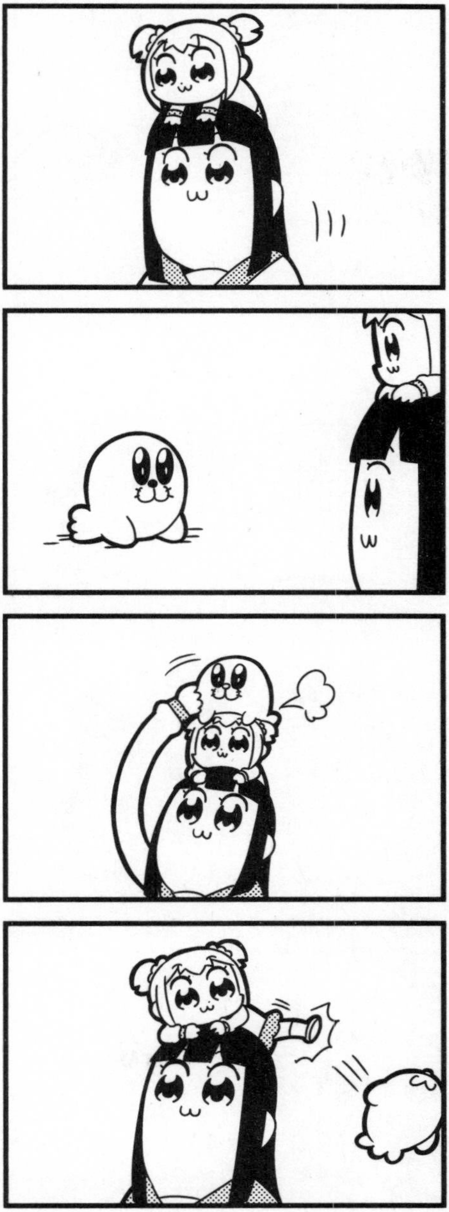

274

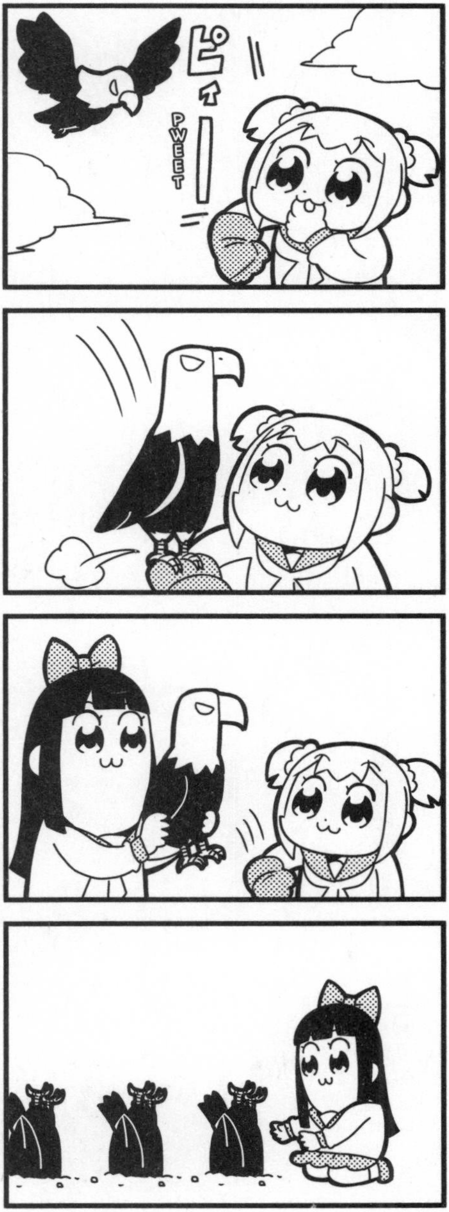
ピィー
PWEET

275

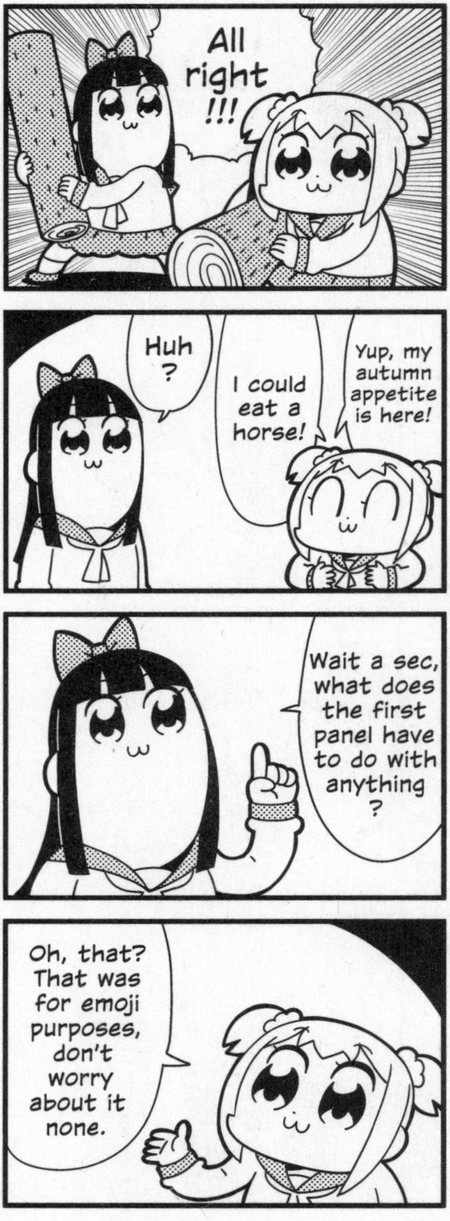
All right !!!
Yup, my autumn appetite is here!
I could eat a horse!
Huh ?
Wait a sec, what does the first panel have to do with anything ?
Oh, that? That was for emoji purposes, don't worry about it none.

276

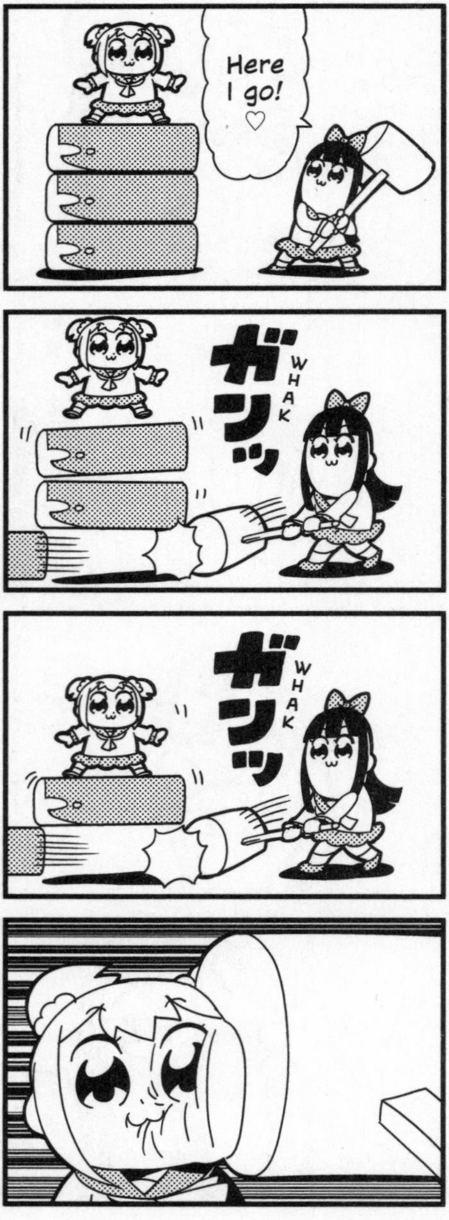
Here I go! ♡
ガツッ
WHAK
ガツッ
WHAK

277

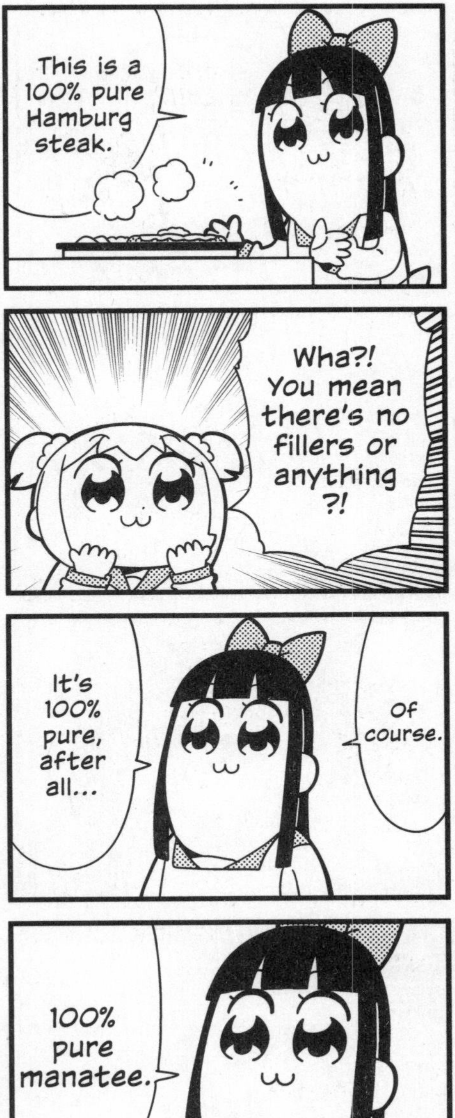

This is a 100% pure Hamburg steak.
Wha?! You mean there's no fillers or anything?!
It's 100% pure, after all...
Of course.
100% pure manatee.

278

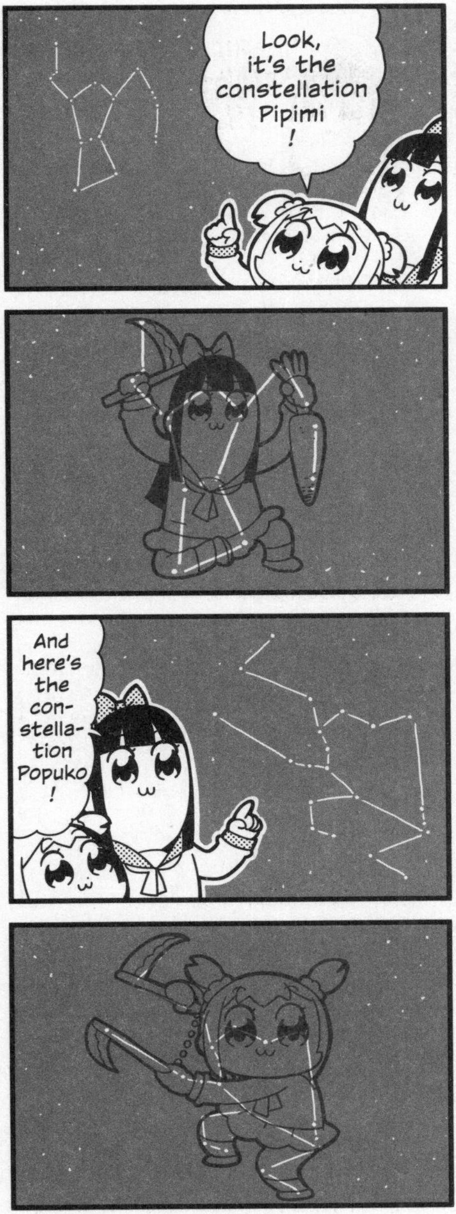

Look, it's the constellation Pipimi!
And here's the con-stella-tion Popuko!

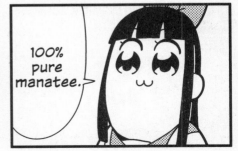

279

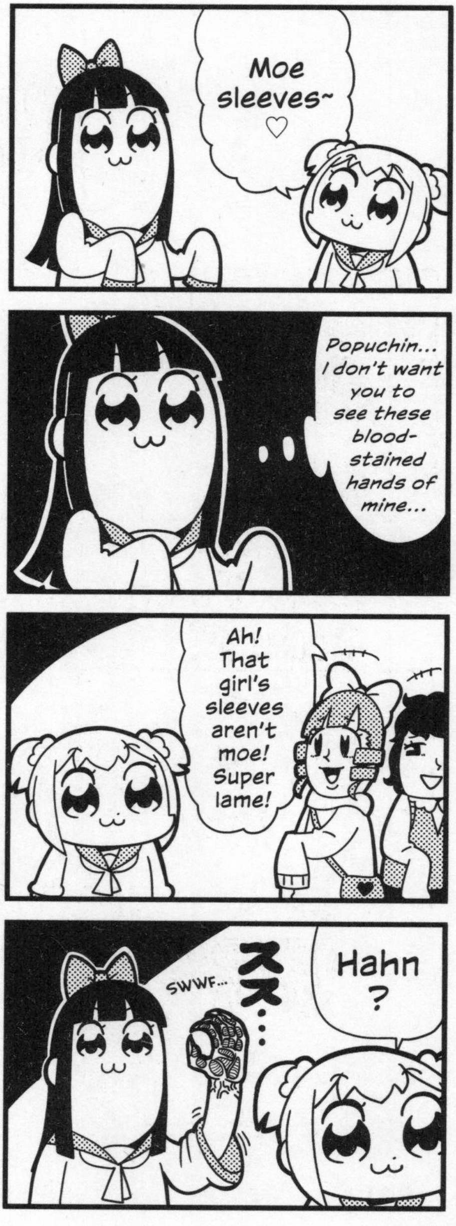
Moe sleeves~ ♡
Popuchin... I don't want you to see these blood-stained hands of mine...
Ah! That girl's sleeves aren't moe! Super lame!
Hahn?
スス…
SWWF...

280

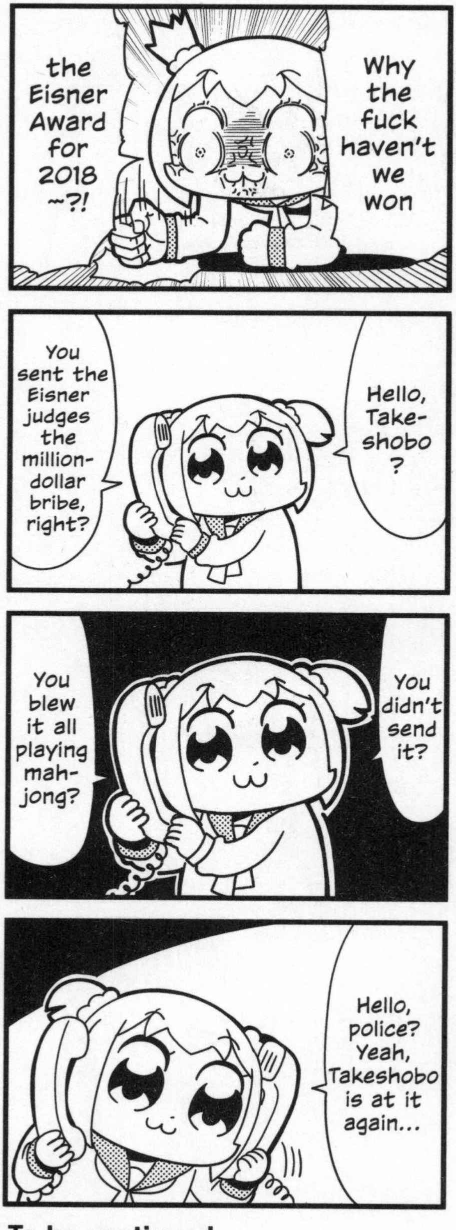
Why the fuck haven't we won
the Eisner Award for 2018 ~?!
Hello, Take-shobo?
You sent the Eisner judges the million-dollar bribe, right?
You didn't send it?
You blew it all playing mah-jong?
Hello, police? Yeah, Takeshobo is at it again...

To be continued...

Extra Charge For Shitty Hipster Girls Now In Effect
Pop Team Epic Café

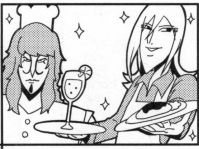

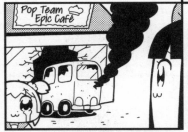

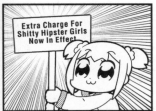

Let's Visit the **Pop Team Epic Café 2!**

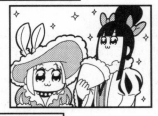

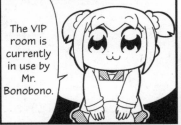

The VIP room is currently in use by Mr. Bonobono.

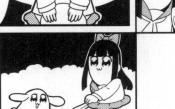

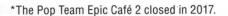

*The Pop Team Epic Café 2 closed in 2017.

My name is Grandpa Woods.
BAMM
KEEP IT DOWN, YA GEEZER !!!! IT'S TOO EARLY FOR YOUR SHIT!!!
SLAM
My name is Grandpa Woods...

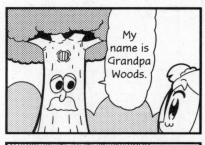

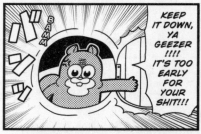

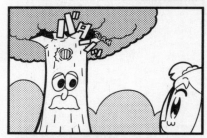

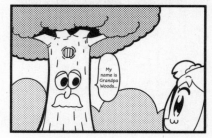

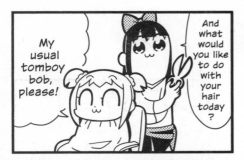

POP TEAM EPIC

Bkub Okawa

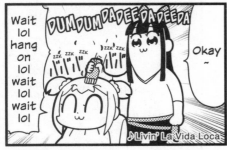

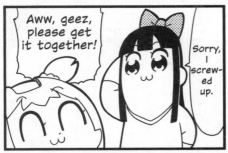

281

And what would you like to do with your hair today?
My usual tomboy bob, please!
DUMDUM DADEE DA DEEDA
Okay ~
Wait lol hang on lol wait lol wait lol
ZZK ZZK ZZK ZZK ZZK
♪Livin' La Vida Loca
Sorry, I screw-ed up.
Aww, geez, please get it together!
DUMDUM DADEE DA DEEDA
Okay ~
Wait lol hang on lol wait lol wait lol
ZZK ZZK ZZK ZZK ZZK
♪Livin' La Vida Loca

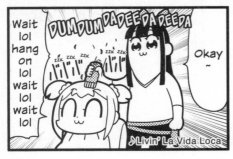

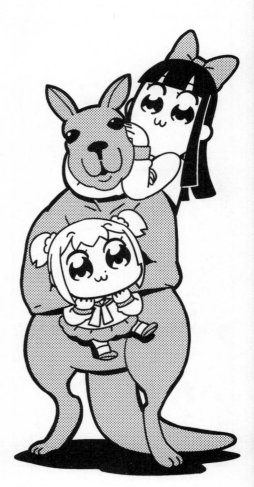

282

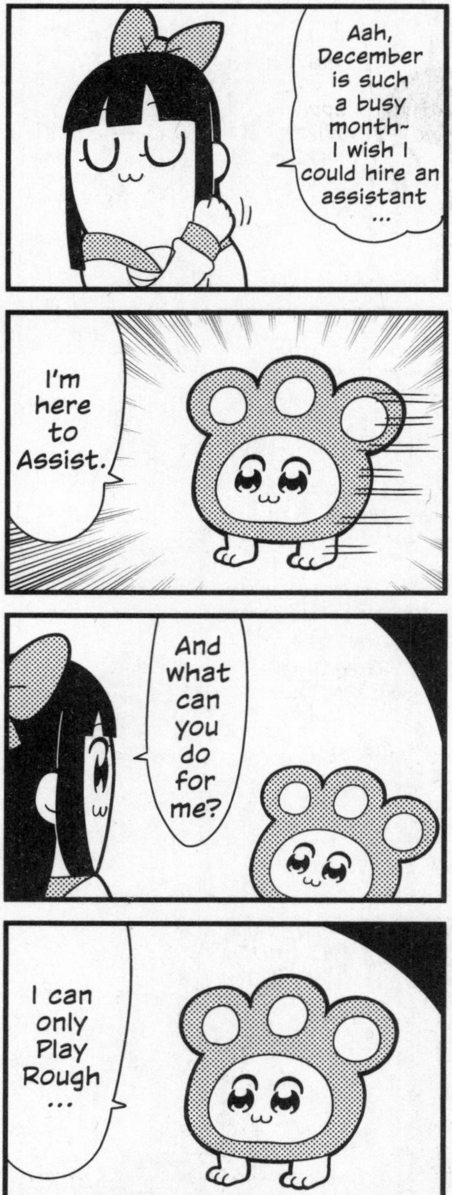
Aah, December is such a busy month~ I wish I could hire an assistant ...
I'm here to Assist.
And what can you do for me?
I can only Play Rough ...

283

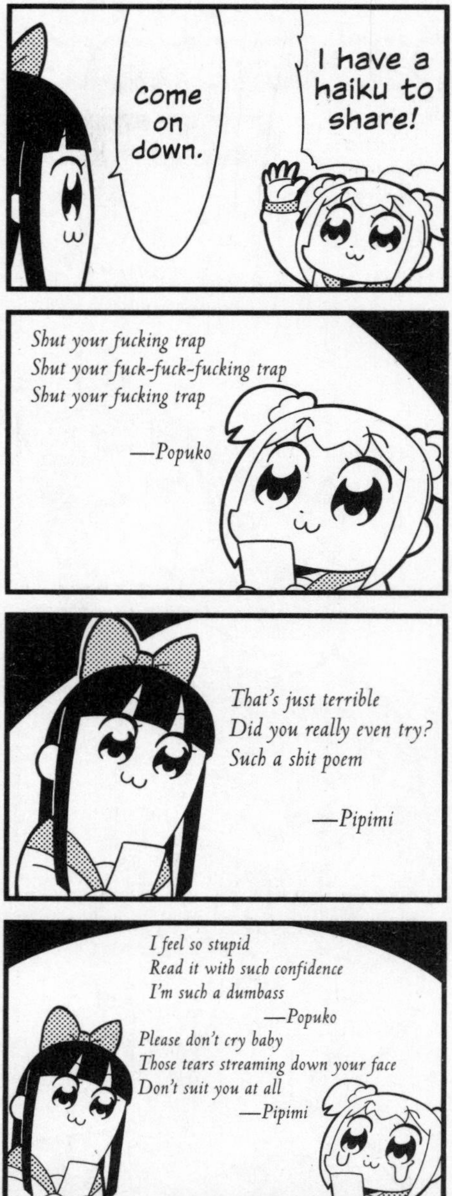
I have a haiku to share!
Come on down.
Shut your fucking trap
Shut your fuck-fuck-fucking trap
Shut your fucking trap
—Popuko
That's just terrible
Did you really even try?
Such a shit poem
—Pipimi
I feel so stupid
Read it with such confidence
I'm such a dumbass
—Popuko
Please don't cry baby
Those tears streaming down your face
Don't suit you at all
—Pipimi

284

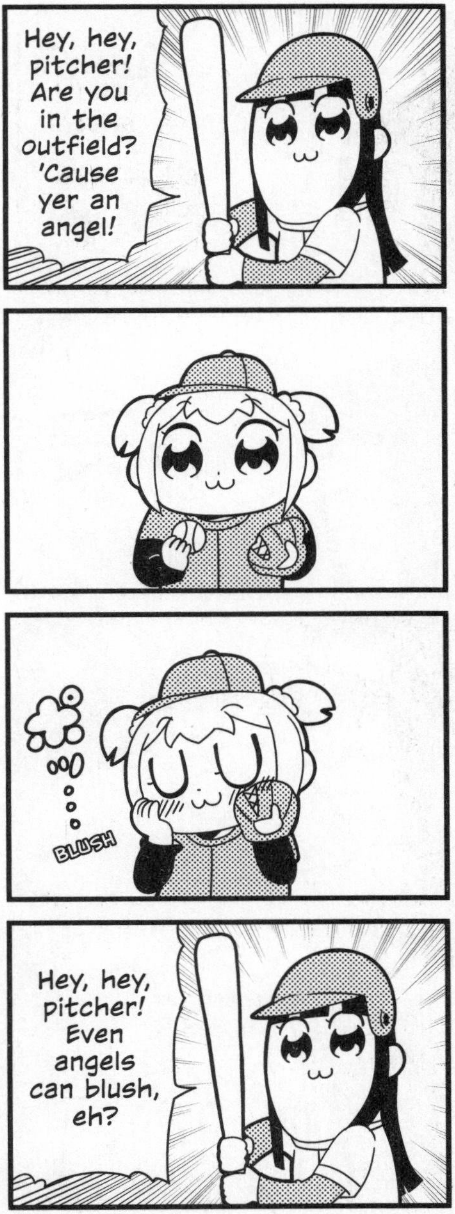

Hey, hey, pitcher! Are you in the outfield? 'Cause yer an angel!
BLUSH
Hey, hey, pitcher! Even angels can blush, eh?

285

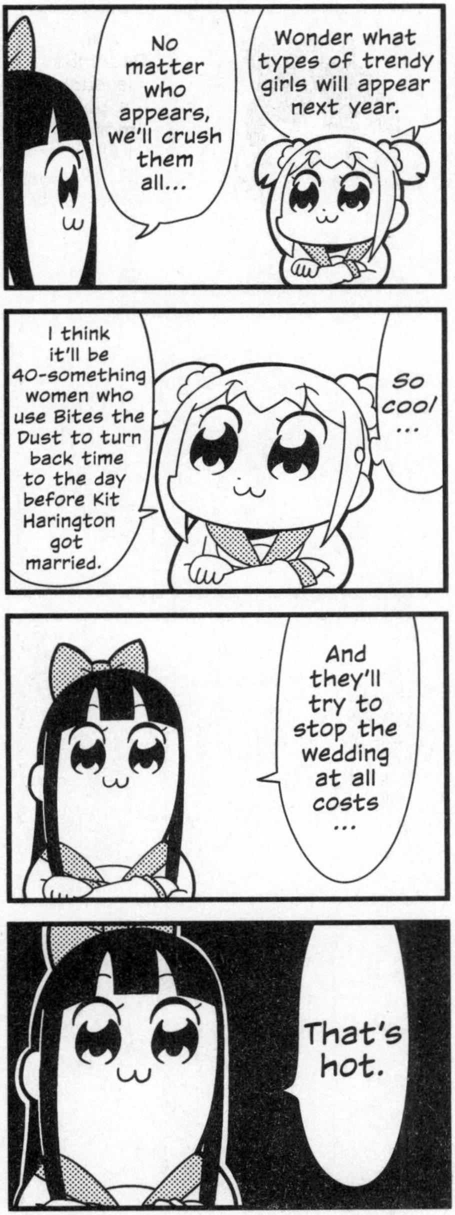

Wonder what types of trendy girls will appear next year.
No matter who appears, we'll crush them all...
So cool ...
I think it'll be 40-something women who use Bites the Dust to turn back time to the day before Kit Harington got married.
And they'll try to stop the wedding at all costs ...
That's hot.

286

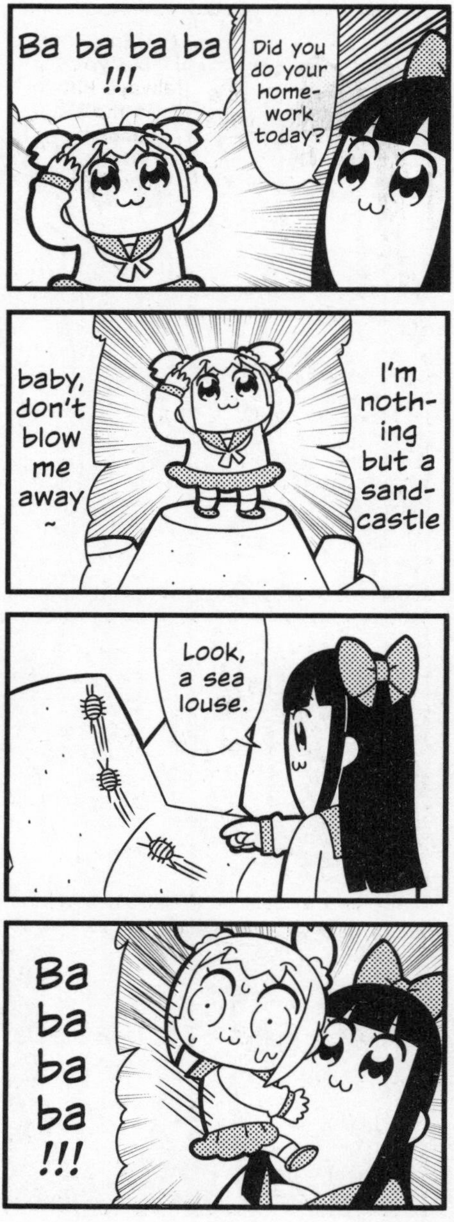
Did you do your home-work today?
Ba ba ba ba !!!
I'm noth-ing but a sand-castle
baby, don't blow me away ~
Look, a sea louse.
Ba ba ba ba !!!

287

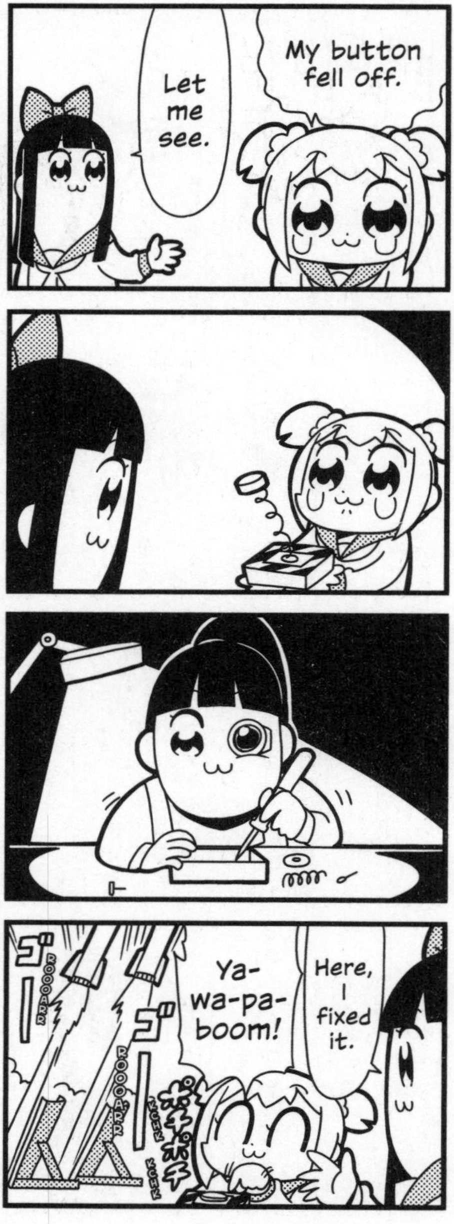
My button fell off.
Let me see.
Here, I fixed it.
Ya-wa-pa-boom!
ポチポチ
KCHK KCHK
ゴー
ROOOARR
ゴー
ROOOARR

288

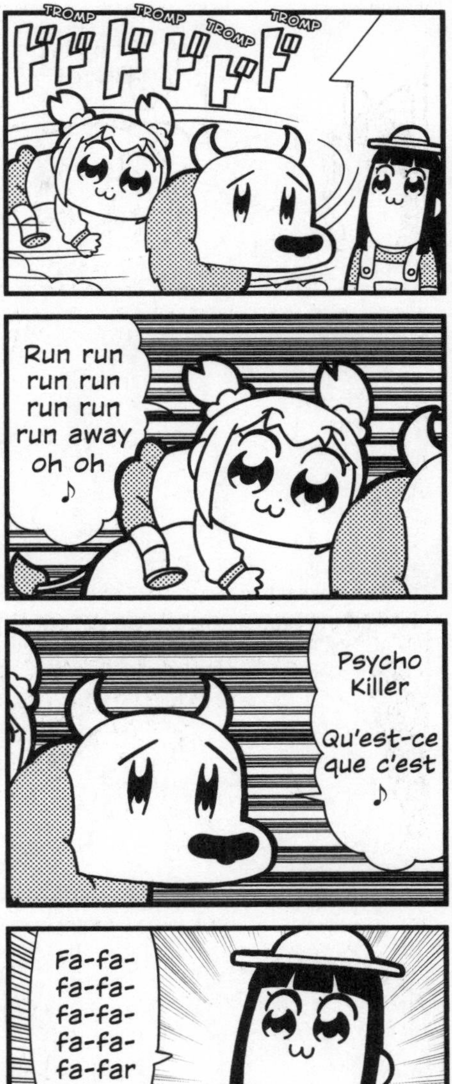
TROMP
TROMP
TROMP
TROMP
Run run run run run run run away oh oh ♪
Psycho Killer
Qu'est-ce que c'est ♪
Fa-fa-fa-fa-fa-fa-fa-fa-fa-fa-fa-far better ♪

289

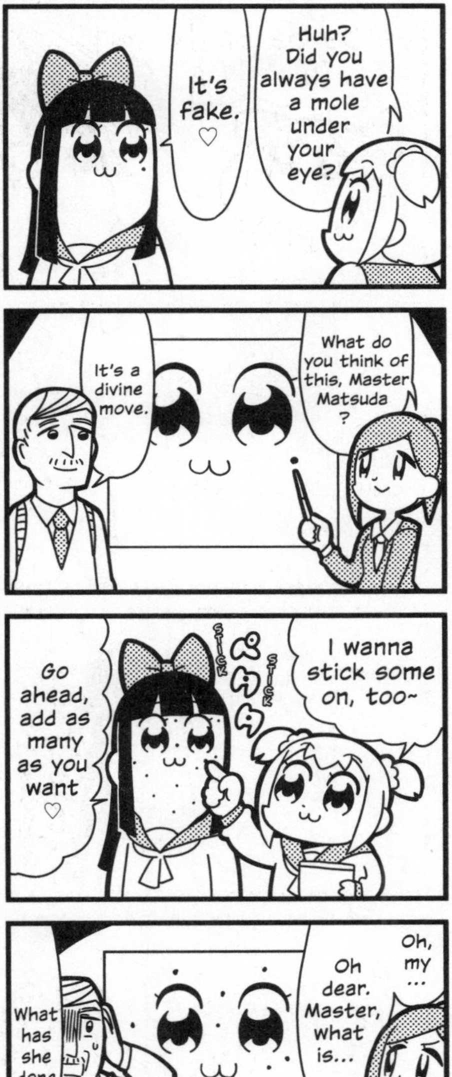
Huh? Did you always have a mole under your eye?
It's fake. ♡
What do you think of this, Master Matsuda?
It's a divine move.
I wanna stick some on, too~
STICK
STICK
Go ahead, add as many as you want ♡
Oh, my …
Oh dear. Master, what is…
What has she done …

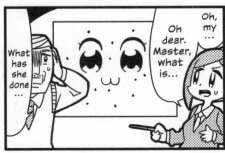

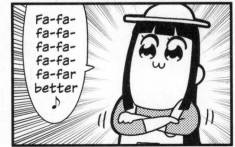

290

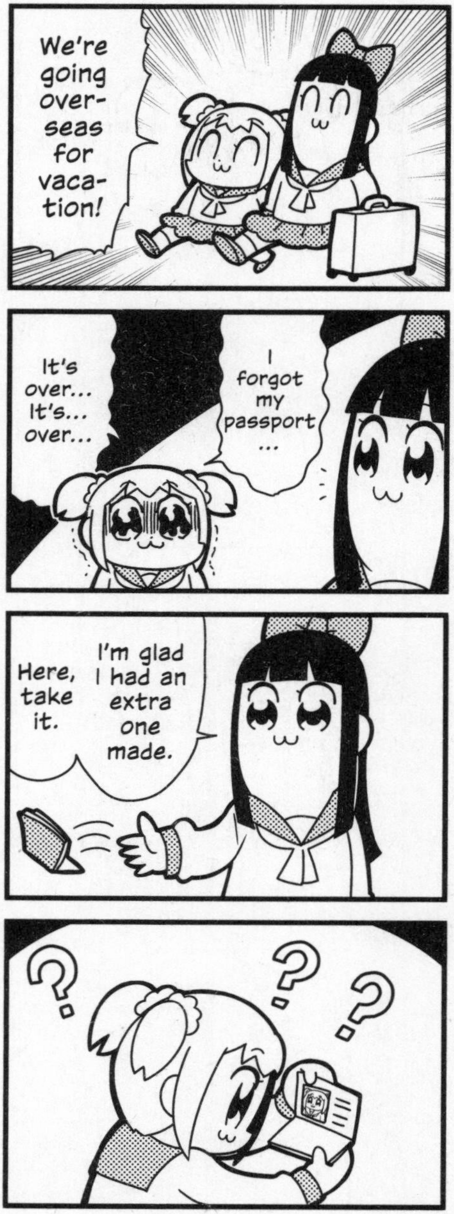
We're going over-seas for vaca-tion!
I forgot my passport...
It's over... It's... over...
I'm glad I had an extra one made.
Here, take it.
? ? ?

291

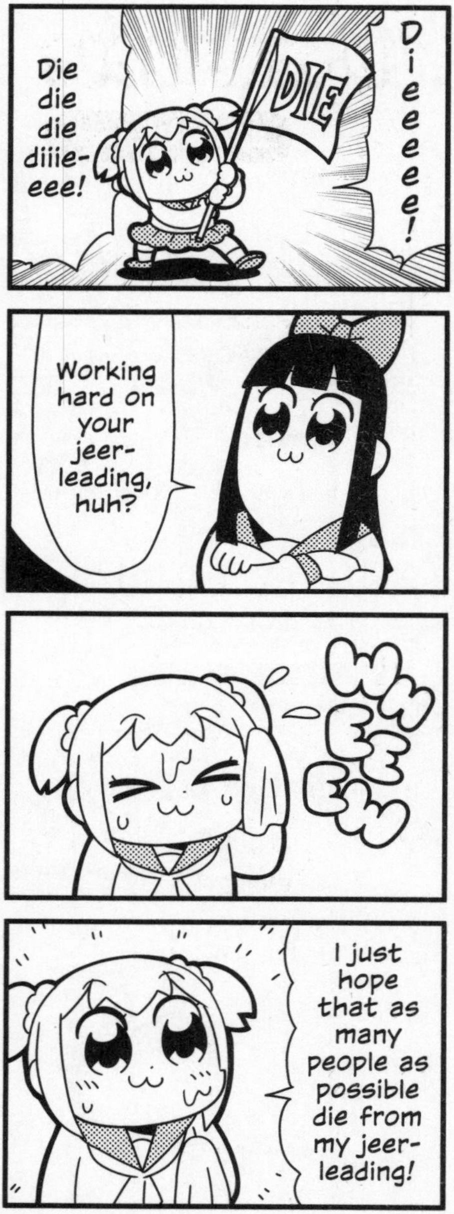
DIE
Dieeeeee!
Die die die diiie-eee!
Working hard on your jeer-leading, huh?
WHEEEW
I just hope that as many people as possible die from my jeer-leading!

To be continued...

292

POP TEAM EPIC

Bkub Okawa

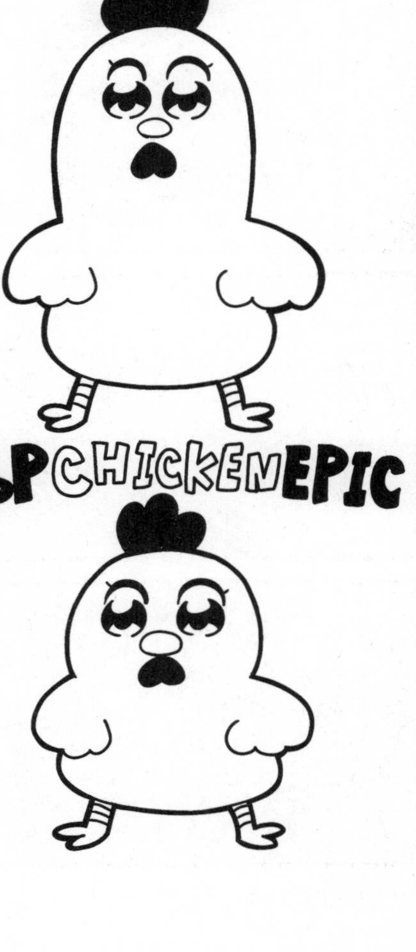
POP CHICKEN EPIC

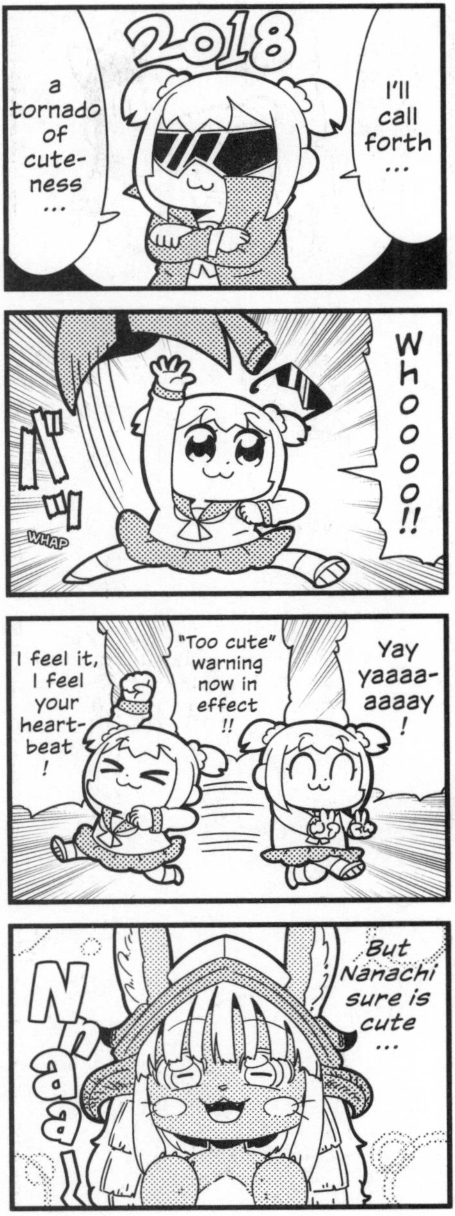
2018
I'll call forth ...
a tornado of cuteness ...
Whoooooo!!
WHAP
Yay yaaaa-aaaay!
"Too cute" warning now in effect !!
I feel it, I feel your heart-beat!
But Nanachi sure is cute ...
Nnaaa!

293

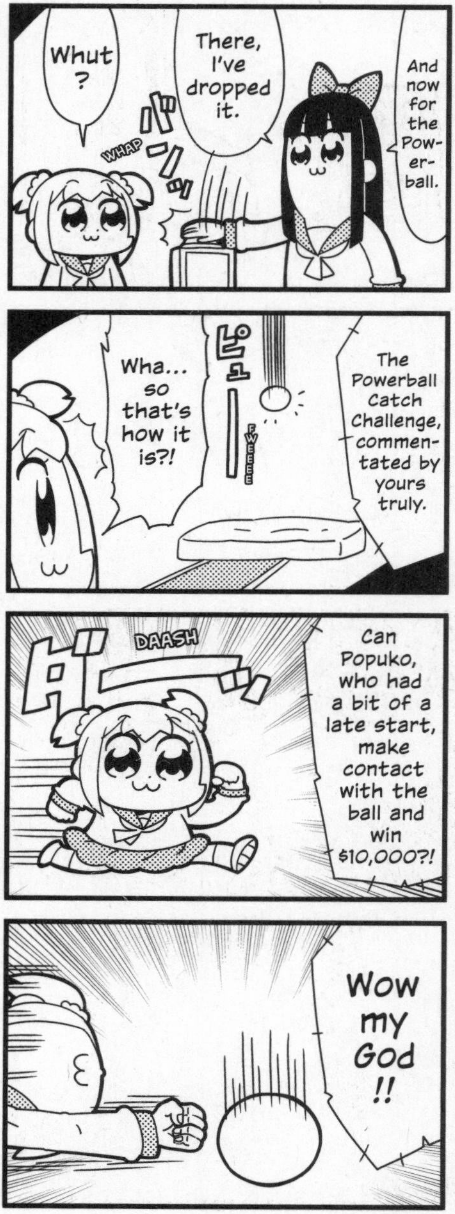
And now for the Pow-er-ball.
There, I've dropped it.
WHAP
Whut?
The Powerball Catch Challenge, commen-tated by yours truly.
Wha... so that's how it is?!
FWEEEE
Can Popuko, who had a bit of a late start, make contact with the ball and win $10,000?!
DAASH
Wow my God !!

294

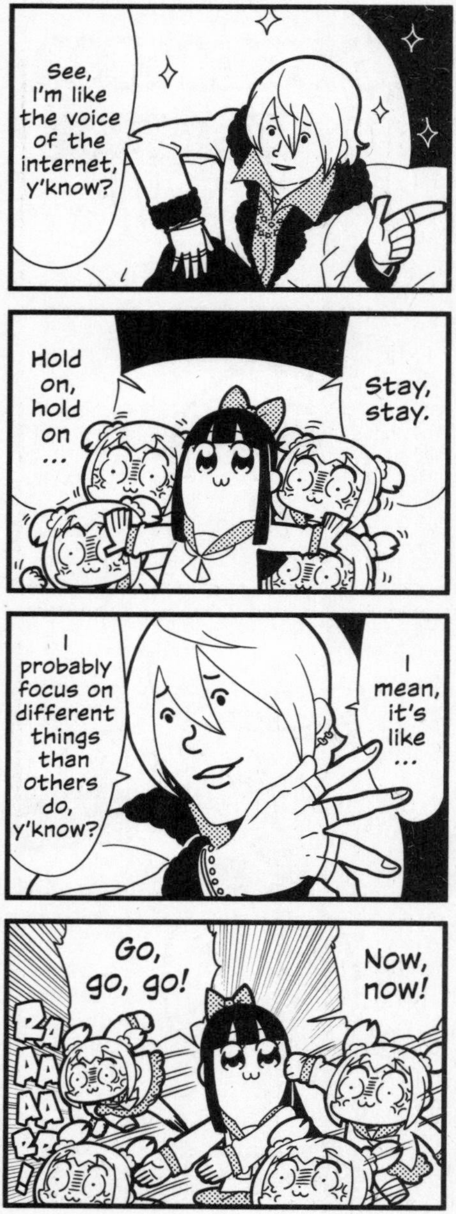
See, I'm like the voice of the internet, y'know?
Stay, stay.
Hold on, hold on ...
I mean, it's like ...
I probably focus on different things than others do, y'know?
Now, now!
Go, go, go!
RAAAAARR!

295

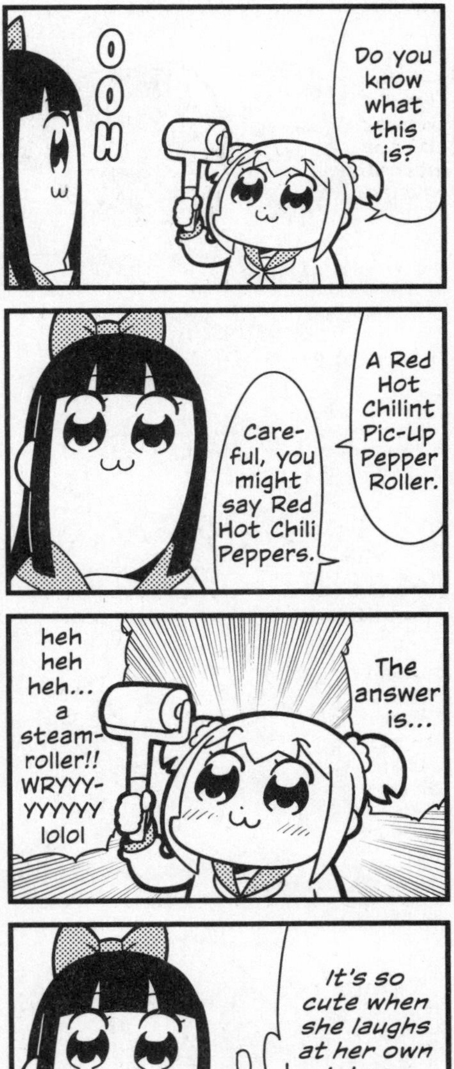
Do you know what this is?
OOH
A Red Hot Chilint Pic-Up Pepper Roller.
Care-ful, you might say Red Hot Chili Peppers.
The answer is...
heh heh heh... a steam-roller!! WRYYY-YYYYYY lolol
It's so cute when she laughs at her own jokes~

296

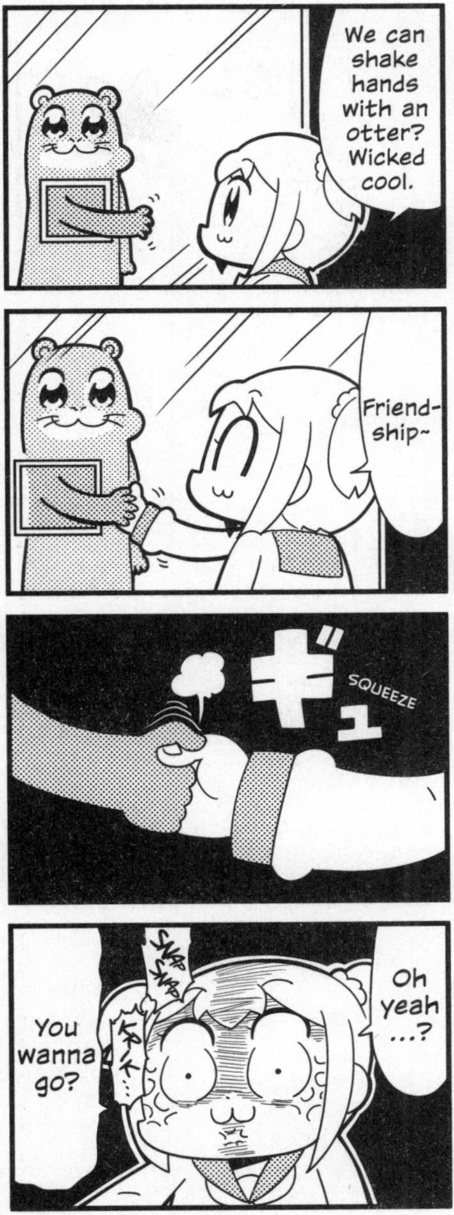
We can shake hands with an otter? Wicked cool.
Friend-ship~
ギュ
SQUEEZE
Oh yeah ...?
SNAP SNAP
You wanna go?

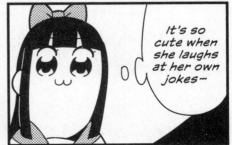

297

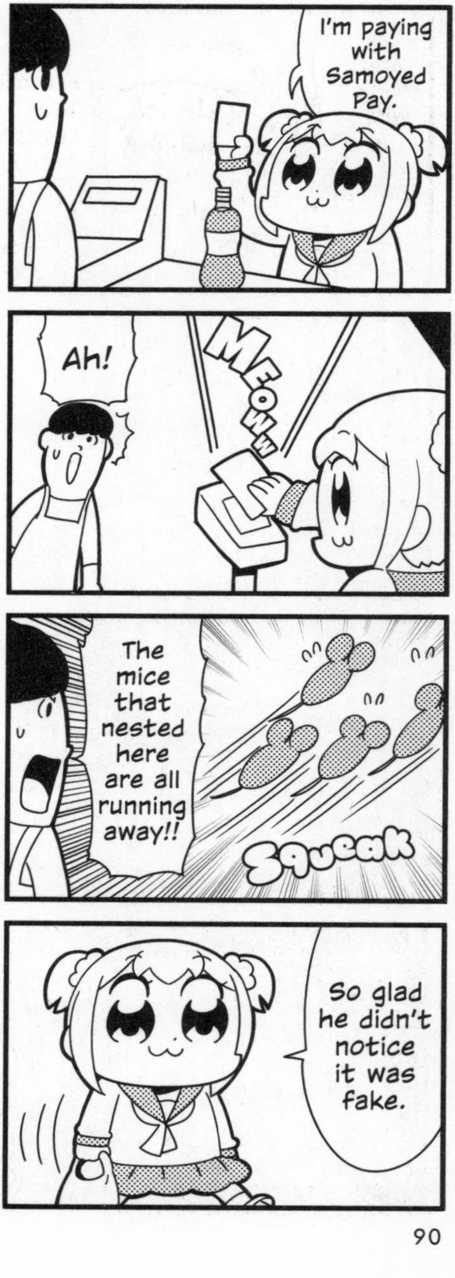
I'm paying with Samoyed Pay.
MEOWW
Ah!
The mice that nested here are all running away!!
Squeak
So glad he didn't notice it was fake.

298

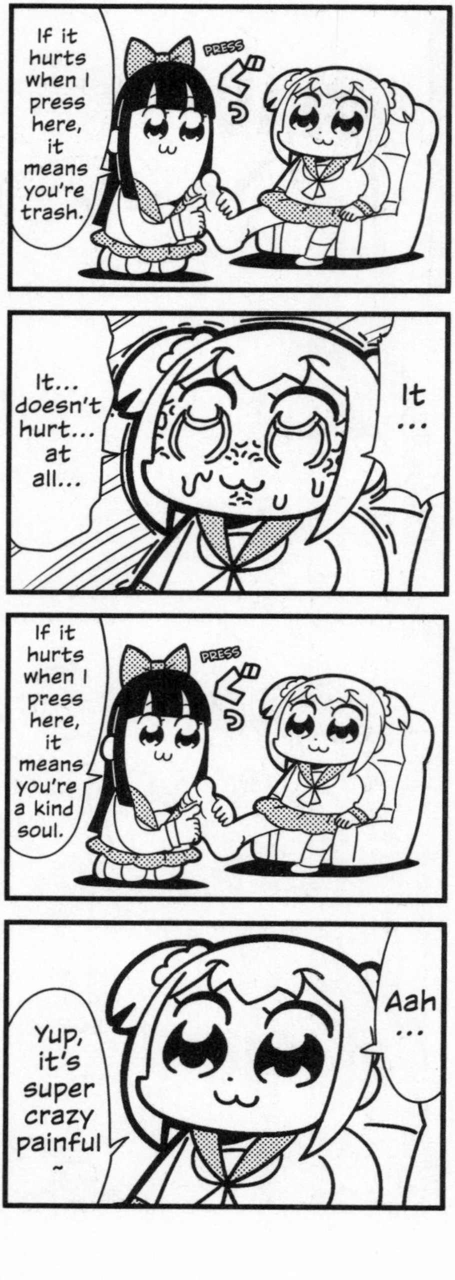
PRESS
If it hurts when I press here, it means you're trash.
It ...
It... doesn't hurt... at all...
PRESS
If it hurts when I press here, it means you're a kind soul.
Aah ...
Yup, it's super crazy painful ~

299

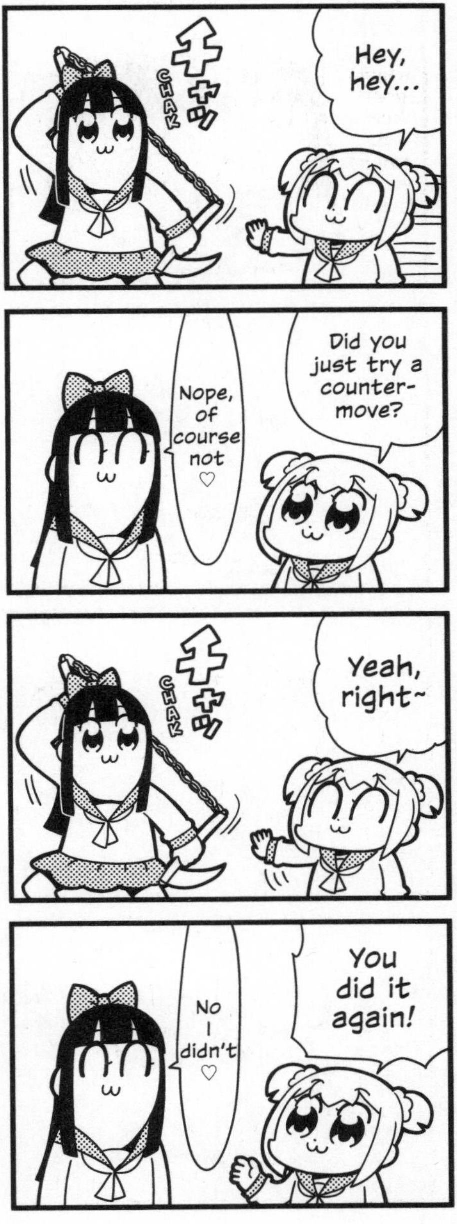
Hey, hey...
チャッ
CHAK
Did you just try a counter-move?
Nope, of course not ♡
Yeah, right~
チャッ
CHAK
You did it again!
No I didn't ♡

300

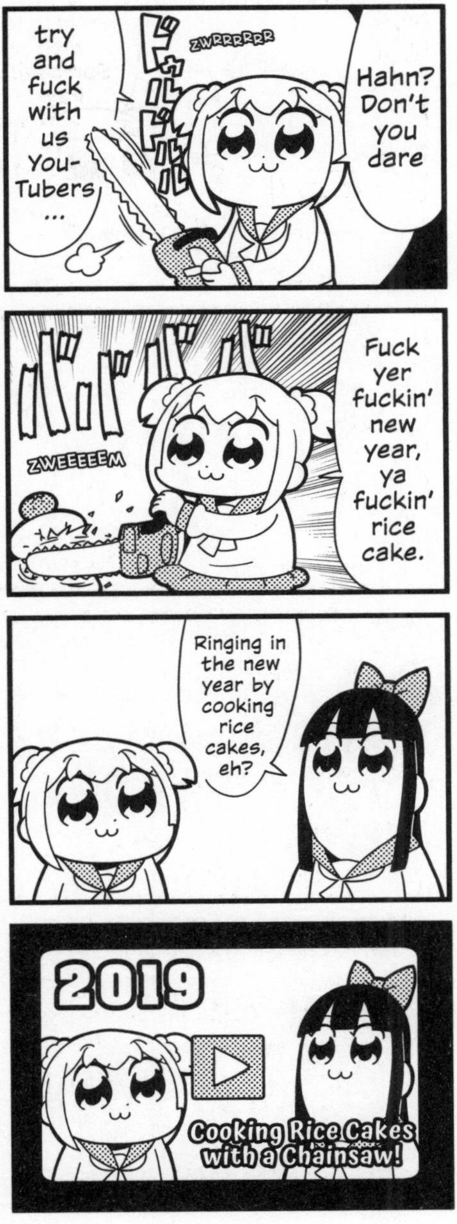
Hahn? Don't you dare
try and fuck with us You-Tubers...
ZWRRRRRR
Fuck yer fuckin' new year, ya fuckin' rice cake.
ZWEEEEEM
Ringing in the new year by cooking rice cakes, eh?
2019
Cooking Rice Cakes with a Chainsaw!

301

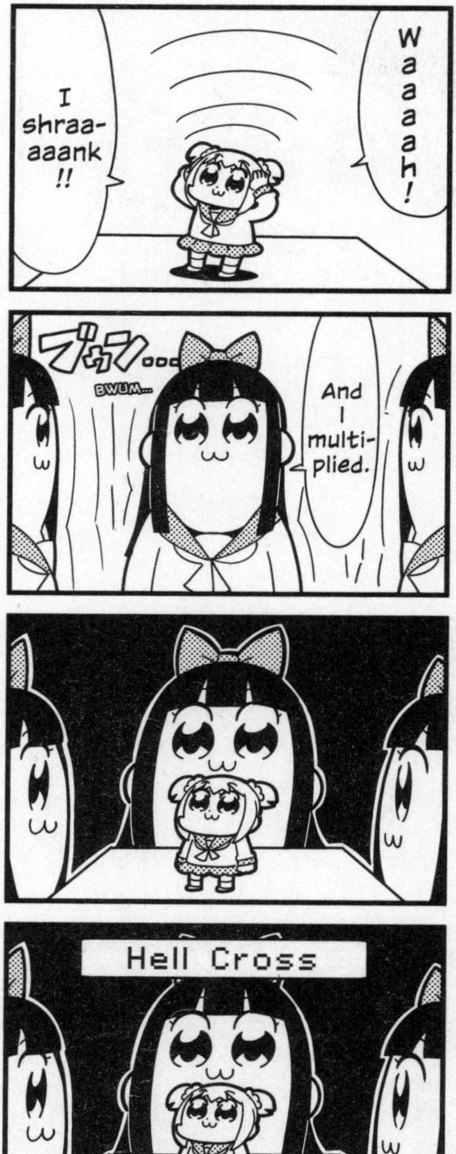
Waaaah!
I shraaaaank!!
ブゥン…
BWUM...
And I multiplied.
Hell Cross

302

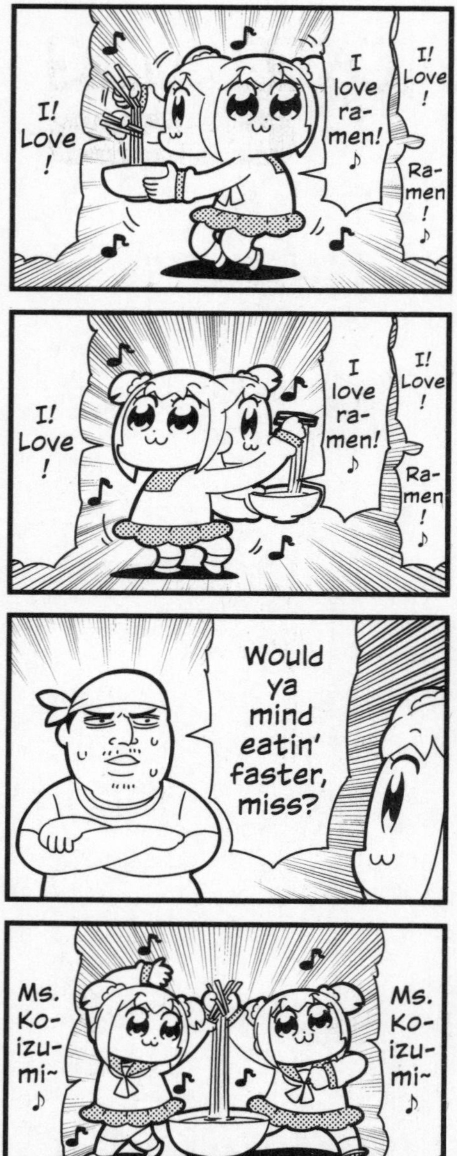
I! Love! Ramen! ♪
I love ramen! ♪
I! Love!
I! Love! Ramen! ♪
I love ramen! ♪
I! Love!
Would ya mind eatin' faster, miss?
Ms. Koizumi~ ♪
Ms. Koizumi~ ♪
I just love it~♪

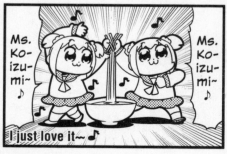

To be continued...

POP TEAM EPIC

Bkub Okawa

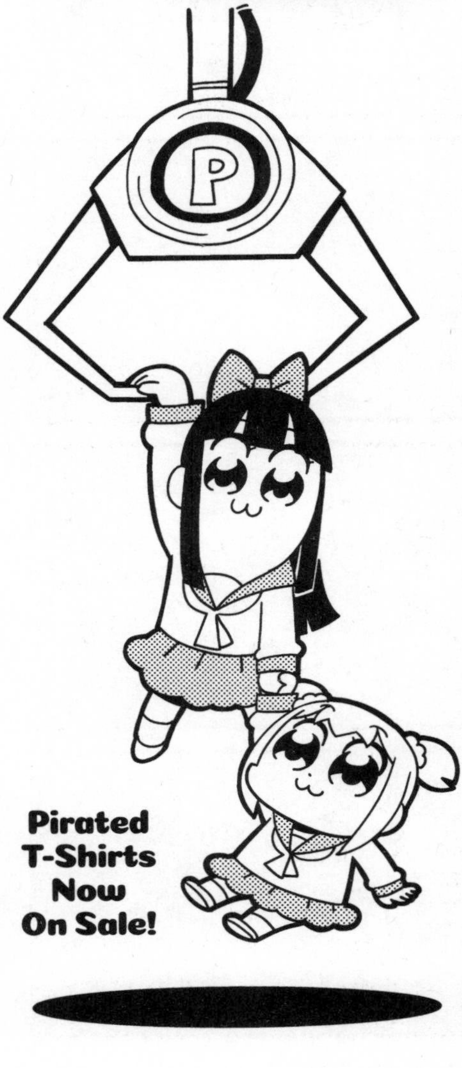
Pirated T-Shirts Now On Sale!

303

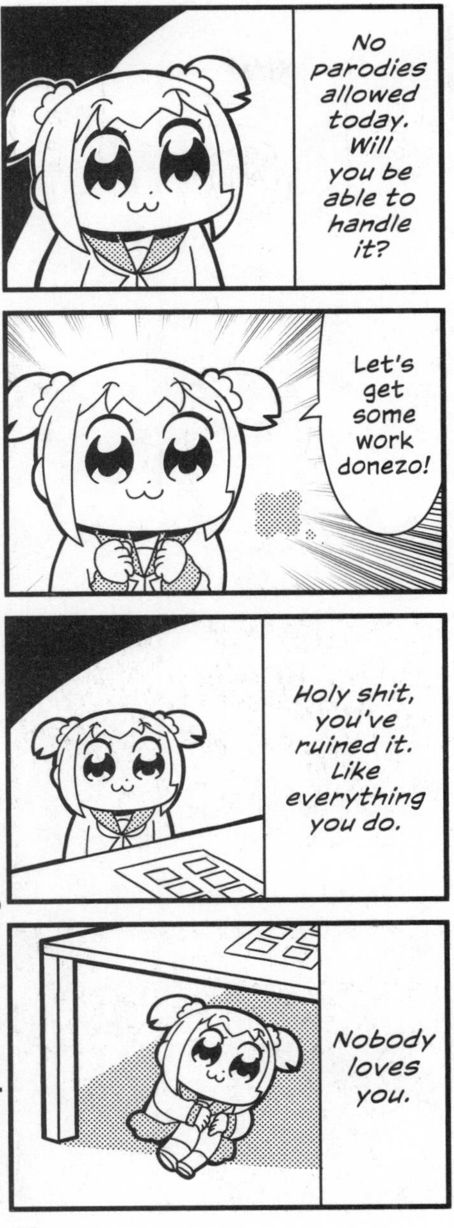
No parodies allowed today. Will you be able to handle it?
Let's get some work donezo!
Holy shit, you've ruined it. Like everything you do.
Nobody loves you.

☆This strip includes no original work.

304

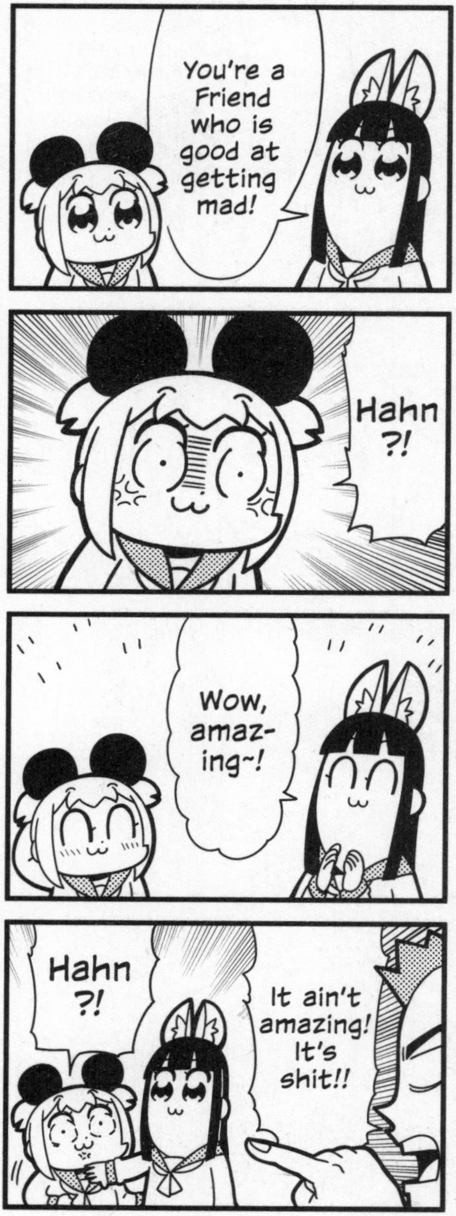
You're a Friend who is good at getting mad!
Hahn ?!
Wow, amazing~!
It ain't amazing! It's shit!!
Hahn ?!

305

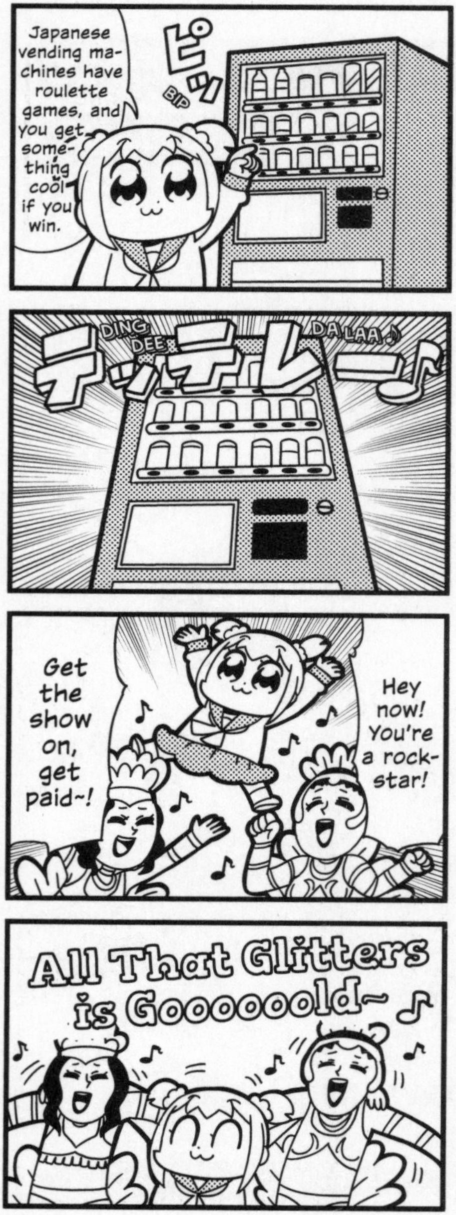
ピッ
BIP
Japanese vending machines have roulette games, and you get something cool if you win.
ティテレー
DING DEE
DA LAA♪
Hey now! You're a rock-star!
Get the show on, get paid~!
All That Glitters is Goooooold~♪

306

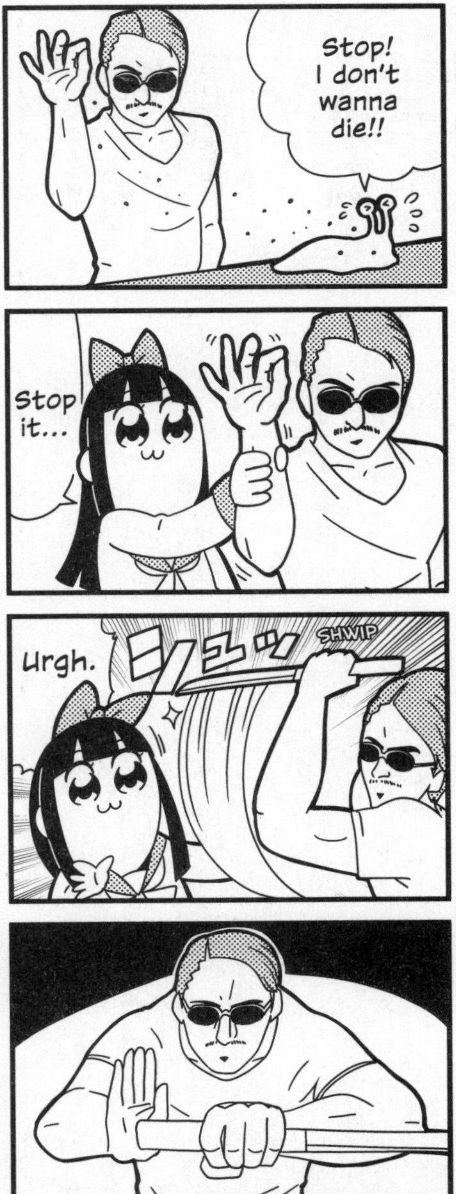
Stop! I don't wanna die!!
Stop it...
SHWIP
シュッ
Urgh.

307

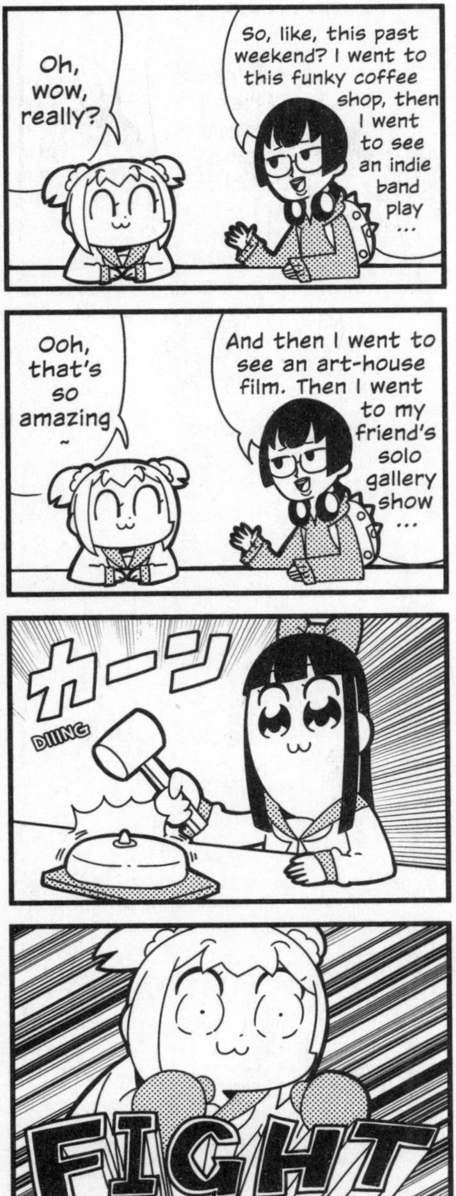
So, like, this past weekend? I went to this funky coffee shop, then I went to see an indie band play ...
Oh, wow, really?
And then I went to see an art-house film. Then I went to my friend's solo gallery show ...
Ooh, that's so amazing ~
カーン
DIIING
FIGHT

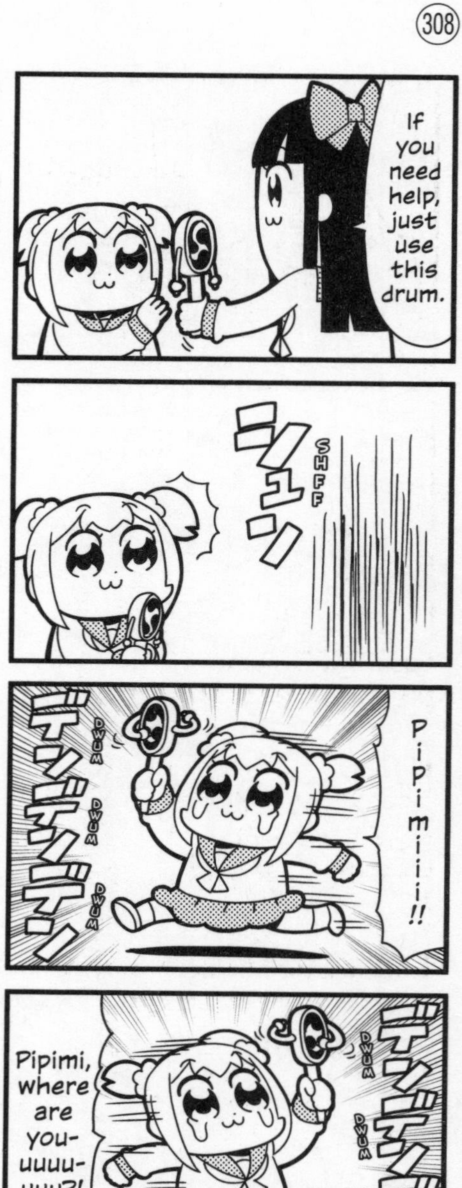
308
If you need help, just use this drum.
シュンッ
SHFF
デンデンデンッ
DWUM
DWUM
DWUM
Pipimiiii!!
デンデンデンッ
DWUM
DWUM
DWUM
Pipimi, where are you-uuuu-uuu?!

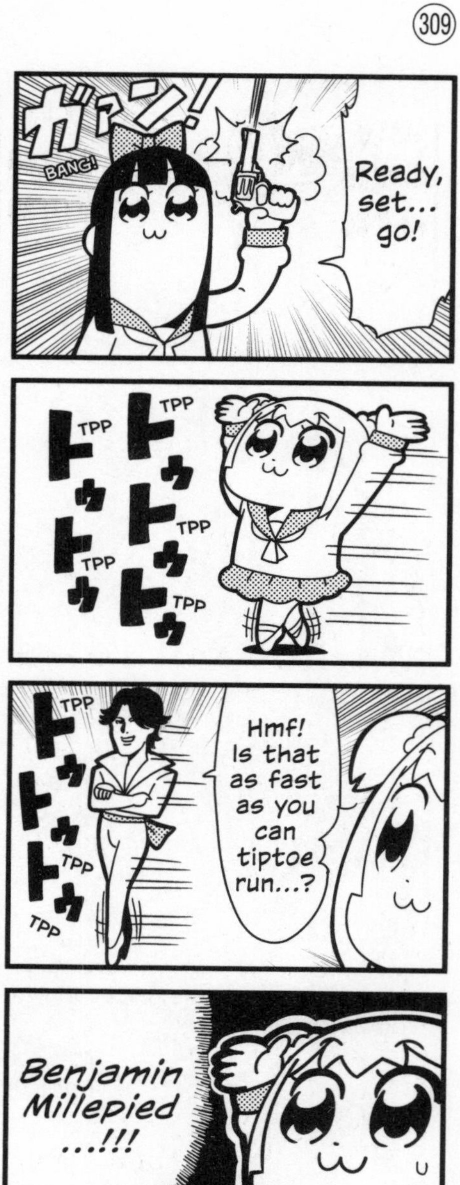
309
ガァンッ!
BANG!
Ready, set... go!
TPP
TPP
TPP
TPP
TPP
Hmf! Is that as fast as you can tiptoe run...?
TPP
TPP
TPP
Benjamin Millepied ...!!!

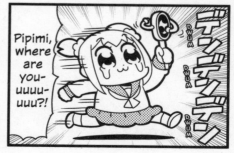

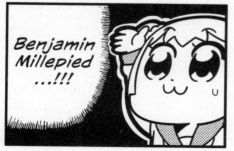

310

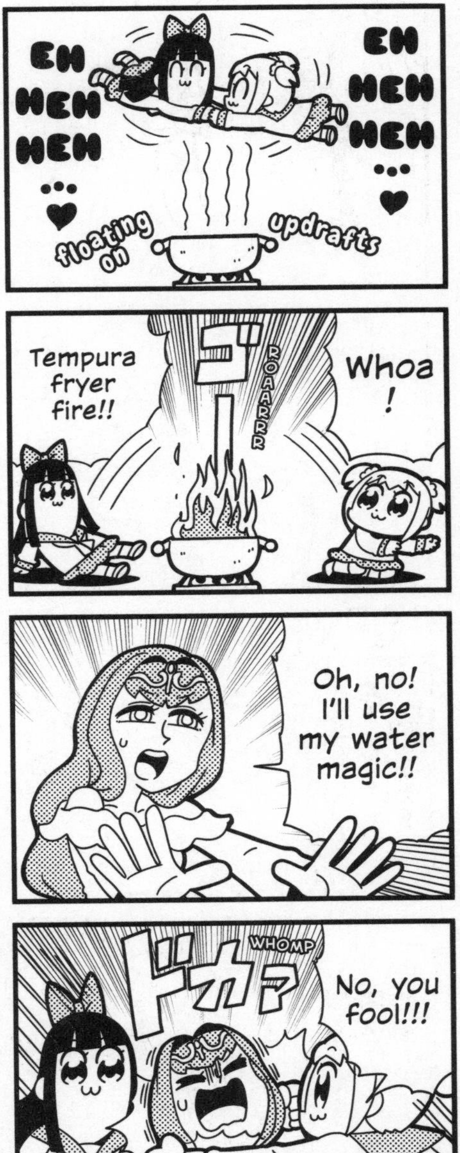
EH HEH HEH...♥
EH HEH HEH...♥
floating on updrafts
Whoa!
ゴ
ROAAARRR
Tempura fryer fire!!
Oh, no! I'll use my water magic!!
No, you fool!!!
ドカァ
WHOMP

311

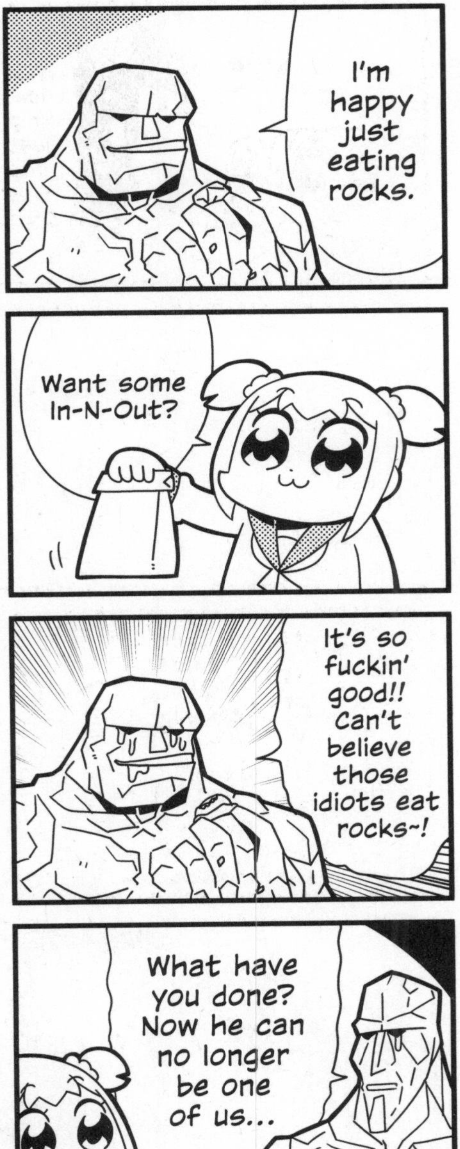
I'm happy just eating rocks.
Want some In-N-Out?
It's so fuckin' good!! Can't believe those idiots eat rocks~!
What have you done? Now he can no longer be one of us...

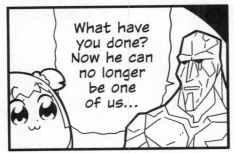

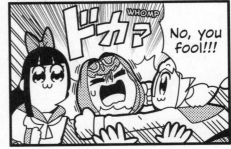

312

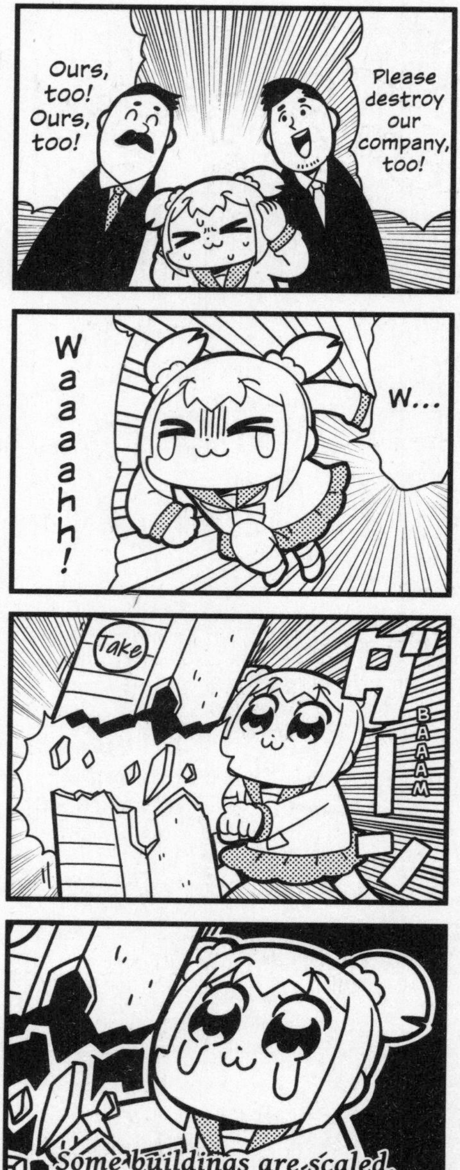
Please destroy our company, too!
Ours, too! Ours, too!
W...
Waaaaahh!
BAAAM
Take
Some buildings are scaled, others are slain...

313

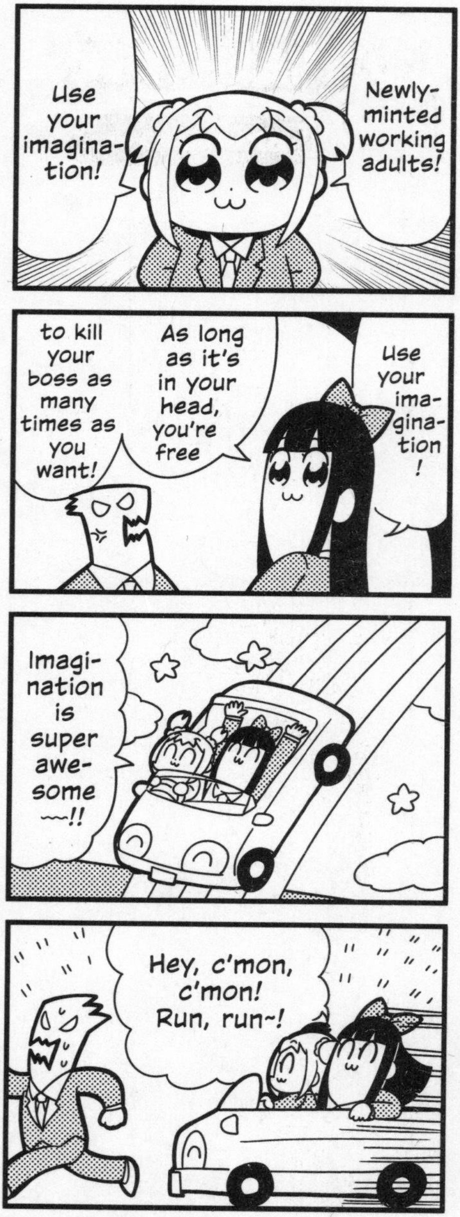
Newly-minted working adults!
Use your imagination!
Use your imagination!
As long as it's in your head, you're free
to kill your boss as many times as you want!
Imagination is super awesome~!!
Hey, c'mon, c'mon! Run, run~!

To be continued...

POP TEAM EPIC

Bkub Okawa

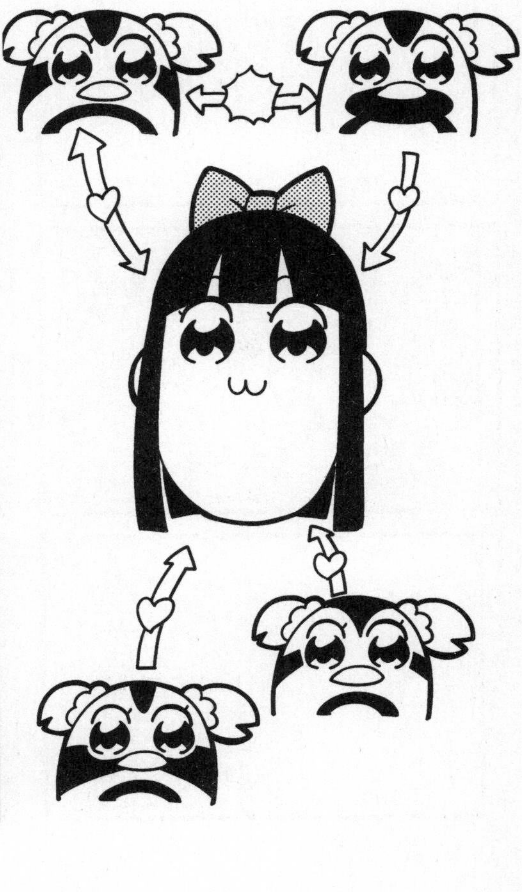

314

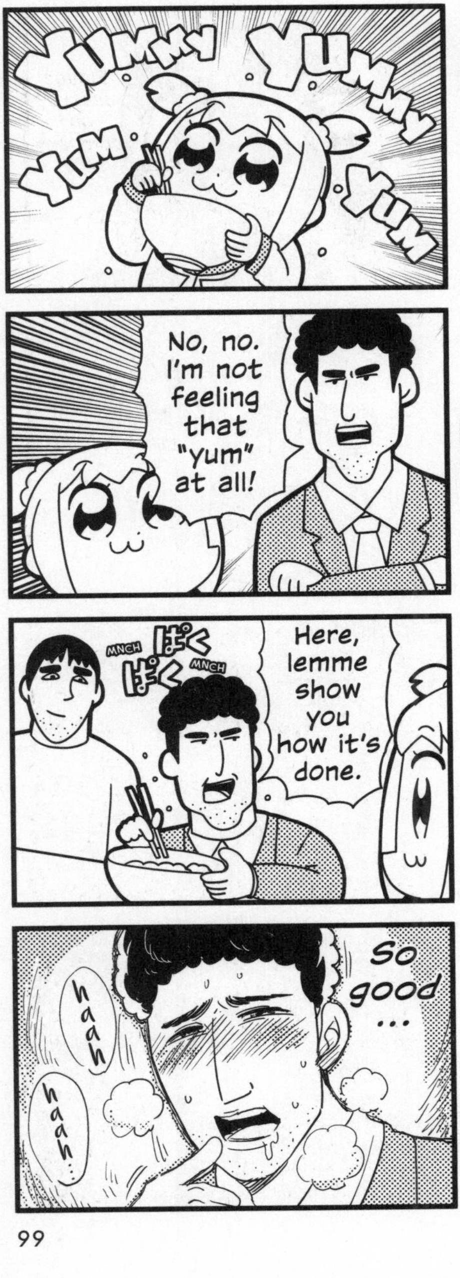
YUMMY
YUMMY
YUM
YUM
No, no. I'm not feeling that "yum" at all!
Here, lemme show you how it's done.
ぱく
MNCH
ぱく
MNCH
So good...
haah
haah...

315

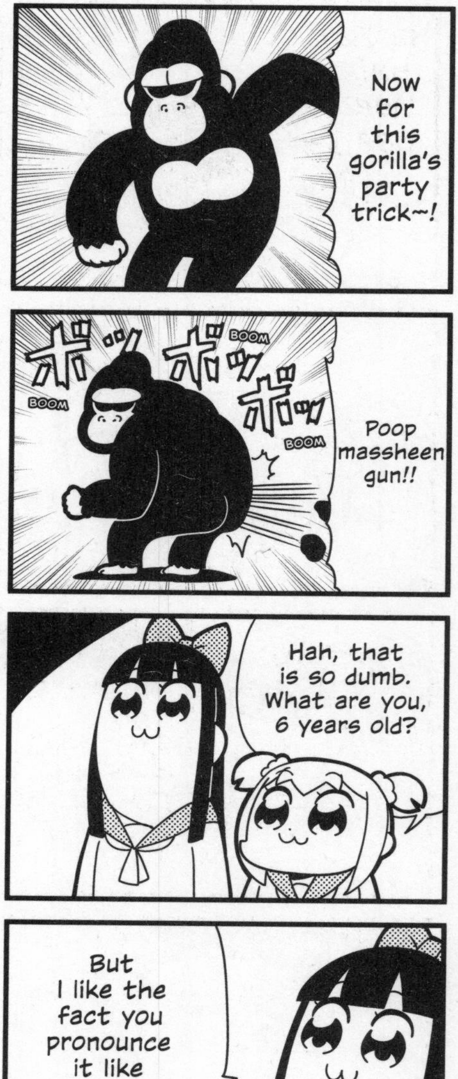
Now for this gorilla's party trick~!
BOOM
BOOM
BOOM
Poop massheen gun!!
Hah, that is so dumb. What are you, 6 years old?
But I like the fact you pronounce it like they do in *Metal Slug*.

316

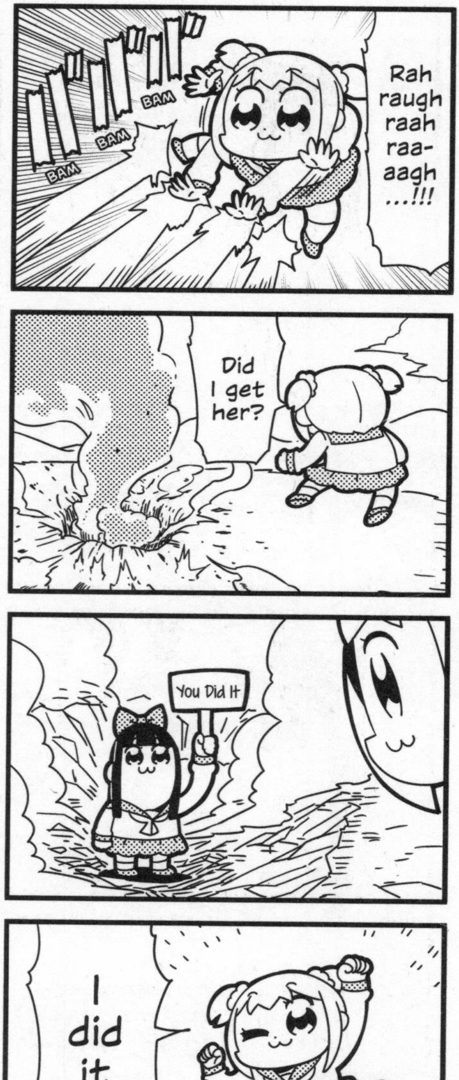
Rah raugh raah raa-aagh ...!!!
BAM
BAM
BAM
Did I get her?
You Did It
I did it !!!

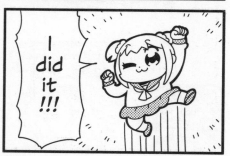

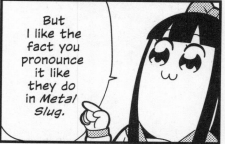

317

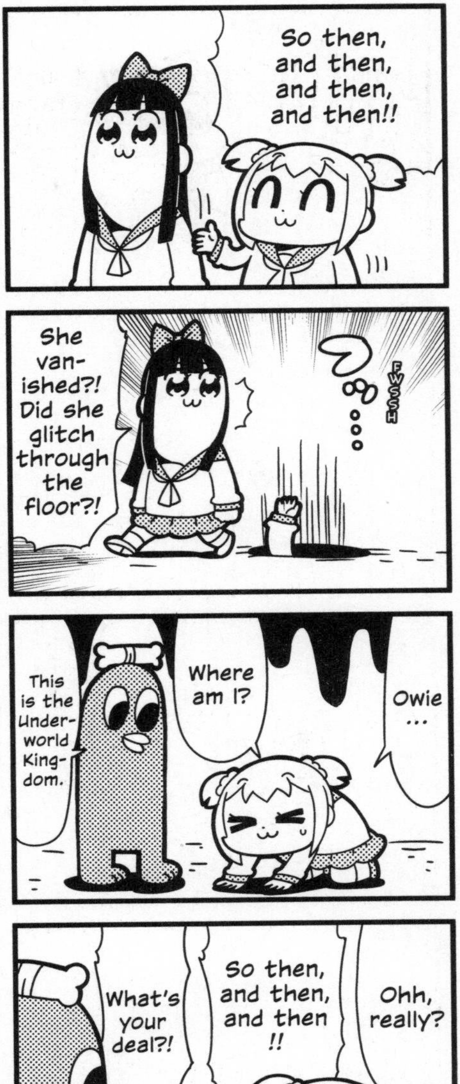
So then, and then, and then, and then!!
FWSSH
She vanished?! Did she glitch through the floor?!
Owie...
Where am I?
This is the Underworld Kingdom.
Ohh, really?
So then, and then, and then!!
What's your deal?!

318

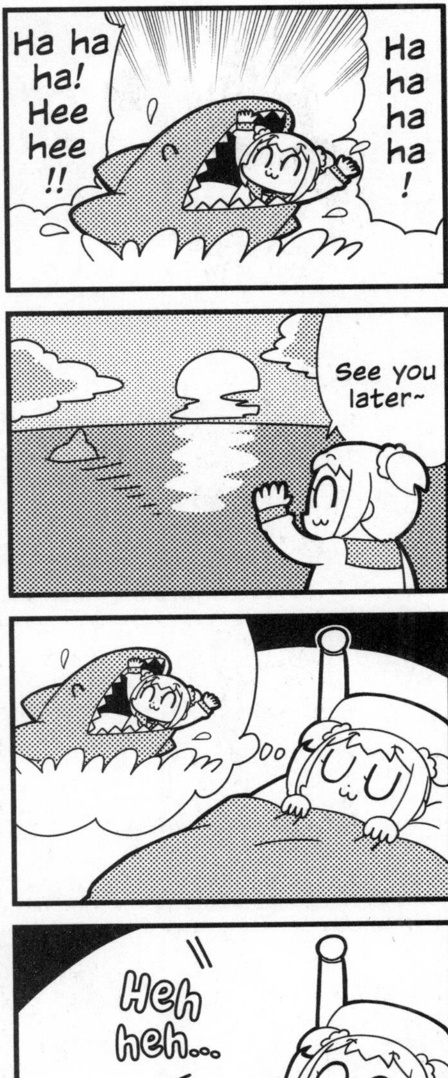
Ha ha ha ha!
Ha ha ha! Hee hee!!
See you later~
Heh heh...

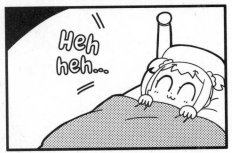

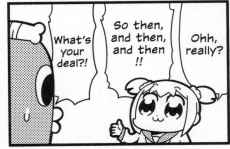

319

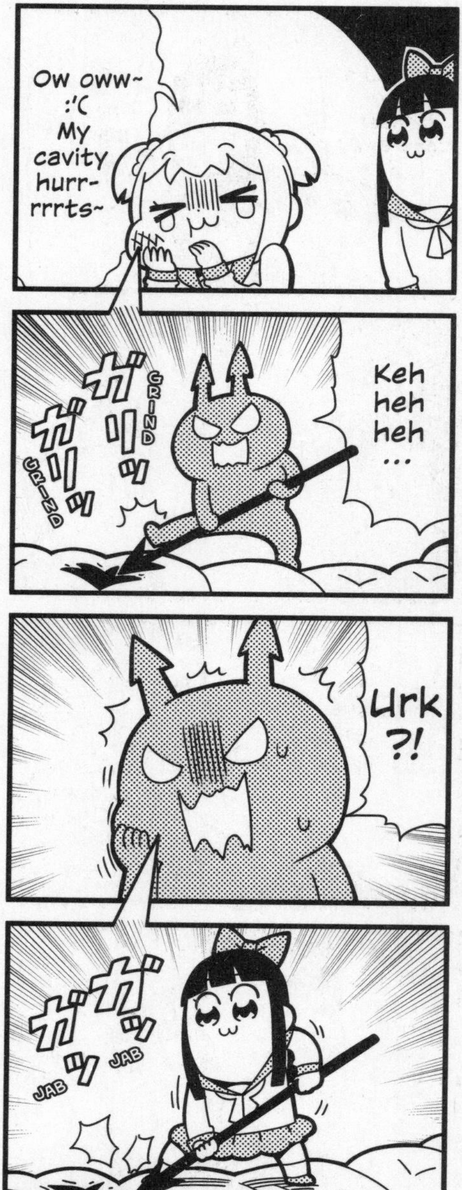
Ow oww~ :'(My cavity hurr-rrrts~
Keh heh heh ...
ガリッ
GRIND
ガリッ
GRIND
Urk ?!
ガッ
JAB
ガッ
JAB

320

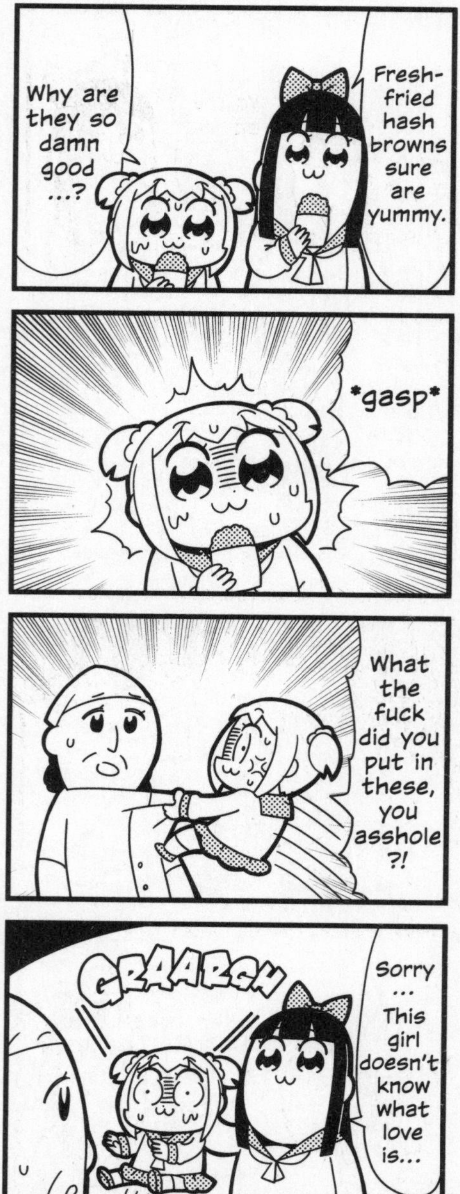
Fresh-fried hash browns sure are yummy.
Why are they so damn good ...?
gasp
What the fuck did you put in these, you asshole ?!
Sorry ... This girl doesn't know what love is...
GRAARGH

321

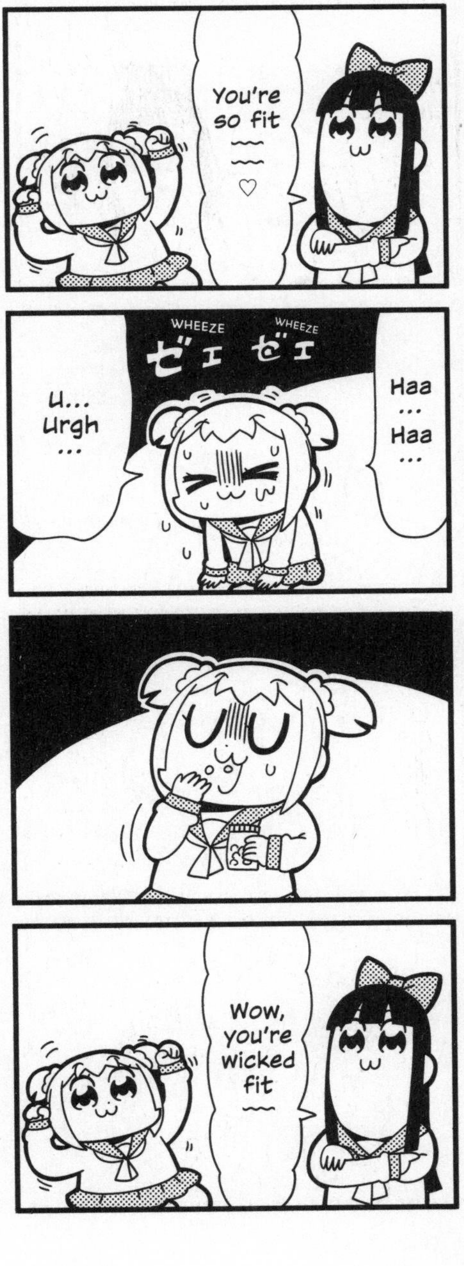
You're so fit ~~~ ~~~ ♡
WHEEZE ゼェ WHEEZE ゼェ
Haa ... Haa ...
U... Urgh ...
Wow, you're wicked fit ~~~

322

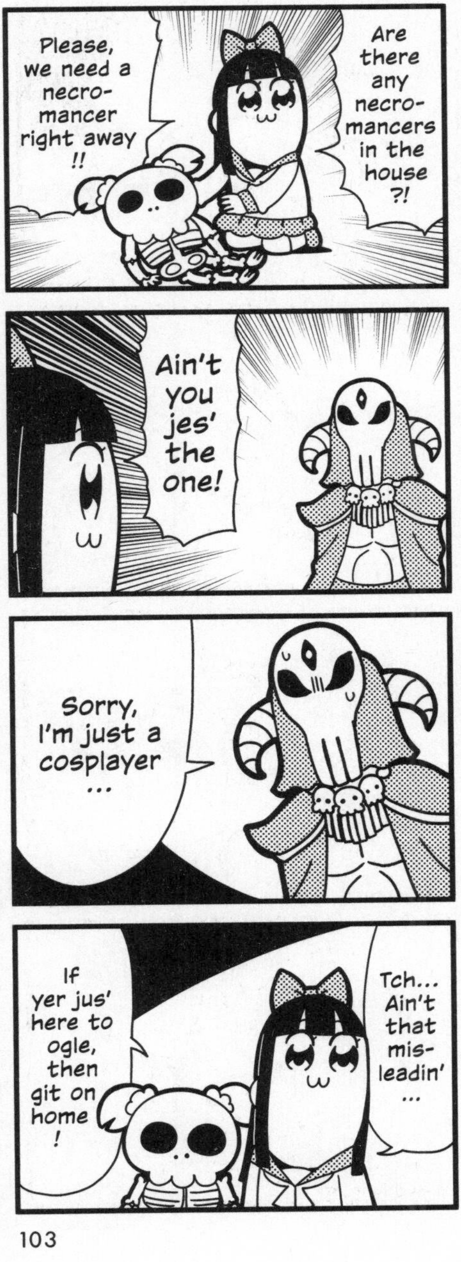
Are there any necro-mancers in the house ?!
Please, we need a necro-mancer right away !!
Ain't you jes' the one!
Sorry, I'm just a cosplayer ...
Tch... Ain't that mis-leadin' ...
If yer jus' here to ogle, then git on home !

☆Next chapter, a major announcement! *Pop Team Epic* is finally getting a...!

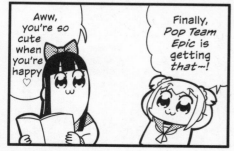

323

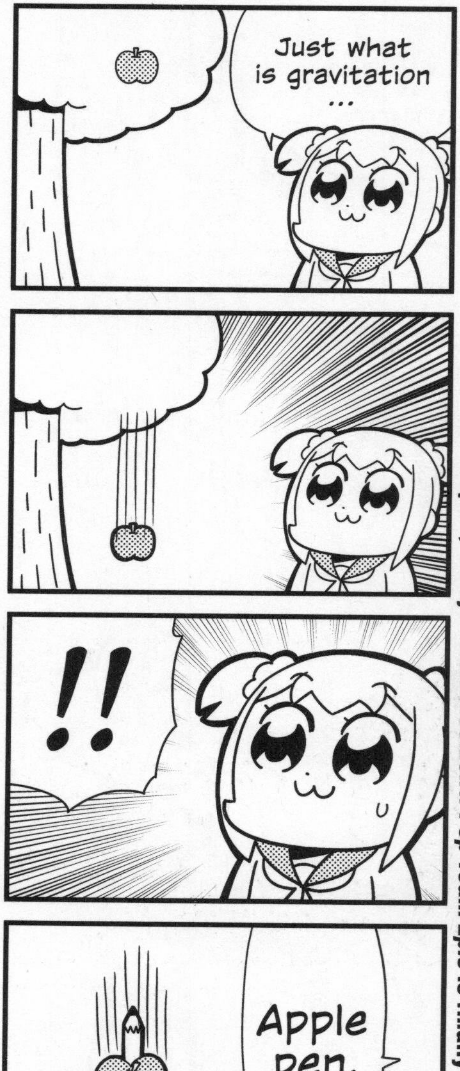
Just what is gravitation ...
!!
Apple pen.

324

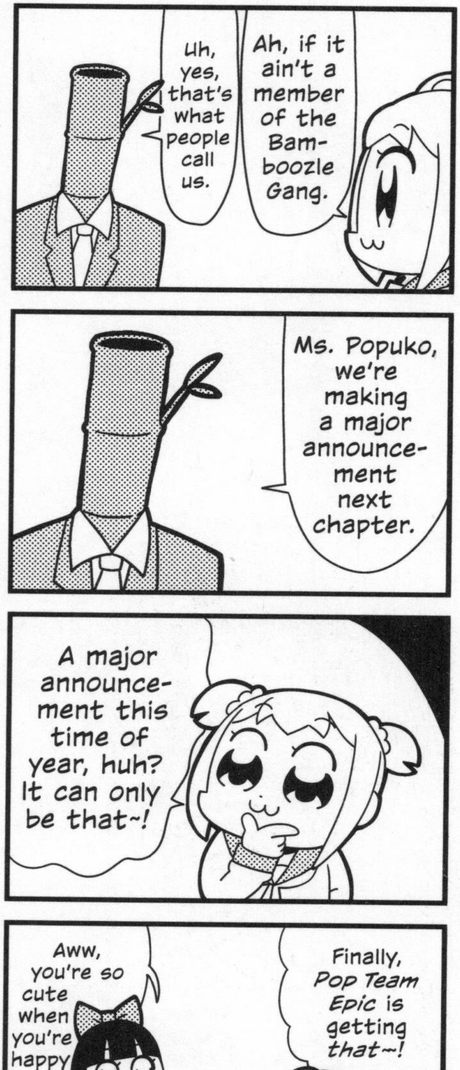
Ah, if it ain't a member of the Bam-boozle Gang.
Uh, yes, that's what people call us.
Ms. Popuko, we're making a major announce-ment next chapter.
A major announce-ment this time of year, huh? It can only be that~!
Finally, *Pop Team Epic* is getting *that*~!
Aww, you're so cute when you're happy ♡

To be continued...

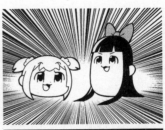

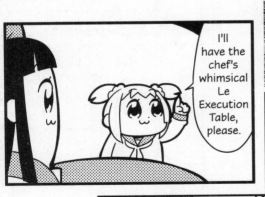

I can't help it, I'm a baby.
I'll have the chef's whimsical Le Execution Table, please.
Terra incog-nita.

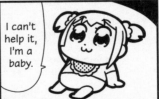

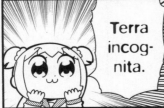

Get cooking.
We are food lovers ...
Where's the beef?
Where's the beef?
Beef ...
It's what's for dinner.
C'mon, give us a good retort, you weird little animal!

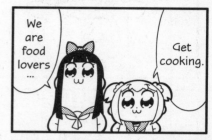

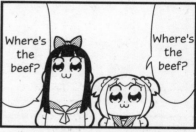

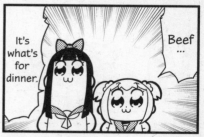

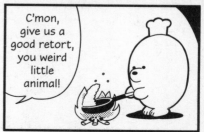

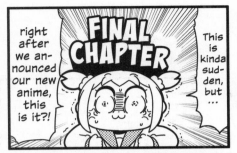

Nothing Can Stop Us!
FINAL CHAPTER

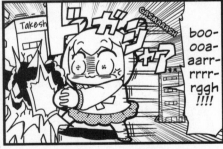

POP TEAM EPIC

Bkub Okawa

This is kinda sudden, but...
FINAL CHAPTER
right after we announced our new anime, this is it?!
VWOOOSH
ゴーーッ
Takeshobo
Take-sho...
GASMAAAASH
ドガシャア
boooooaaarrrrrrrggh!!!!
Takesh
Takeshobo
Chairman! She figured out that it was a dummy building!
I... Impossible...!!

☆Major announcement! *Pop Team Epic* is finally getting a... final chapter!

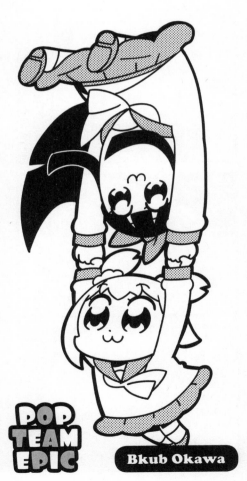

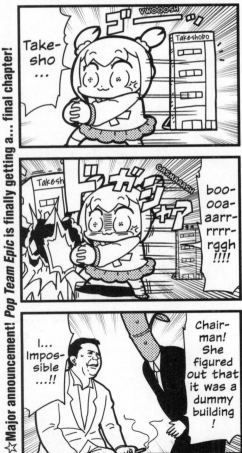

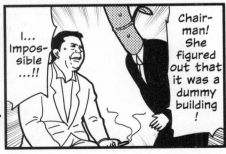

326

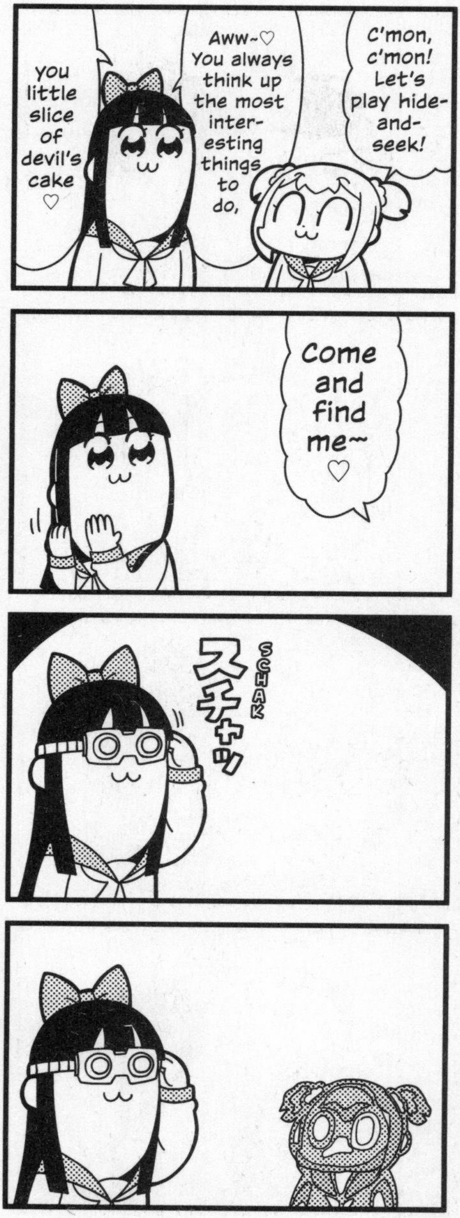
C'mon, c'mon! Let's play hide-and-seek!
Aww~♡ You always think up the most interesting things to do,
you little slice of devil's cake ♡
Come and find me~ ♡
スチャッ
SCHAK

327

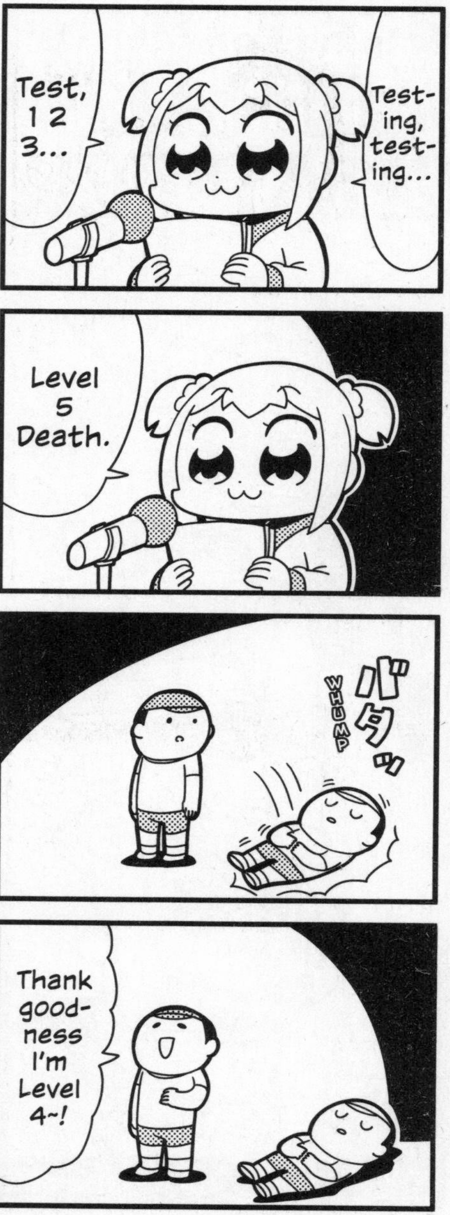
Testing, testing...
Test, 1 2 3...
Level 5 Death.
バタッ
WHUMP
Thank goodness I'm Level 4~!

328

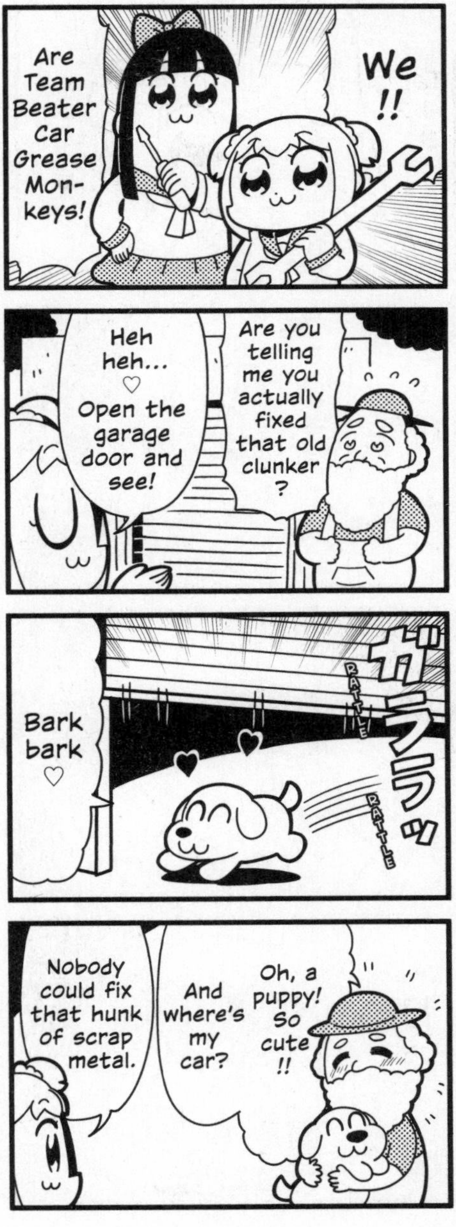
We !!
Are Team Beater Car Grease Mon-keys!
Are you telling me you actually fixed that old clunker ?
Heh heh... ♡ Open the garage door and see!
ガララッ
RATTLE RATTLE
Bark bark ♡
Oh, a puppy! So cute !!
And where's my car?
Nobody could fix that hunk of scrap metal.

329

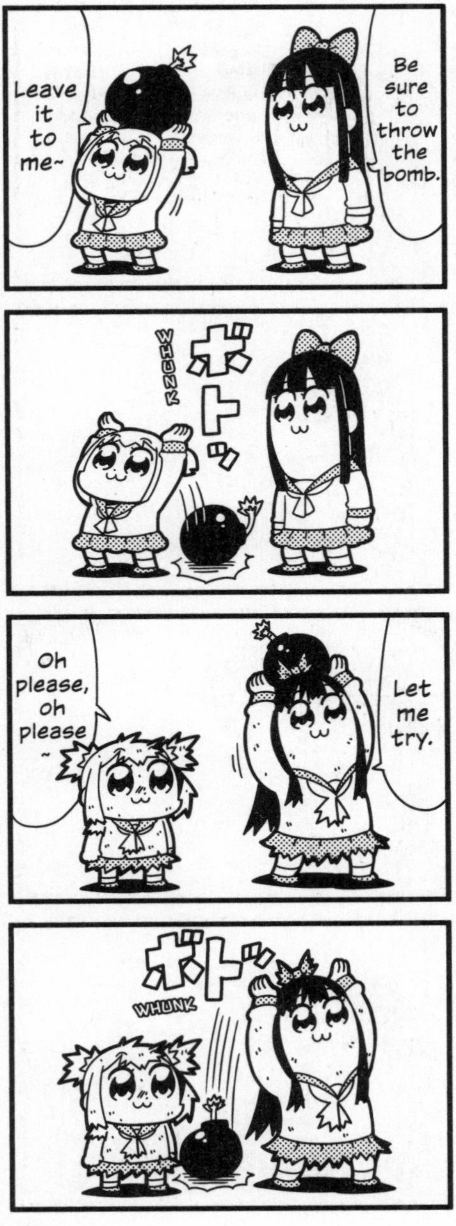
Be sure to throw the bomb.
Leave it to me~
ボトッ
WHUNK
Let me try.
Oh please, oh please ~
ボトッ
WHUNK

330

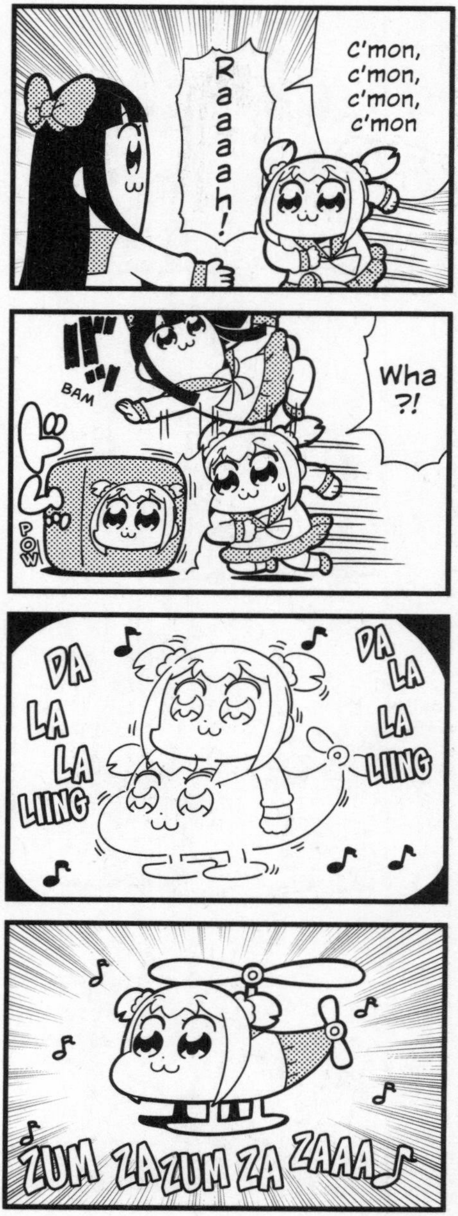
C'mon, c'mon, c'mon, c'mon
Raaaah!
Wha ?!
BAM
POW
DA LA LA LIING
DA LA LA LA LIING
ZUM ZA ZUM ZA ZAAA

331

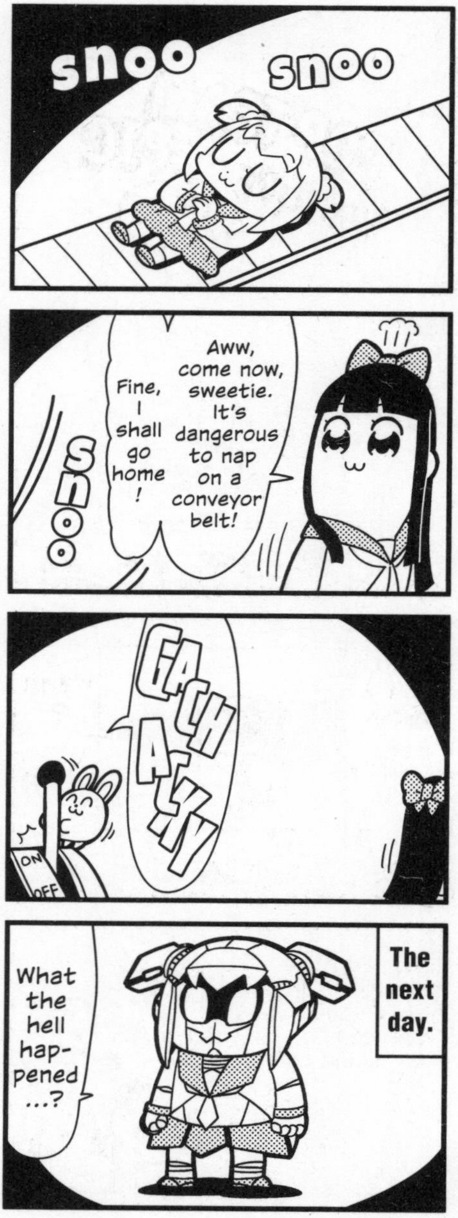
snoo
snoo
Aww, come now, sweetie. It's dangerous to nap on a conveyor belt!
Fine, I shall go home!
snoo
GACH ACLK
ON
OFF
The next day.
What the hell hap-pened ...?

332

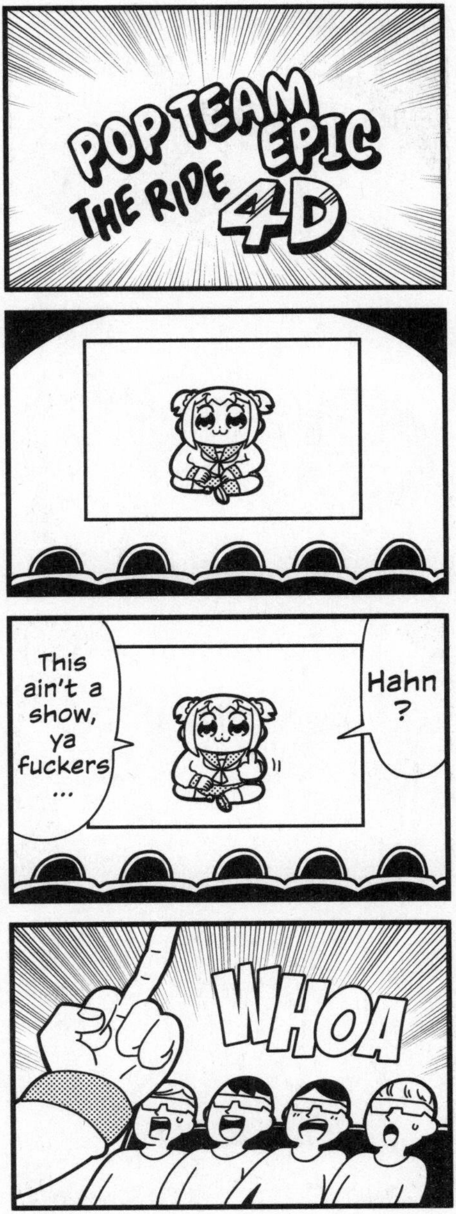
POP TEAM EPIC THE RIDE 4D
Hahn?
This ain't a show, ya fuckers...
WHOA

333

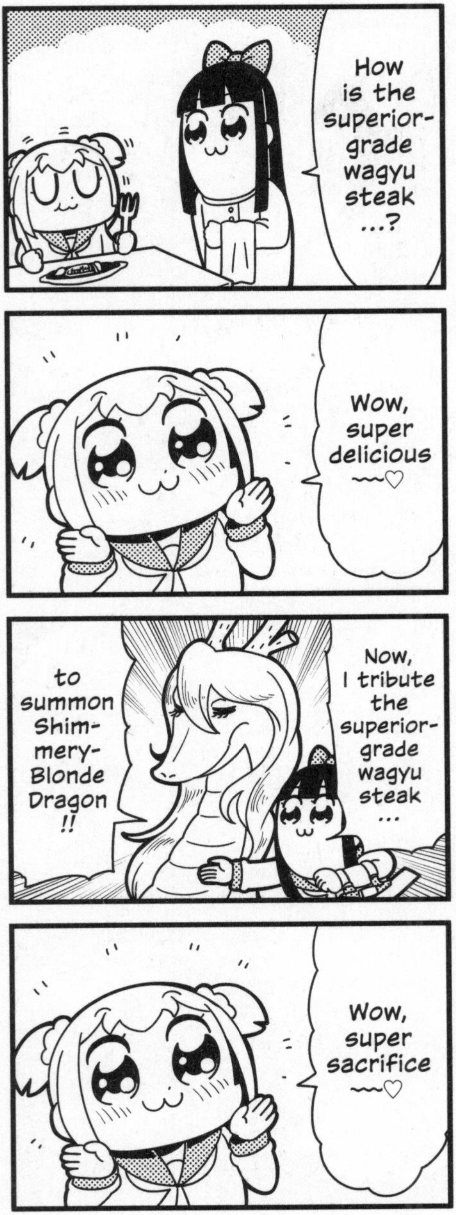
How is the superior-grade wagyu steak...?
Wow, super delicious ~~♡
Now, I tribute the superior-grade wagyu steak...
to summon Shimmery-Blonde Dragon!!
Wow, super sacrifice ~~♡

334

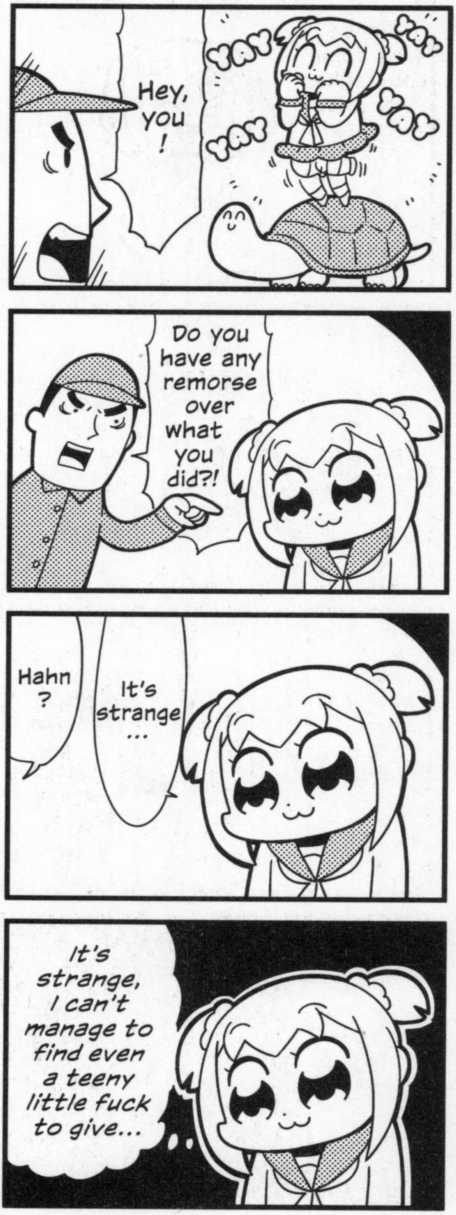
YAY YAY
YAY YAY
Hey, you!
Do you have any remorse over what you did?!
It's strange ...
Hahn?
It's strange, I can't manage to find even a teeny little fuck to give...

335

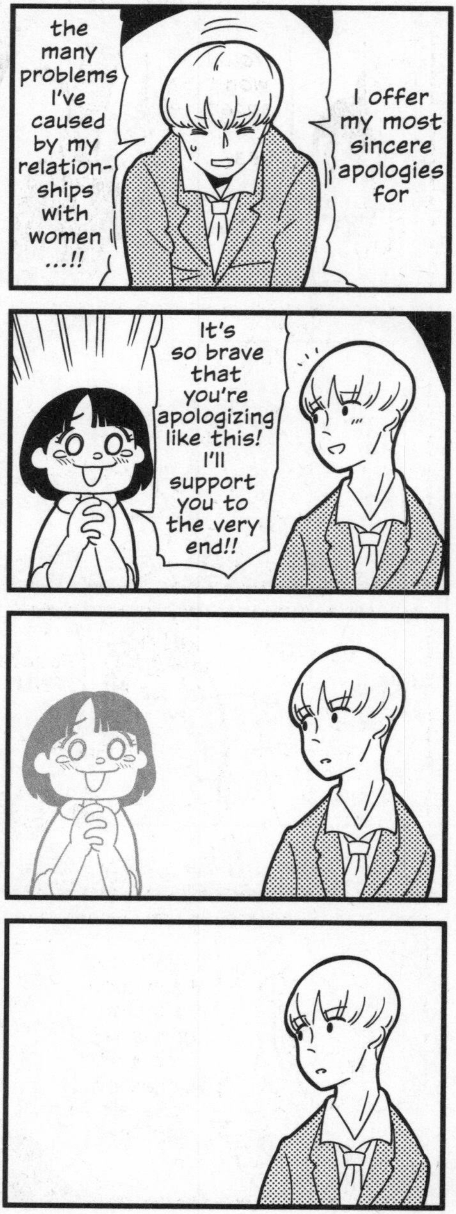
I offer my most sincere apologies for
the many problems I've caused by my relationships with women ...!!
It's so brave that you're apologizing like this! I'll support you to the very end!!

336

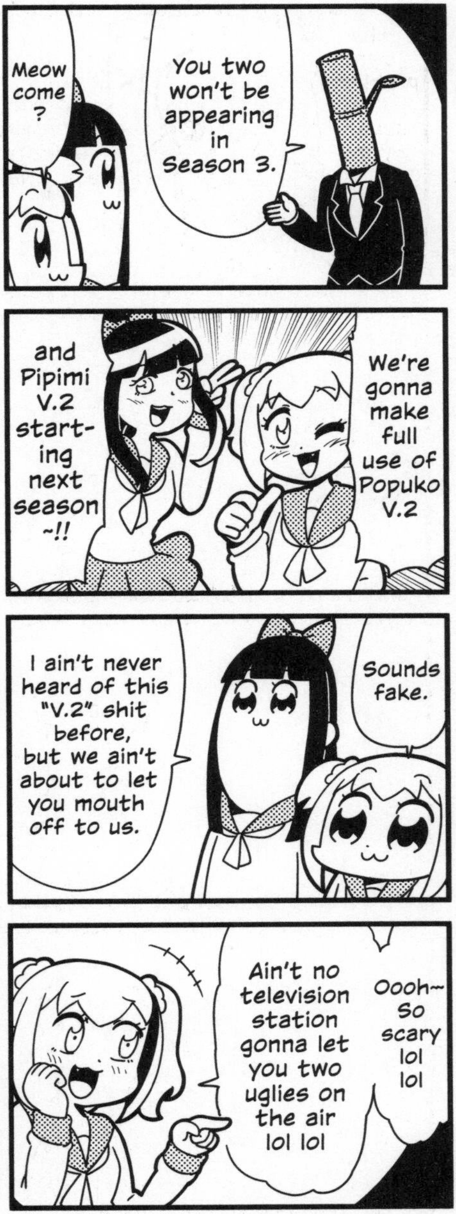
You two won't be appearing in Season 3.
Meow come ?
We're gonna make full use of Popuko V.2
and Pipimi V.2 starting next season ~!!
Sounds fake.
I ain't never heard of this "V.2" shit before, but we ain't about to let you mouth off to us.
Oooh~ So scary lol lol
Ain't no television station gonna let you two uglies on the air lol lol

337

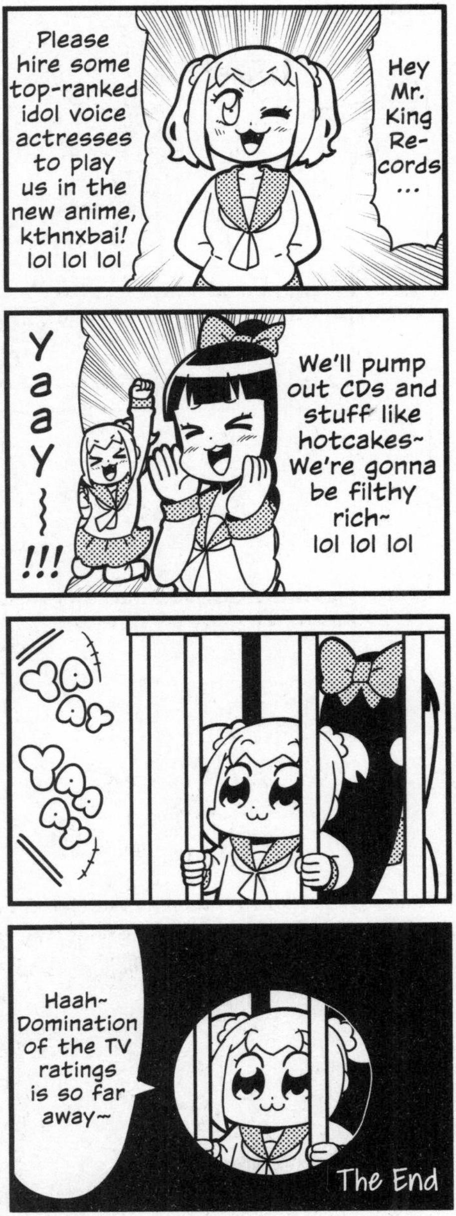
Hey Mr. King Re-cords ...
Please hire some top-ranked idol voice actresses to play us in the new anime, kthnxbai! lol lol lol
We'll pump out CDs and stuff like hotcakes~ We're gonna be filthy rich~ lol lol lol
Yaaay~~!!!
YAY YAY YAAAY
Haah~ Domination of the TV ratings is so far away~
The End

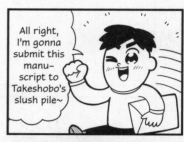

All right, I'm gonna submit this manu-script to Takeshobo's slush pile~
EAM PUBLISH
Nah, don't do it, man~~!
Don't bother sub-mitting to such a crap publish-er...
Work with us and you can debut right away!!
We'll make an anime version right away!!
And you'll have voice actresses waiting on you hand and foot!
FOR REAL?! I'LL GO WITH YOU! WHO WOULD EVER CHOOSE TAKESHOBO? THEY'RE TOTAL GARBAGE!!
And nobody ever saw him again...

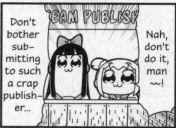

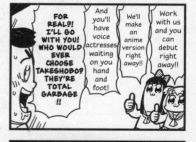

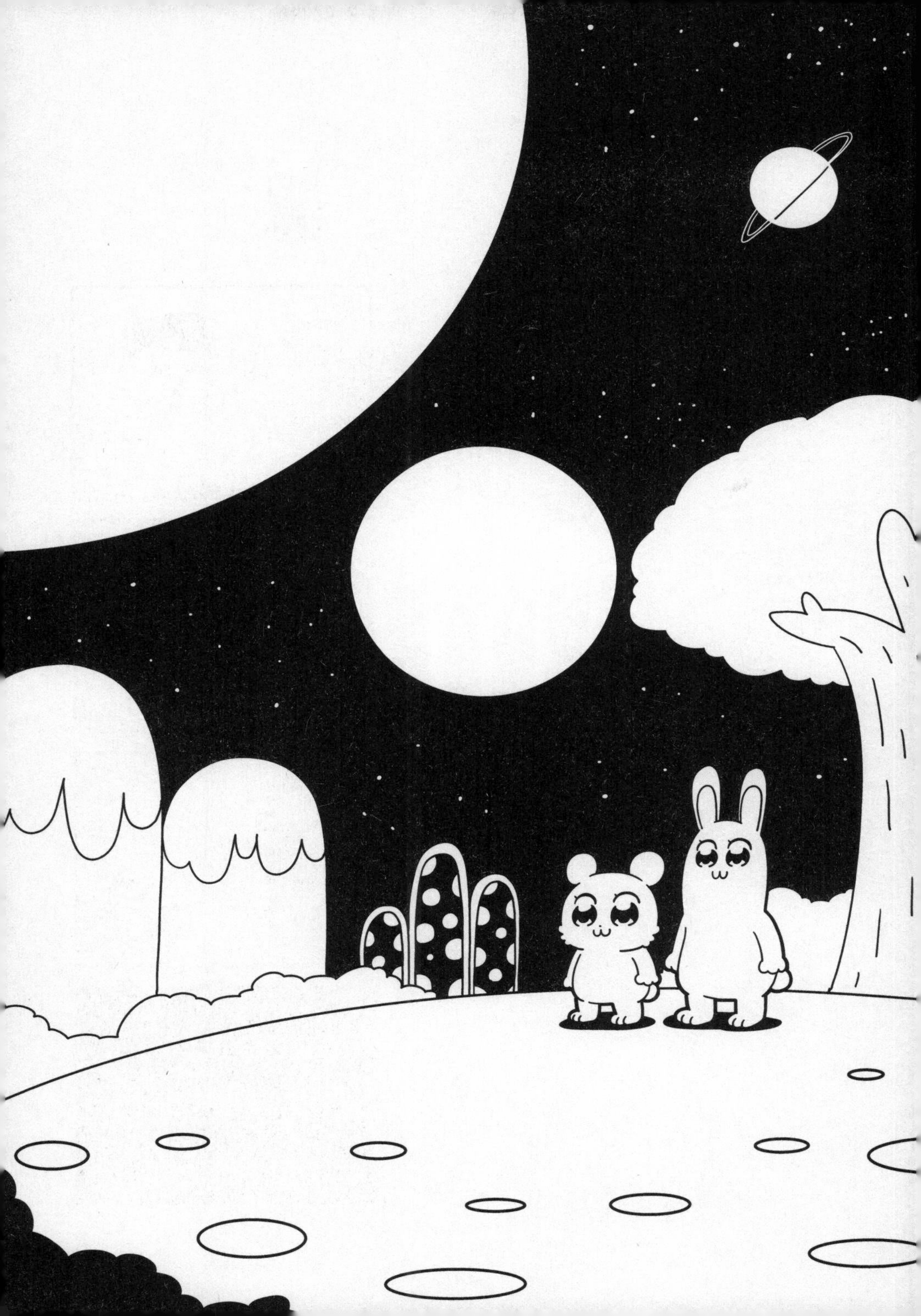

POP TEAM EPIC

POP
TEAM
EPIC

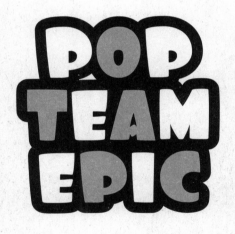

OWN IT NOW

BLU-RAY & DIGITAL
FUNIMATION.COM/POPTEAMEPIC

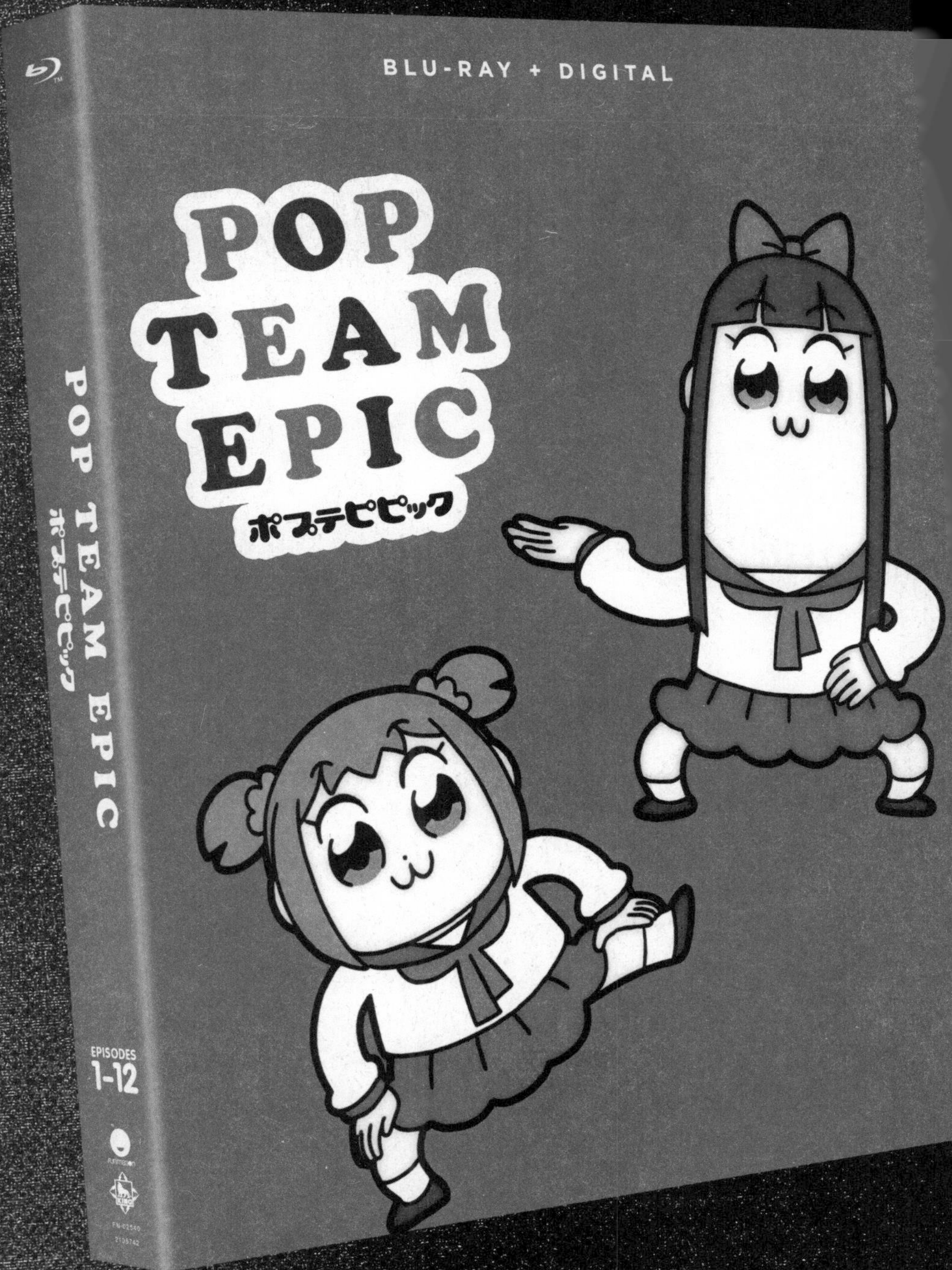
BLU-RAY + DIGITAL
POP TEAM EPIC
ポプテピピック
POP TEAM EPIC
ポプテピピック
EPISODES 1-12

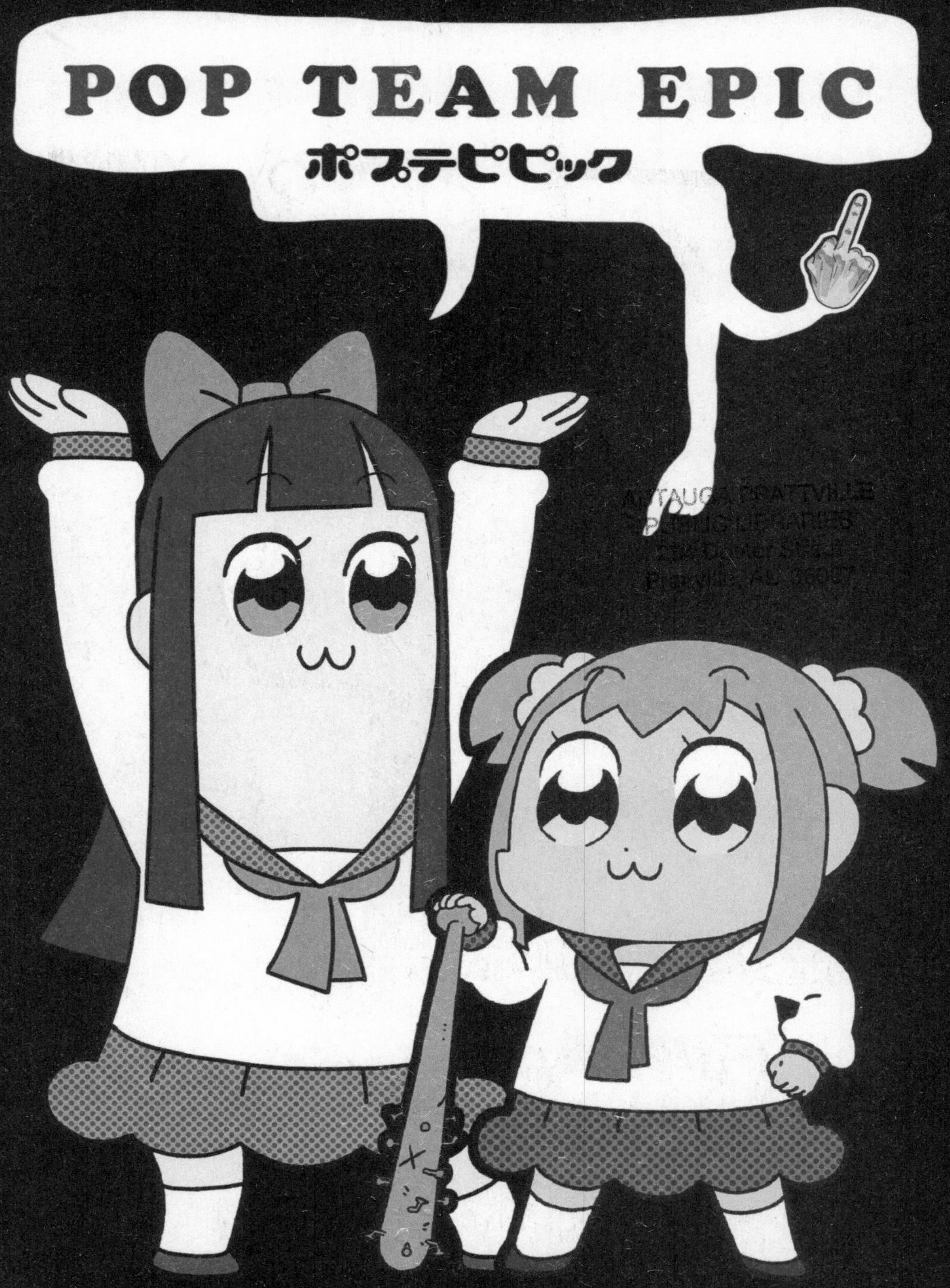
POP TEAM EPIC
ポプテピピック

POP TEAM EPIC
SECOND SEASON

A Vertical Comics Edition

Translation: Yota Okutani
          Maya Rosewood
Production: Grace Lu
          Nicole Dochych

© 2017 bkub OKAWA
First published in Japan in 2017 by Takeshobo Co. Ltd.
English translation rights arranged with Takeshobo Co. Ltd.
through TUTTLE-MORI AGENCY, INC., Tokyo.

Translation provided by Vertical Comics, 2018
Published by Vertical Comics, an imprint of Vertical, Inc., New York

Originally published in Japanese as *Poputepipikku Second Season*
by Takeshobo Co., 2017
Poputepipikku first serialized in *Manga Life WIN,* Takeshobo Co., 2014-

This is a work of fiction.

ISBN: 978-1-947194-25-0

Manufactured in Canada

First Edition

Vertical, Inc.
451 Park Avenue South
7th Floor
New York, NY 10016
www.vertical-comics.com

Vertical books are distributed through Penguin-Random House Publisher Services.